Lecture Notes in Computer Science 2649

Edited by G. Goos, J. Hartmanis, and J. van Leeuwen

T0226170

Springer
Berlin
Heidelberg
New York
Barcelona
Hong Kong
London
Milan
Paris
Tokyo

Bernhard Westfechtel   André van der Hoek (Eds.)

Software Configuration Management

ICSE Workshops SCM 2001 and SCM 2003
Toronto, Canada, May 14-15, 2001
and Portland, OR, USA, May 9-10, 2003
Selected Papers

 Springer

Series Editors

Gerhard Goos, Karlsruhe University, Germany
Juris Hartmanis, Cornell University, NY, USA
Jan van Leeuwen, Utrecht University, The Netherlands

Volume Editors

Bernhard Westfechtel
RWTH Aachen, Informatik III
52056 Aachen, Germany
E-mail: westfechtel@cs.rwth-aachen.de

André van der Hoek
University of California, School of Information and Computer Science
444 Computer Science Building, Irvine, CA 92697-3425, USA
E-mail: andre@ics.uci.edu

Cataloging-in-Publication Data applied for

A catalog record for this book is available from the Library of Congress

Bibliographic information published by Die Deutsche Bibliothek
Die Deutsche Bibliothek lists this publication in the Deutsche Nationalbibliographie;
detailed bibliographic data is available in the Internet at <http://dnb.ddb.de>.

CR Subject Classification (1998): K.6.3, K.6, D.2

ISSN 0302-9743
ISBN 3-540-14036-0 Springer-Verlag Berlin Heidelberg New York

Springer-Verlag Berlin Heidelberg New York
a member of BertelsmannSpringer Science+Business Media GmbH

http://www.springer.de

© Springer-Verlag Berlin Heidelberg 2003
Printed in Germany

Typesetting: Camera-ready by author, data conversion by Christian Grosche, Hamburg
Printed on acid-free paper   SPIN: 10929407   06/3142   5 4 3 2 1 0

Preface

The discipline of software configuration management (SCM) provides one of the best success stories in the field of software engineering. With the availability of over 100 commercial SCM systems that together form a billion-dollar marketplace, and the explicit recognition of SCM by such standards as the CMM and ISO-9000, the discipline has established itself as one of the essential cornerstones of software engineering.

While SCM is a well-established discipline, innovative software engineering approaches constitute new challenges that require support in the form of new or improved tools, techniques, and processes. These challenges emerge in component-based development, distributed systems, dynamically bound and reconfigured systems, embedded systems, software architecture, Web-based systems, XML, engineering/product data management, system engineering, process support, concurrent and cooperative engineering, etc.

Since the first SCM workshop was held in 1988, the workshop series has provided a recurring forum for researchers and practitioners to present technical contributions, to exchange and discuss ideas, and to establish contacts for further cooperation. The current volume contains papers from two workshops which were both co-located with the International Conference on Software Engineering, but differed in their formats and goals.

SCM-10 was held as an ICSE workshop at Toronto, Canada in May 2001. It was deliberately decided to have an informal workshop in order to open a forum for discussing new practices, new challenges, and new boundaries for SCM. This was achieved by a blend of invited talks, talks on selected position papers, and lively discussions. Originally, informal proceedings were produced which were delivered to the workshop participants. Later on, 5 out of 22 submissions were selected for publication in this joint volume. All authors were asked to extend their contributions to full papers and to revise them thoroughly.

While the SCM-10 experiment proved very successful, the SCM community felt that it should go for a formal workshop once again. In fact, this would open up the opportunity to document current research and fertilize the development of this discipline. As a consequence, the follow-up workshop SCM-11 was held as a co-located event with ICSE at Portland, Oregon in May 2003. The Call for Papers received a lively response with 36 submissions, out of which 15 were accepted for publication (12 long and 3 short papers). These papers appear in the second part of this volume, ordered by topic. In addition to paper presentations, the workshop provided sufficient time for inspiring discussions.

The chairs of both workshops would like to acknowledge the invaluable contributions of all authors and speakers, the program committees, the organizers of the ICSE conferences, and Springer-Verlag.

May 2003

Bernhard Westfechtel
André van der Hoek

Program Committee of SCM 2003

Geoff Clemm, Rational, USA
Reidar Conradi, NTNU Trondheim, Norway
Ivica Crnkovic, Malardalen University, Sweden
Wolfgang Emmerich, University College London, UK
André van der Hoek, University of California, Irvine, USA
Annita Persson, Ericsson AB, Mölndal, Sweden
Bernhard Westfechtel (Chair), RWTH Aachen, Germany
Jim Whitehead, University of California, Santa Cruz, USA
Andreas Zeller, University of Saarbrücken, Germany

Program Committee of SCM 2001

Geoff Clemm, Rational, USA
Ivica Crnkovic, Malardalen University, Sweden
Wolfgang Emmerich, University College London, UK
Jacky Estublier, LSR-IMAG, France
André van der Hoek (Chair), University of California, Irvine, USA
Jeff Magee, Imperial College, London, UK
Bernhard Westfechtel, RWTH Aachen, Germany
Jim Whitehead, University of California, Santa Cruz, USA
Andreas Zeller, University of Saarbrücken, Germany

SCM Workshops

SCM-1, Grassau, Germany (1988)
SCM-2, Princeton, USA (1990)
SCM-3, Trondheim, Norway (1991)
SCM-4, Baltimore, USA (1993)
SCM-5, Seattle, USA (1995)
SCM-6, Berlin, Germany (1996)
SCM-7, Boston, USA (1997)
SCM-8, Brussels, Belgium (1998)
SCM-9, Toulouse, France (1999)
SCM-10, Toronto, Canada (2001)
SCM-11, Portland, Oregon (2003)

Table of Contents

Best Papers of SCM 2001

Defining and Supporting Concurrent Engineering Policies in SCM 1
   Jacky Estublier, Sergio García, and Germán Vega

Configuration Management in Component Based Product Populations 16
   Rob van Ommering

Software Architecture and Software Configuration Management 24
   Bernhard Westfechtel and Reidar Conradi

Supporting Distributed Collaboration through Multidimensional Software
Configuration Management 40
   Mark C. Chu-Carroll and James Wright

Software Configuration Management Related to the Management of
Distributed Systems and Service-Oriented Architectures 54
   Vladimir Tosic, David Mennie, and Bernard Pagurek

Version Models I

Uniform Comparison of Configuration Management Data Models 70
   E. James Whitehead, Jr. and Dorrit Gordon

Towards Intelligent Support for Managing Evolution of Configurable
Software Product Families 86
   Tero Kojo, Tomi Männistö, and Timo Soininen

Integrating Software Construction and Software Deployment 102
   Eelco Dolstra

Version Models II

Data Product Configuration Management and Versioning in Large-Scale
Production of Satellite Scientific Data 118
   Bruce R. Barkstrom

Merging Collection Data Structures in a Content Management System 134
   Axel Wienberg

Compatibility of XML Language Versions 148
   Daniel Dui and Wolfgang Emmerich

Architecture

Using Federations for Flexible SCM Systems 163
  Jacky Estublier, Anh-Tuyet Le, and Jorge Villalobos

Dissecting Configuration Management Policies 177
  Ronald van der Lingen and André van der Hoek

Concurrency and Distribution

Improving Conflict Detection in Optimistic Concurrency Control Models . . 191
  Ciaran O'Reilly, Philip Morrow, and David Bustard

Data Topology and Process Patterns for Distributed Development 206
  Darcy Wiborg Weber

Component-Based Systems

Managing the Evolution of Distributed and Interrelated Components 217
  Sundararajan Sowrirajan and André van der Hoek

A Lightweight Infrastructure for Reconfiguring Applications 231
  Marco Castaldi, Antonio Carzaniga, Paola Inverardi,
  and Alexander L. Wolf

Education

A Software Configuration Management Course 245
  Ulf Asklund and Lars Bendix

New Applications

Applications of Configuration Information to Security 259
  Dennis Heimbigner

Towards Software Configuration Management for Test-Driven
Development 267
  Tammo Freese

Author Index

Author Index 275

Defining and Supporting
Concurrent Engineering Policies in SCM

Jacky Estublier, Sergio García, and Germ‡n Vega

LSR-IMAG, 220 rue de la Chimie, BP53
38041 Grenoble Cedex 9, France
{jacky.estublier,sergio.garcia,german.vega}@imag.fr

Abstract. Software Configuration Management addresses roughly two areas, the first and older one concerns the storage of the entities produced during the software project; the second one concerns the control of the activities performed for the production / change of these entities. Work space support can be seen as subsuming most of the later dimension. Indeed, work space is the place where activities take place; controlling the activities, to a large extent, is work space control. This short paper presents our concurrent engineering experience in Dassault Syst•mes, as well as our new approach in the modeling and support of concurrent engineering for large teams.

1   The Problem

The Dassault Syst•mes Company develops a family of large systems, notably Catia, the world leader in computer aided design CAM. This system alone contains more than 4 millions LOCs, is developed simultaneously by 1000 engineers which produce a new release every 4 months. The last two numbers show that Dassault Syst•mes experiences very high concurrent engineering constraints. Indeed, the time where a software engineer was ÒowningÓ the set of files needed for his job, for the duration of his job is far away. Take the Dassault Syst•mes example:

In average, at any point in time, there exist about 800 workspaces each containing in average 2000 files. Obviously each file may be present in more than one workspace at a given point in time; our numbers show that a given file is contained in 50 to 100 different workspaces simultaneously. The consistency of data submitted to concurrent access is known for long by the data base community, which have established the transaction consistency criteria. In our case, consistency would mean that a file could be changed in a single workspace at a time. Unfortunately, the duration of a activity can be days and weeks: a file would be locked for too long and severe dead lock would occur.

In the Dassault Syst•mes context, this hypothesis has been measured. At any point in time, in average, a file is changed simultaneously in 3 workspaces, with maximum around 30; but most files are not changed at all. In average, a few hundred files are changed in a workspace before it is committed. Thus, still in average, a workspace conflicts permanently with about 100 other workspaces. Not allowing simultaneous

B.Westfechtel, A. van der Hoek (Eds.): SCM 2001/2003, LNCS 2649, pp. 1-15, 2003.
© Springer-Verlag Berlin Heidelberg 2003

changes for a file would reduce concurrent engineering almost to null, most of the 1000 engineers being forced to wait.

The direct consequence of this is that merges occur frequently, depending on the policy and the kind of software. The average for an application file is 2 merges a year, for a kernel file 0.4 a year. These numbers may seem low, but averages are meaningless because most files are not changed or merged at all. Conversely, files under work are subject to many changes and merges. We have records of more than 200 merges a year for the same file, which means about 1 merge per workday. Globally, about one thousand merges occur each day at Dassault Syst•mes.

We think these numbers clearly show that concurrent change does exist on a very serious scale. Controlling this situation is a real critical issue. For us concurrent engineering control means:

Merge control (what is to be merged, when...)
Activity structuring and control.
High level policy modeling and enforcement.

We will see shortly theses topics. For more info on activity structuring and control see [11][12][15][18].

1.1 Merge Control

The above values apply to files whereas, in this work and at Dassault Syst•mes, we deal with objects (files are atomic attributes in our object model). Our experience shows that concurrent changes to the same attribute of different objects (typically the source code) as well as changes to different attributes of the same object (like responsible, state, name, file name, protection etc.) are very common. Merging must address both cases. For example, restructuring, renaming and changing files are common but may be independent activities undertaken by different persons. Raising the granularity from file to object makes appear new kinds of concurrent changes, which may produce new kinds of merges (typically composition changes). It is our claim that objects concurrent change control subsumes traditional file control and provides homogeneous and elegant solutions to many difficulties that currently hamper concurrent software engineering.

Suppose we denote by A0, A1,... Ai the different values of an attribute A, and Ai = Ci(A) the value of A after change Ci is performed. The classic (ACID) transaction concept says that Ci and Cj are performed in transaction if the result A3 = Cj (Ci (A)) or A3 = Ci (Cj (A)). We extend that definition saying that, given an object A, changes Ci and Cj on the that object can be performed in a concurrent way if there exists a function M (merge) such that M (C1(A0), C2(A0)) = Ci(Cj(A0)) = Cj(Ci(A0)) = M (C2(A0), C1(A0)) .

This means that the result of a merge is the same as if changes Ci and Cj were performed in sequence on A0, irrespective of the order. If an exact merge function existed for each attribute, concurrent engineering would always lead to consistent results! Unfortunately, for a given attribute, such a merge function either (1) exists, (2) is an approximation, or (3) does not exist at all. Typically, the composition attribute has an exact merge, sourceFile merge is an approximate function (the usual merges), and most attributes like fileName have no merge at all.

2   High Level Concurrent Engineering Policies

Experience shows that customers find extremely difficult to design their own concurrent engineering strategies. Our claim is that planning and implementing different strategies is a hard task in existent SCM tools because of the lack of an adequate level of abstraction. Any decision made using classic SCM concepts (branches and revisions) is error prone, due the unexpected effects it might have.

We propose a basic work model (the group) and a set of operations on which concurrent engineering policies can be easily designed. This vision allows us to take CE policies conception to a more adequate level, using abstractions that are more natural to concurrent work (groupÕsworkspaces and operations among them) instead of the traditional low level ones (branches, revisions and merges). We have defined a language that lets us express the most common forms of group based C.E. policies in a simple straightforward way.

2.1   Product Data Model

A product is a typed and named object composed of attributes (name-value pairs) and a complex object representing the document in a domain or tool specific format. Attributes are either *common* or *versionable*; document formats can be data based schema, XML, or any other, but most often it is a simple file system representation i.e. a hierarchy of files and directories, where each file is seen as operating system attributes (name, author, rights É) and a content.

2.2   Workspaces

A workspace contains one or more documents. A workspace is made of two parts: the *working area*, and the workspace *local history*.

The *working area* is a repository in which documents are represented following their original format, and under the tool required for their management; and attributes can be seen and changed through our specific attribute management tool. In Dassault Syst•mes the working workspace is simply a FS containing the documents. [4]

The workspace *local history* is a repository in which is stored some *states* of the associated workspace (i.e. its value at a given point in time). The local history is meant to be local to the participantÕsmachine and therefore can be used while working off-line. A workspace manager is responsible of providing the mapping operations between the working workspace and the local history repository.

In a large development environment it is possible to have different policies regarding the frequency and the motivation of creating new versions; it is also possible to have different version managers according to the different versioning requirements and different emplacements. Our system doesnÕtaddress the problem of versioning; it is capable to work with heterogeneous version managers, s long as a few functions are available (i.e. the CI and CO functions) [5]. In our simple CE tool, the local history can be either CVS or Zip, and the working workspace is a FS containing the documents, plus the attribute management tool.

From the Òoutside worldÓ only a single workspace state is visible, it is always one of the states stored in the local history; not necessarily the latest one. The working workspace is not directly visible.

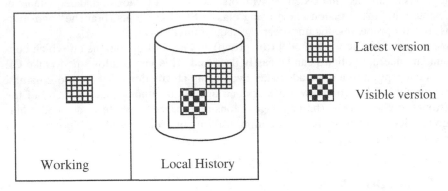

Fig. 1. Workspace

2.3   Groups

A group is a set of workspaces working on the same products to achieve a common goal. One of them, the *parent* workspace, is in charge of synthesize and integrate the work made by the child workspaces. The *child* workspaces can only communicate with the parent.

Comparing with databases, the parent workspace plays the role of the central DB and the Childs the role of the cache for the concurrent transactions.

The complete group behaves as its Parent alone; from outside, the Parent is a "normal" workspace in which is performed the whole job of the group. It is thus possible to build groups where Childs can be parent of a lower level group. The work structure is therefore a tree where nodes are either parent or child workspaces, and arrows the containment relationships. Containment between two groups may mean either work decomposition into concurrent activities (each group performing a different task), or different level of validation (top level nodes being more validated that leaves).

In practice, companies use both approaches simultaneously; Dassault Syst•mes uses currently at least a 6 level work space hierarchy; the 3 top level being called GA (general availability), BSF (Best So Far), and Integration which represent different levels of validation, while the 3 (or more) lowest levels represent a decomposition in task and sub-task for the current work to do.

It is also interesting to point out that a group defines de facto a cluster of highly related work spaces; the Parent work space playing the role of global repository for the group. It allows for a real distribution of repositories as shown in [6]; there is no longer any need for a common central repository; distributed and remote work is handled that way. It is our belief that concurrent engineering of very large teams cannot be handled without such a distribution of repositories, not found in classic SCM tools [9].

CE policies are defined for a group, a whole hierarchy of groups can have different polices reflecting the different methodologies and consistency constraints of each level. Typically, the groups closer to the top level, which can be seen as holding the official copies of the documents, have more restrictive policies then the ÒbottomÓ groups, who need higher concurrency levels.

2.4   CE Global Policies

A product is a composite entity that has a number of internal consistency constraints. In a similar way as transactions, a number of changes must be done before a product recovers a new consistent state; this means that only complete new consistent states can be communicated to other workspaces, not only a sub sets of changes. Therefore operations between workspaces involve only complete product states.

Provided a group with Parent workspace P and a child workspace W, these operations are the following:

Synchronize (W,D): If Document D does not exist in workspace W, it is copied from P. Otherwise, the currently visible D version of P, is integrated in W working workspace. In other words, changes made on D in P since last synchronize operation, are integrated in W.

Integrate (W,D): All modifications made on the visible version of D in workspace W are integrated into the D in the ParentÕs working workspace. In practice, it means that changes performed in W, since last Integrate, are propagated in P.

These operations are critical for any CE policy. It is important to know who is entitled to decide to synchronize or integrate two workspaces (the Child or the Parent one (ÒwÓ or ÒpÓ), and if the synchronization or integration are performed interactively (ÒiÓ), or ÒbatchÓ (ÒbÓ), as well as to decide the level of consistency of such critical operations.

By default, interactive merging allows unsynchronised integrations (s), merges (m) and conflicts (c), and batch (b) do not. For example ÒIÓ alone means that integration is initiated by the Parent workspace, in interactive mode, merges and conflicts allowed. Unsynchronised (s) means that the receiving workspace is the current common ancestor, which means the operation is simply a copy of the current workspace to the receiving one.

ÒIbsmÓ means that the integrate operation (I) is asked by the Parent workspace in batch mode(b); it can involve merges (m) but not conflicts. For example, CVS enforces ÒIwsÓ and ÒSbmcÓ assuming the Parent WS is the CVS repository; i.e. Integration is at the child initiative (w), in batch mode (b), and allows no merge nor conflict; while Synchronize are batch (b), but accept merges (m) and conflicts (c).

Of course ÒmÓ implies ÒsÓ, and ÒcÓ implies ÒmÓ, thus ÒsmcÓ and ÒcÓ are equivalent. In order to make policies more readable, by convention ÒIpÓ is equivalent to ÒIÓ and ÒSwÓ to ÒSÓ; and ÒSÓ and ÒPÓ alone is interpreted as ÒSwismcÓ and ÒIpismcÓ.

The other possible operations are:

Publish (D): The integrator stores its working state of document D in the local history and made it visible. All child workspaces are notified that there is a new visible version to synchronize from.

<u>Propose (W, D)</u>: Workspace W stores its working state of document D in the local history; that version becomes the visible version, and the integrator is notified that there is a new version of D, on the workspace W ready to be integrated.

<u>Change (C, D, W)</u>: Pseudo operation Change means workspace W *is allowed* to perform a modification on document D, this is, it can modify its attributes.

2.5   Policy Definition

Defining a policy means defining the valid history of operations a workspace can perform on a given product. This can be made by defining a state machine representing the different valid operations (the inputs of the state machine) for a given state of the workspace (a particular step in the work cycle of the workspace). A global policy defines the rules for a particular child workspace and on a particular product. We can then define a global policy using the following conventions for the operations:

I : Integrate, as discussed above (with possibly suffixes p, w, i, s, b, m, c)
S : Synchronize, as discussed above (with possibly suffixes p, w, i, s, b, m, c)
Pu : Publish
Pr : Propose
C : Change

The parameters of the operations are the workspace and the product for which the policy is being defined. We use regular expressions syntax as the base for our language. For examples:

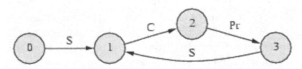

Fig. 2. (S C Pr)*

In this simple global policy, a workspace must first to Synchronize (S) to have the current visible version of the product in Parent, and only then it can start its work, modifying what it needs to change(C), and finally, propose (Pr) its working version to be integrated. The cycle then starts again. Integrate is not indicated, it means that the Parent workspace decides, based on the Childs ready for integration, which one to integrate. But, in this policy, integration may involve merges and conflicts that the user working in the Parent workspace will have to solve.

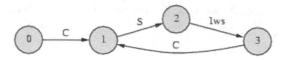

Fig. 3. (C S Iwbs)*

In this policy, the workspace starts working on the product (C) followed by a synchronize (S) and an integrate (I), both executed at the current workspace initiative. Since S is performed right before I, merges, if any, are performed in the child workspace during the S operation. This is consistent since S alone stands for Swismc i.e. interactive with merges and conflict allowed. In this policy, Integrate will not involve any merges; this is why it is often used.

The Change Operation
The pseudo operation C indicates when, in the execution of a policy, modifications can be made. This does not means that actual changes on the product attributes are mandatory, but only the possibility to perform them. We then always interpret C as (C)? meaning a change is always optional.

Integrator Initiated Operations and Behavior of the Integrator Workspace
The user working in the Parent workspace (when existing) plays the role of group manager. He/she manages the reference version of the group, he/she decides what product to integrate (if ÒIiÓ), notifies when new versions are available (PuÓ). It will be seen later that he/she has also special role in managing locks, solving conflicts and handling failures, using for that purpose, special operations.
The global policy defines the behaviour of a single child workspace. For a given state, only some operations are allowed, and its execution fires the transition to the next state, where new operations are allowed. Some of the group operations, however, are not under the control of child workspaces, but are initiated by the integrator. It is desirable to clarify some aspects of the interaction between integrator and child workspaces, such as the fact a newly integrated version has to be immediately published, or that a workspace must wait for a Publish to continue working.
Our strategy is to gather all these details in a single global policy, in order to have a single place to look to know the policy.

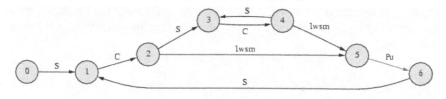

Fig. 4. ((S C)+ Iwsm Pu)*

In this policy, a workspace can synchronize and modify a product several times, but it needs to do at least one synchronization/modification cycle(Ò(S C)+Ó). When the workspace integrates its work, at its initiative (Iwsm), a publish is automatically executed, to notify all workspaces that a new version is available in the integrated workspace.

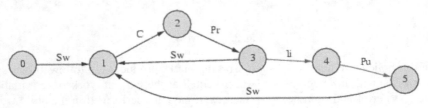

Fig. 5. (S C Pr (Ipic Pu) ?)*

In this policy, the workspace does not need to wait for ÒpublishÓ; after proposing a modification (pr), it can synchronize again and continue to work. A new ÒproposeÓ will however replace the visible version with the new visible state of the product in the workspace. When the user working in the Parent workspace integrates one of the proposed versions, it is published immediately.

2.6   Local Policies

The global policy assumes all attributes can be changed and that conflicts, if any, are solved during the ÒsynchronizeÓ or ÒintegrateÓ operations. According to the nature of the attribute, merge functions may not exist, in which case the work will be lost during synchronization. If the merge function is approximate, the merge operation is risky and may require manual intervention. Even if perfect, merges may be not desirable without control.

Sensible data can be protected using the consistency constraints for S and I operations defined in the global policy. An operation that violates the imposed constraints is banned, and a special recovery mechanism must be applied. This is an optimistic strategy, while recovery might be an expensive operation; violations of the consistency constraints are expected not to occur often. In local policies a pessimistic approach using locks can be used to protect consistency of the data held by the most sensible attributes.

Local policies have a name and are defined for families of attributes, for examples:

AttributeName => PolicyName

Standard expansion rules for files and directories apply, with the product directory as the root directory. Operating system file attributes are precised using Ò:Ó after the file expansion. :

FileSuffix:FileAttributeName => PolicyName

Examples:

Date => Policy1

src/*.c:name => Policy2

Which means that the ÒDateÓ attribute is managed following the Policy1 policy, and the name of C files Ò*c:nameÓ found under the ÒsrcÓ directory are managed following the Policy2 policy.

Local Operations

Reserve (W, P, A) : A lock is set on attribute A of product P by workspace W, if there is no lock already. When a lock is set, only the workspace that owns it can modify the attribute.

Free(W, P, A) : A lock is removed on attribute A of product P by workspace W, if W owns that lock.

Correctness

The complex nature of the data manipulated, the semantic dependences among the attributes, and the long duration of the tasks in concurrent engineering make global notions of correctness such as serializability and atomicity inconvenient. Instead, user defined correctness criteria based on semantic knowledge of the attributes; their relationships and the tasks performed must be allowed. Studies on cooperative transactions have found in patterns and conflicts a natural way to specify different correctness criteria. Patterns define the operations that must happen, and the order in which they must happen for a transaction to be correct. On the other side, conflicts specify the forbidden interleaving between different transactions [1][2][3][10][16].

We have not defined a general language for defining any possible correctness criteria for any cooperative transaction, as proposed in [1], where the defined grammar can take into account all possible interleaving among transactions. This would make policy definition difficult, and threaten the dynamic nature of our system where new groups and policies can be easily created as the development advances. Instead we propose a tiny set of interpretations of the local policies corresponding to different levels of consistency, inspired by typical consistency constraints found in Software Engineering.

Our global policy defines the pattern of behaviour for all attributes, for example in the policy Ò(S C I)*Ó states that a synchronization, modifications and integration, in that order, are necessary for a workspace to correctly finish a cycle of work. Introducing Reserve and Free operations in the local policies we define the conflicts, reducing the possible interleaving to a sub-set that enforces our correctness criteria:

Very Strict Policies

Very strict policy execution might be desirable for groups of attributes that are related by strong consistency constraints.

An example is the name of the files composing a software module. Restructuring that module involves changing file names, and clearly this task should be undertaken in a single workspace at a time.

A group of attributes under a very strict policy can only be modified by a single workspace, thus locking the whole group of attributes before starting the transaction.

Module_names = very_strict: (R S C I F)*

We protect the source file names of certain module with the local policy:

/project/libxyz/*.java:name : Module_names

If a workspace tries to modify the name of a java file in the module libxyz, it needs to reserve all the name attributes, synchronize, modify and integrate, and finally all attributes are freed.

Strict Policies

A very-strict policy guarantees consistency of relationships among attributes within a group, but prohibits any concurrent work. In some cases concurrent modifications on different workspaces is still considered consistent as long as the set of attributes modified are not overlapping.

For example, a given word files should not be edited concurrently in different workspaces, but it is no problem to edit different word files concurrently. It corresponds to a strict interpretation of policy like:

$$EditDoc = strict: (R\ Swismc\ C\ Ipismc\ F)*$$
$$/project/stat/*.xls : EditDoc$$

EditDoc policy means that all Excel documents that are to be changed in a session are to be first reserved, then a synchronize is performed (thus getting in the current version of the documents), then editing of the document is allowed; the session ends by integrating all the changed documents.

Flexible Policies

The strict interpretation requires an a-priori knowledge of all the documents that are involved in a session; it is not possible to try to reserve a new document as soon as the editing session is started. For most purposes, this is too strict.

For a given attribute A, $\grave{O}R ... S ... C\acute{O}$ is equivalent to $\grave{O}S ... R ... C\acute{O}$ if between synchronization and reserve the attribute value did not change in the Parent workspace.

This property is at the base of flexible policies. In a flexible policy, the reserve is automatically attempted when the attribute is to be changed; this reserve succeeds only if the value of that attribute did not changed in the Parent WS since last operation S. Therefore the policy

$$EditDocFlex = flexible: (R\ S\ C\ I\ F)*$$
$$/project/doc/*.doc : EditDocFlex$$

looks similar to EditDoc presented above, but here, as soon as a new word document is about to be changed, a reserve operation is attempted. There is no need to perform explicit reserve operations. This is much more flexible indeed, but there is two drawbacks, with respect to a strict policy:

There is a risk of inconsistency, if some documents have strong semantic consistency constraints, and one of them is not reserved,

There is a risk of dead locks if two concurrent sessions require an overlapping set of documents.

Reservation Propagation

Reserving an attribute in a group means reserving that attribute for all the group workspaces, including the Parent. But reserving the attribute in the parent may reserve it in the group to which the parent pertains, and successively. Thus, reserving an attribute may propagate to a large number of workspaces, especially because higher level groups have stricter policies, and are more likely to define policies with locks.

Optimistic and Controlled Strategies without Locks
The major reason to use locks, is to make sure that an integrate operation will not involve any merge and conflict. But our specialization of operation I and S allows such a control, a posteriori, i.e. an optimistic controlled policy, as opposed to locking strategies which correspond to pessimistic ones; the different lock interpretations ranging from very pessimistic (very-strict), to relaxed-pessimistic (flexible).

For example
$$Pesimistic= strict: (R\ Swismc\ C\ Iwb\ Pu\ F)*$$
is similar to
$$Optimistic= (\ Swismc\ C\ Iwb<\&S>\ Pu\ )*$$

The difference is that in the Optimistic policy ÒIwbÓ may fail, if there are merges or conflict involved. If case of failure, the policy indicates that an operation synchronize must be performed, and Integrate attempted again Ò<&S>Ó.

Implementation
We translate the policies, including their correctness criteria, into a state machine. Our implementation is efficient, because a single state machine is sufficient for a group of attribute, whatever the number of actual attributes in the group, and the state machine interpretation is straightforward. Policy interpretation is very cheap. Further, these state machines are created and executed on the workspace machine, and need little interaction with other work space to be executed. Reserve and free are those operations, as well as a delayed reserved (to check the attribute value in the parent); but in all cases, only the parent workspace is involved.

2.7   Summary

The language is based on the distinction between global and local policies. Global policies come from the fact consistency requires a product to be managed as an atomic entity; local policies come from the fact each attribute may have different consistency constraints, either technical (related to the availability of reliability of their merge function) or logical (sensitivity and criticality of the attribute, semantic relationships, and so on). The system allows for both and enforces the consistency of the whole.

The language is also fairly independent from a given data model. Indeed, it is based on attributes of entities and can therefore be adapted to almost any data model, even if the tool we have built works on a very pragmatic one: file system attributes and a number a specific attributes.

The central issue in concurrent engineering is always to find the compromise between high concurrent work (and thus very optimistic policies, or no policy at all), and reliability (and thus restrictive policies). We address this issue first, allowing different policies for different attributes, second allowing a large range of pessimistic-optimistic policies.

The optimistic / pessimistic range is split in two. In the pessimistic side, we use locks, and we provide three different interpretations of the lock instruction: very-strict, strict, and flexible. But locks propagate and may seriously reduce concurrency.

In the optimist side, we provide a number of restriction in operations Synchronize and Integrate (batch/interactive, parent/child, synchronized/unsynchronised, merge/no_merge, conflict/no_conflict) which allows to avoid problems, still retaining maximum concurrency, but in this case, the policy must include failure recovery.

Altogether, the language covers a very wide spectrum of concurrency policies, going much farther than traditional database strategies, and capable to represent many database strategies (including, ACID, dirty read, non repeatable read, 2PL and others). Nevertheless, the language does not allow for any and all concurrency policy, but do correspond to actual practices in software engineering. It is our goal to propose a very simple language, intuitive enough for users to define easily the policies they need, not to define anything, thus this selection of interpretations, which corresponds to best practices.

3   The CE Tool

We have built a prototype implementing the ideas presented above. Our system exposes the following features:

It contains an interpreter of our language that runs locally to each workspace, enforcing the policies defined for the group that contains the workspace. An efficient implementation of the interpreter has been
It implements the basic synchronization services
It implements a distributed locking system.
It manages dynamic creation of new groups as development evolves

Special attention is paid to the awareness capabilities of the tool. Awareness is characterized as Òan understanding of the activities of others, which provide a context for your own activityÓ [7]. The assumption is that providing the users with the appropriate contextual information allows them to make more sophisticated local decisions. The awareness concept has been long studied and proved beneficial in the CSCW domain, but has never gained the same popularity in SCM systems.

For the vision of context to be useful it must provide only the information relevant for the user to take decisions based on it, without the unimportant information introducing noise. We use the group model to filter all the information coming from all the workspaces to the subset that is useful for each user.

The most basic contextual information needed for cooperative work is group membership, our CE Tool provides every user with a vision of the workspaces in his group, as shown in figure 6, this list is synchronized with the actual state of the group held by the integrator. Additionally, the user can find what documents each user has proposed.

The tool also provides a vision of the state of the documentÕs attributes. Based on the operationsÕ history in a group, the attributes of a child workspace version of a document can be in one of the following states:

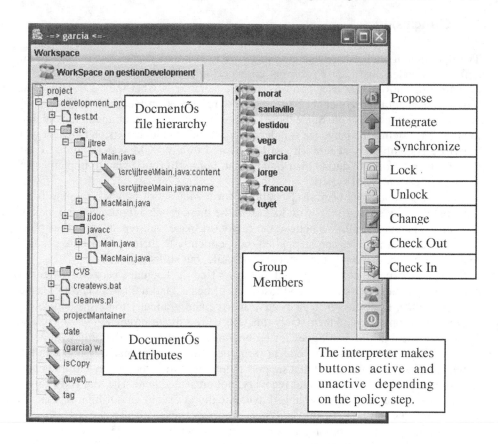

Fig. 6. The CE tool

Obsolete: The attribute has changed in the parent workspace and not in the child workspace.

Updated: The attribute has the same value in the child workspace than in the parent workspace.

Modified: The attribute has been modified in the child workspace and not in the parent workspace.

Conflict: The attribute has been modified both in the parent workspace and in the child workspace.

Currently, the system can run using CVS or our home-grown zip version manager as the tools to store the local history, but integration with other version managers should be not difficult.

4   Conclusion

The intention of such a language is to propose, to non-expert users, a simple way to define and understand their concurrent engineering policies. Indeed the language is based on operations that user know very well, since it is what they use daily, and hides implementation concepts like branches, revisions, predecessor relationship, common ancestor and so on. Since these operations are, in a way or another, available in all SCM systems, the language is independent from any single version manager and therefore is completely general; it can be adapted to any SCM system, and at least used by team leaders to define their policy first, before to find a way to implement it using their current SCM system.

The language; despite been simple, allows for a wide set of policies, ranging from the most restrictive (very-strict with locks), to the more relaxed (optimistic, no locks), or even no policies at all. We believe the fact workspaces are typed, as well as policies, the fact that policies can be applied independently to different attribute groups, makes the system extremely powerful and versatile, but still simple.

Indeed the experience so far proved that users find the language very convenient to define the policies; users understand fast what it means, and it allows them to reason on their policy, to discuss their respective merits, and gradually to define and select the one most convenient to them. Only this is already a major progress.

We believe that this work goes a step beyond, deriving from the policy an automatic implementation, still independent from the actual version manager in use in the company. We have built a tool that support policy definition and policy enforcement, including the special operations for recovery, not presented here. The tool is dynamic, in that groups are created and changed dynamically at execution. Of high interest, is the fact policies can be statically analysed, and properties statically derived. Among the properties, we can mention that we know if merges are possible or not, we know where and who is the common ancestor and we know which files will be involve in next Synchronize and Integrate. From these properties, optimisations can be performed including the determination of the files involved in the next Synchronize / Integrate, the computation of deltas before hand, and the avoidance of useless checks like changes or merges. Indeed, in many cases, most of the work involved in the heavy operations Synchronize and Integrate can be computed before hand. This is important since experience shows that users feel that Synchronize and Integrate are operations that slow down their work; our optimisations make these operations much faster from the user point of view and improve significantly user comfort.

The properties are also used to improve awareness strategies. Indeed our tool includes awareness facilities only sketched in this paper.

Altogether, we believe that our system improves the state of the art of concurrent engineering in many dimensions, both from theoretical and practical point of views. From conceptual point of view, we found a language simple, powerful, with well-defined semantics. From the practical point of view, this system improves user understanding of CE issues, improves the enforcement of these policies, improves the independence between policies and versioning tools, improves efficiency of the system, and improves user comfort and awareness.

References

[1] M. Nodine, S. Ramaswamy, and S. Zdonik. ÒA Cooperative Transaction Model for Design DatabasesÓ. Edited by A.Elmagarmid. ÒDatabase Transaction ModelsÓChapter 3, pages 54-85, Morgan Kauffman Publishers, Inc.

[2] S. Heiler, S. Haradhvala, S. Zdonik. B. Blaustein, and A. Rosenthal ÒA Flexible Framework for Transaction Management in Engineering EnvironmentsÓ. Edited by A. Elmagarmid. ÒDatabase Transaction ModelsÓ. Chapter 88-121, Morgan Kauffman Publishers, Inc.

[3] A. Skarra. ÒLocalized correctness specifications for cooperating transactions in an object-oriented databaseÓ. Office Knowledge Engineering, 4(1):79-106, 1991

[4] J. Estublier. ÒWorkspace Management in Software Engineering EnvironmentsÓ. In SCM-Workshop. LNCS 1167, Springer-Verlag, Berlin, Germany, March 1996

[5] J. Estublier and R. Casallas. ÒThree Dimensional VersioningÓ. In SCM-4 and SCM-5 Workshops. J. Estublier (editor), September, 1995. LNCS 1005, Springer-Verlag, Berlin, Germany

[6] J. Estublier. ÒDistributed Objects for Concurrent EngineeringÓ. In SCM-9. Toulouse, France. September 1999

[7] P. Dourish and V. Belloti: ÒAwareness and Coordination in Shared Work SpacesÓ. Proceedings of the ACM Conference on Computer Supported Cooperative Work (CSCW'92)

[8] C. Neuwirth, D. Kaufer, R. Chandhok, and J. Morris, ÒIssues in the design of Computer Support for Co-authoring and CommentingÓ, Proc. CSCWÕ90 Computer Supported Cooperative Work (Los Angeles, Ca., October 1990)

[9] J. Estublier and R. Casallas. ÒThe Adele Software Configuration ManagementÓ. Configuration ManagementÓ.Configuration Management. Edited by W. Tichy; J. Wiley and Sons. 1994. Trends in software

[10] A. Skarra. Concurrency control for cooperating transactions in an object-oriented database. SIGPLAN Notices, 24(4), April 1989

[11] J. Estublier, S. Dami, and M. Amiour. ÒAPEL: A graphical yet Executable Formalism for Process ModellingÓ. Automated Software Engineering, ASE journal. Vol. 5, Issue 1, 1998

[12] J. Estublier, S. Dami, and M. Amiour. High Level Processing for SCM Systems. SCM 7, LNCS 1235. pages 81-98, May, Boston, USA, 1997

[13] P. Molli, H. Skaf-Molli, and C. Bouthier: ÒState Treemap: an Awareness Widget for Multi-Synchronous GroupwareÓ. 7th International Workshop on Groupware (CRIWG'01). September 2001

[14] P. Dourish and S. Blay, ÒPortholes: Supporting Awareness in Distributed Work GroupsÓ, Proc. CHIÕ92 Human Factors in Computer Systems (Monterey, CA, May 1993)

[15] C. Godart, F. Charoy, O.Perrin, and H. Skaf-Molli: ÒCooperative Workflows to Coordinate Asynchronous Cooperative Applications in a Simple WayÓ. 7th International Conference on Parallel and Distributed Systems (ICPADSÕ00). Iwate, Japan, July 2000

[16] M. Franklin, M, Carey, and M. Livny: ÒTransactional Client-Server Cache Consistency: Alternatives and PerformanceÓ. ACM Transactions on Database Systems, Vol. 22, No. 3. September 1997

[17] C. Godart, G. Canals, F. Charoy, and P. Molly. ÒAbout some relationships between configuration management, software process and cooperative work: The COO EnvironmentÓ. In 5th Workshop on Software Configuration and Maintenance, Seatle, Washington D.C. (USA), LNCS 1005, Springer-Verlag, Berlin, Germany, April 1995

[18] C. Godart, O. Perrin, and H. Skaf. ÓCoo: A Workflow operator to improve cooperation modeling in virtual enterprisesÓ. In 9th IEEE International Workshop on Research Issues in Data Engineering Information Technology for Virtual EnterprisesÓ (RIDE-VEÕ99), 1999

Configuration Management in Component Based Product Populations

Rob van Ommering

Philips Research Laboratories,
Prof. Holstlaan 4, 5656AA Eindhoven, The Netherlands
Rob.van.Ommering@philips.com

Abstract. The ever-increasing complexity and diversity of consumer products drives the creation of product families (products with many commonalties and few differences) and product populations (products with many commonalties but also with many differences). For the latter, we use an approach based on composition of software components, organized in packages. This influences our configuration management approach. We use traditional CM systems for version management and temporary variation, but we rely on our component technology for permanent variation. We also handle build support and distributed development in ways different from the rest of the CM community.

1 Introduction

Philips produces a large variety of consumer electronics products. Example products are televisions (TVs), video recorders (VCRs), set-top boxes (STBs), and compact disk (CD), digital versatile disk (DVD) and hard disk (HD) players and recorders. The software in these products is becoming more and more complex, their size following Moore's law closely [1]. Additionally, the market demands an increasing diversity of products. We have started to build small software product families to cope with the diversity within a TV or VCR family. But we believe that our future lies in the creation of a product population that allows us to integrate arbitrary combinations of TV, VCR, STB, CD, DVD, and HD functionality into a variety of products.

This paper describes the configuration management approach that we devised to realize such a product population. We first define the notion of product family and product population, and then describe some of our technical concepts. We subsequently discuss five aspects of configuration management, and end with some concluding remarks.

B.Westfechtel, A. van der Hoek (Eds.): SCM 2001/2003, LNCS 2649, pp. 16-23, 2003.

2   Product Family and Population

We define a product *family* as a (small) set of products that have many commonalties and few differences. A software product family can typically be created with a single variant free architecture [9] with explicit variation points [2] to control the diversity. Such variation points can be defined in advance, and products can be instantiated by 'turning the knobs'. Variation points can range from simple parameters up to full plug-in components. An example of a product family is a family of television products, which may vary - among other things - in price, world region, signal standard and display technology.

We define a product *population* as a set of products with many commonalties but also with many differences [4]. Because of the significant differences, a single variant free architecture no longer suffices. Instead we deploy a composition approach, where products are created by making 'arbitrary' combinations of components. An example product population could contain TVs, VCRs, set-top boxes, CD, DVD, and HD players and recorders, and combinations thereof. These products have elements in common, e.g. a front-end that decodes broadcasts into video and audio signals. These products are also very different with respect to for instance display device and storage facility.

It is true that any product population of which *all* members are known at initiation time, can in principle be implemented as a product family, i.e. with a single variant free architecture. In our case, two reasons prevent us from doing so. First of all, our set of products is dynamic - new ideas for innovative products are invented all the time. Secondly, different products are created within different sub organizations, and it is just infeasible - both for business as well for social reasons - to align all developments under a single software architecture.

3   Technical Concepts

In this section we briefly describe the software component model that we use, and show how components are organized into packages and into a component based architecture.

3.1   The Koala Component Model

We use software components to create product populations. Our component model, Koala, is specifically designed for products where resources (memory, time) are not abundant [5, 6]. Basic Koala components are implemented in C, and can be combined into compound components, which in turn can be combined into (more) compound components, until ultimately a product is constructed. The Koala model was inspired by Darwin [3].

Koala components have explicit provides *and* requires interfaces. Provides interfaces allow the environment of the component to use functionality implemented within the component; requires interfaces allow the component to use functionality implemented in the environment. All requires interfaces of a component must be bound explicitly when instantiating a component. We find that making all requires interfaces both explicit and third-party bindable, greatly enhances the reusability of such components.

Provides and requires interfaces of components are actually instances of reusable *interface definitions*. We treat such interface definitions as first class citizens, and define them independently from components. Such interface definitions are also common in Java, and correspond with abstract base classes in object-oriented languages.

Diversity interfaces, a special kind of requires interfaces, play an important role in Koala. Such interfaces contain sets of parameters that can be used to fine-tune the component into a configuration. We believe that components can only be made reusable if they are heavily parameterized, otherwise they either become too product specific, or they become too generic and thus not easily or efficiently deployable.

Note that the Koala terminology slightly differs from that used by others. A Koala component *definition*, or more precisely a component *type* definition, corresponds closely with the notion of *class* in object-oriented languages. A Koala component *instantiation* corresponds with an *object*. What Szyperski calls a *component*, a binary and independently deployable unit of code [10], resembles mostly a Koala package as described in the next section, i.e. a set of classes and interfaces. It is true that we distribute source code for resource-constrained reasons, but users of a package are not allowed to change that source code, only compile it, which inherently is what Szyperski meant with 'binary'.

3.2 Packages

We organize component and interface definitions into *packages*, to structure large-scale software development [7]. A package consists of public and private component and interface definitions. Public definitions can be used by other packages - private definitions are for use in the package itself only. This allows us to manage change and evolution without overly burdening the implementers and users of component and interface definitions.

Koala packages closely resemble Java packages, where component definitions in Koala resemble classes in Java, and interface definitions in Koala resembling interfaces in Java. Unlike in Java, the Koala notion of package is *closed*; users of a package cannot add new elements to the package.

3.3 The Architecture

With Koala we have created a component-based product population that consists of over a dozen packages, each package implementing one specific sub domain of functionality [8]. Products can be created by (1) selecting a set of packages appropriate for the product to be created, (2) instantiating the relevant public component definitions of those packages, and (3) binding the diversity and (4) the of those packages, and (3) binding the diversity and (4) the other requires interfaces of those components. Product variation is managed by making choices in steps (1) - (4).

4   Configuration Management

We now come to the configuration management aspects of our product population development. We distinguish five issues that are traditionally the domain of configuration management systems, and provide our way of dealing with these issues. These issues are:

- Version management.
- Temporary variation.
- Permanent variation.
- Build support.
- Distributed development.

The issues are discussed in subsequent subsections.

4.1   Version Management

In the development of each package, we use a conventional configuration management system to maintain a version history of *all* of the programming assets in that package, such as C header and source files, Koala component and interface definitions, Word component and interface data sheets, et cetera. Each package development team deploys its own configuration management system - see also the section that describes our distributed development approach.

A package team issues formal *releases* of a package, where each release is tagged with a version identification (e.g. 1.1b). The version identification consists of a major number, a minor number, and a 'patch letter'. The major and minor version numbers indicate regular releases in the evolution of the package - the 'patch letter' indicates bug-fix releases for particular users of the package.

Each formal release of a package must be internally consistent. This means that in principle *all* components should compile and build, and run without errors. In practice, not every release is tested completely, but it is tested sufficiently for those products that rely on this specific version of this package.

Customers of a package only see the formal releases of the package. They will download the release from the intranet (usually as ZIP file), and insert it in their local configuration management system. This implies that they will only maintain the formal release history of the package, and will not see all of the detailed (intermediate) versions of the files in the package.

Each release of a package must be backward compatible with the previous release of that package. This is our *golden rule*, and it allows us to simplify our version management - only the last release of each package is relevant. Again in practice, it is sometimes difficult to maintain full backward compatibility, so sometimes we apply our *silver rule*, which states that all existing and relevant clients of the package should build with the new release of the package.

4.2 Temporary Variation

For temporary variation we use the facilities of traditional configuration management systems. We recognize two kinds of temporary variation.

Temporary variation *in the small* arises if one developer wants to fix a bug *while* another developer adds a feature. By having developer-specific branches in the CM system, developers do not see changes made by other developers *until* integration time. This allows them to concentrate on their own change before integrating changes made by others into their system.

Temporary variation *in the large* arises just before the release of a product utilizing the package. Note that packages are used by multiple products - this is what reuse is all about. We cannot run the risk of introducing bugs into a product coming out soon when adding features to a package for a product to be created somewhere in the future. This is why we create a branch in the package version history for a specific product just before it is being released. Bug fix releases for such a product are tagged with 'patch letters', e.g. 1.2a, 1.2b, et cetera. As a rule, no features may be added in such a branch, only bugs may be fixed.

Although the branch may live for a number of weeks or even months - it may take that long to fully test a product - we still call this a temporary branch since the branch should be closed when the product has been released. All subsequent products should be derived from the main branch of the package. There is also *permanent variation* in our product population, but we handle that completely *outside* of the scope of a configuration management system, as described in the next section.

4.3 Permanent Variation

For permanent variation, i.e. the ability to create a variety of products, we do not deploy a traditional configuration management system, but rely instead on our component technology. We have a number of arguments for doing so:

- It makes variation explicit in our architecture, instead of hiding it in the CM system.
- It allows us to make a late choice between compile-time diversity and run-time diversity, whereas a CM system typically only provides compile-time diversity.
- It allows us to exercise diversity outside the context of our CM system (see also the section on **Build Support**).

The second item may require further clarification. Koala diversity interfaces consist of parameters that can be assigned values (expressions) in the Koala component description language. The Koala compiler can evaluate such expressions and translate the parameters into compile-time diversity (#ifdefs) if their value is known at compile-time, or run-time diversity (if statements) otherwise. This allows us to have a *single* notion of diversity in our architecture. We can then still decide at a late time whether to generate a ROM for a *single* product (with only the code for that product), or a ROM for a set of products (with if statements to choose between the products). Note that always generating a ROM for a single product complicates logistics, but on the other hand always generating a ROM for multiple products increases the ROM size and hence the bill of material.

Put differently, we expect that once (binary) components are commonplace, the whole configuration issue will be handled at run-time, and not by a traditional CM system.

With respect to the first item mentioned above, we have four ways of handling diversity [7]:

- Create a single component that determines by itself in which environment it operates (using *optional* interfaces in Koala, modeled after *QueryInterface* in COM).
- Create a single component with diversity interfaces, so that the *user* of the component can fine-tune the component into a configuration.
- Create two different (public) components in the same package, so that the *user* of the package can select the right component.
- Create two different packages for different implementations of the same sub domain functionality, so that *users* may select the right package (before selecting the right public component, and then providing values to diversity parameters of that component).

It depends on individual circums tances which way is used in which part of the architecture.

4.4 Build Support

The fourth issue concerns build support, a task normally also supported by traditional CM systems. We deliberately uncoupled the choice of build environment from the choice of CM system, for a number of reasons.

First of all, we cannot (yet) *standardize* on one CM tool in our company. And even if different groups have the same CM system, they may still utilize incompatible versions of that system. So we leave the choice of a CM system open to each development group (with a preferred choice of course, to reduce investments). This implies that we must separate the build support from the CM system.

Secondly, we do not *want* to integrate build support with CM functionality, because we want to buy the best solution for each of these problems, and an integrated solution rarely combines the best techniques. So our build support currently utilizes our Koala compiler, off-the-shelf C compilers and a makefile running on multiple versions of make. We deploy Microsoft's Developer Studio as our IDE.

Thirdly, we want to be able to compile and link products while *outside* the context of a CM system, e.g. when in a plane or at home, or in a research lab. Although not a compelling argument, we find this approach in practice to be very satisfying, because it allows us to do quick experiments with the code at any place and at any time.

4.5 Distributed Development

The fifth and our final issue with respect to configuration management concerns distributed development. Recently, many commercial CM systems provide support to distribute the CM databases over the world. We are not in favor of doing that for the following reasons.

First of all, it forces us to standardize again on *one* CM system for the entire company, and we have shown the disadvantages of this in the previous section.

Secondly, we want to be able to utilize our software *outside* the context of the CM system, and relying on a distributed CM system does not help here.

Thirdly, we think this approach doesn't scale up. We envisage a 'small company approach' for the development of packages in our company. You can 'buy' a package, and download a particular release of that package, *without* having to be integrated with the 'vendor' of that package in a single distributed CM system. Imagine that in order to use Microsoft Windows, you would have to be connected to their CM system!

This concludes the five issues that we wanted to tackle in this paper.

5 Concluding Remarks

We have explained our component-based approach towards the creation of product populations. We briefly sketched our Koala component model and the architecture that we created with it. We then listed five configuration management issues, some of which we may have tackled in different ways than is conventional. The issues are:

- Version management of files and packages;
- Temporary variation for bug fixes, feature enhancements and safeguarding products;
- Permanent variation as explicit issue in the architecture;
- Build support separated from configuration management;
- Distributed development using a 'small company model' rather than a distributed CM system.

The approach sketched in this paper is currently being deployed by well over a hundred developers within Philips, to create the software for a wide range of television products.

References

1. Remi Bourgonjon, *The Evolution of Embedded Software in Consumer Products* , International Conference on Engineering of Complex Computer Systems, (unpublished keynote address), Ft. Lauderdale, FL, 1995
2. Ivar Jacobson, Martin Griss, and Patrick Jonsson, *Software Reuse – Architecture, Process and Organization for Business Success*, Addison Wesley, New York, 1997

3.   Jeff Magee, Naranker Dulay, Susan Eisenbach, and Jeff Kramer, *Specifying Distributed Software Architectures*, Proc. ESEC'95, Wilhelm Schafer, Pere Botella (Eds.) LNCS 989, Springer-Verlag, Berlin, Heidelberg, 1995, pp. 137-153

4.   Rob van Ommering, *Beyond Product Families: Building a Product Population?*, Proceedings of the 3rd international workshop on the development and evolution of software architectures of product families, Las Palmas, March 2000

5.   Rob van Ommering, *Koala, a Component Model for Consumer Electronics Product Software*, Proceedings of the Second International ESPRIT ARES Workshop, Springer-Verlag, Berlin Heidelberg, 1998

6.   Rob van Ommering, Frank van der Linden, Jeff Kramer, and Jeff Magee, *The Koala Component Model for Consumer Electronics Software*, IEEE Computer, March 2000, pp. 78-85

7.   Rob van Ommering, *Mechanisms for Handling Diversity in a Product Population*, Fourth International Software Architecture Workshop, June 4-5, 2000, Limerick, Ireland

8.   Rob van Ommering, *A Composable Software Architecture for Consumer Electronics Products*, XOOTIC Magazine, March 2000, Volume 7, no 3, also to be found at URL: http://www.win.tue.nl/cs/ooti/xootic/magazine/mar-2000.html

9.   Dewayne E. Perry, *Generic Architecture Descriptions for Product Lines*, Proceedings of the Second International ESPRIT ARES Workshop, LNCS 1429, Springer-Verlag, Berlin Heidelberg, 1998, pp. 51-56

10. Clemens Szyperski, *Component Software, Beyond Object-Oriented Programming*, Addison-Wesley, ISBN 0-201-17888-5, 1997

Software Architecture and Software Configuration Management

Bernhard Westfechtel[1] and Reidar Conradi[2]

[1] Lehrstuhl für Informatik III, RWTH Aachen
Ahornstrasse 55, D-52074 Aachen
bernhard@i3.informatik.rwth-aachen.de
[2] Norwegian University of Science and Technology (NTNU)
N-7034 Trondheim, Norway
Reidar.Conradi@idi.ntnu.no

Abstract. This paper examines the relations between software architecture and software configuration management. These disciplines overlap because they are both concerned with the structure of a software system being described in terms of components and relationships. On the other hand, they differ with respect to their focus — specific support for programming-in-the-large, versus general support for the management of evolving software objects throughout the whole life cycle. Several problems and alternatives concerning the integration of both disciplines are discussed.

1 Introduction

Software architectures play a central role in the development and maintenance of a software system. A *software architecture* description defines the structure (high-level design) of a software system in terms of components and relationships. It describes the interfaces between components and serves as the blueprint of the system to be implemented. It can be used for generating implementations (complete ones or frames to be filled in by programmers), makefiles to drive system building, overall test plans, etc.

Software configuration management (SCM) is the discipline of managing the evolution of complex software systems. To this end, an SCM system provides version and configuration control for all software objects created throughout the software life cycle. In addition, it supports system building (creation of derived objects from their sources), release management, and change control.

These disciplines overlap considerably. In particular, both software architectures and software configurations describe the structure of a software system at a coarse level. On the other hand, they differ with respect to their focus (specific support for programming-in-the-large versus general support to manage software objects throughout the whole life cycle).

In this paper, we examine the relation between software architecture and SCM. We discuss this relation not only at a conceptual level; we also address tool support for software architecture and SCM, respectively. We identify several problems and alternatives concerning the integration of both disciplines. By summarizing our findings and views with the help of a set of theses, we hope to raise discussions and motivate further research in the intersection of software architecture and SCM.

B. Westfechtel, A. van der Hoek (Eds.): SCM 2001/2003, LNCS 2649, pp. 24–39, 2003.

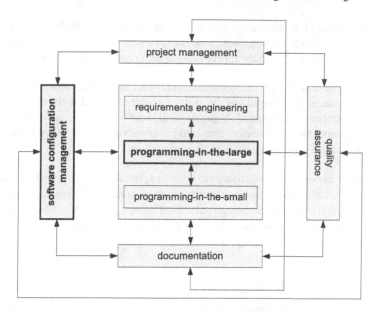

Fig. 1. Software process

2   Software Process

There is a great variety of software processes. Numerous *life cycle models* have been proposed, including the waterfall model, the spiral model, several incremental process models for object-oriented software development, etc. However, in order to discuss the relationships between software architecture and SCM, we have to make some minimal assumptions on the overall software process. Therefore, we briefly introduce a core life cycle model to establish the context of our subsequent discussion (Figure 1). Requirements engineering addresses the problem domain (what has to be built). Programming-in-the-large belongs to the solution domain (how the system is to be built). Here, the software architecture is defined, and then realized in programming-in-the-small. SCM is concerned with the management of all software objects (requirements definitions, software architecture models, component implementations, test data, etc.) created throughout the entire software life cycle. Project management deals with coordination issues such as planning, organizing, staffing, controlling, and leading software projects. Quality assurance comprises activities such as validation, verification, inspections, testing, etc. Finally, documentation includes both technical and user documentation.

3   Software Architecture

3.1   Definition

Although not being a new invention, the discipline of software architecture has recently attracted much attention [1]. Unfortunately, there is no definition of this discipline which has been accepted universally. This became evident at a Dagstuhl Seminar held in 1995 [2] and has not changed significantly since then. The Software Engineering Institute has collected a large set of definitions [3]. Below, we quote one of these definitions [4] which we consider appropriate in the context of this paper:

> An architecture is the set of significant decisions about the organization of a software system, the selection of the structural elements and their interfaces by which the system is composed, together with their behavior as specified in the collaborations among these elements into progressively larger subsystems, and the architectural style that guides this organization.

Terms such as organization, structure, behavior, interfaces, composition, and interaction indicate what is addressed by software architecture. While software architecture is concerned with the overall organization of a software system, this does not imply that details do not have to be considered. In contrast, the design of interfaces and collaborations is an essential part of software architecture.

3.2   Architectural Languages

A variety of languages have been proposed and used to describe software architectures. We will categorize all of them as *architectural languages*, even though they vary considerably from each other. Deliberately, we do not go into debates on the choice of the "best" modeling abstractions for software architectures.

The term *module interconnection language* [5] denotes a group of languages that were developed from the mid 70s to the mid 80s. The first module interconnection languages were designed to add architectural information that could not be expressed in contemporary programming languages. Later on, modular programming languages such as Modula-2 and Ada were developed, parts of which were dedicated to specifying module interconnection. Module interconnection languages address the structure and partly the evolution of software systems, but they do not deal with behavior. Software architectures are described in terms of modules and their export and import interfaces, where modules may be composed into subsystems. Some module interconnection languages offer version control, e.g., multiple realization versions for the same interface.

Object-oriented modeling languages can be used for expressing software architectures, but they usually cover requirements engineering as well. Today, the Unified Modeling Language (UML) [4] dominates the scene. The UML provides a comprehensive set of diagram types that may be used to model both the structure and behavior of software systems, e.g., class, object, collaboration, sequence, and state diagrams. Models may be structured into packages which may be nested. Model evolution is supported e.g. by subclassing and by allowing for multiple classes realizing the same interface.

Loosely defined, "an *architecture description language* for software applications focuses on the high-level structure of the overall application rather than the implementation details of any specific source module" [6]. According to a survey conducted by Medvidovic and Taylor [7], an architecture description language models architectures in terms of components, connectors, and configurations. A component is a unit of computation or a data store. Components communicate with their environment through a set of ports. Connectors are architectural building blocks used to model interactions between components. The interfaces of connectors are called roles, which are attached to ports of components. An architectural configuration is a connected graph of components and connectors that describe architectural structure. For the sake of scalability, complex components and connectors may be refined by subconfigurations. In addition to structure, architecture description languages address behavior of architectural elements, by using e.g. state diagrams, temporal logic, CSP, etc.

3.3   Tools

With respect to tool support, we may distinguish among the language categories introduced above. Tools for module interconnection languages are concerned with analysis and system construction. Analysis refers to syntax and static semantics of module interfaces. System construction comprises version selection and code generation.

Object-oriented modeling languages are supported by integrated CASE tools which provide graphical editors, analysis tools, code generators, and interpreters (if the modeling language is executable). Many commercial CASE tools are available, including e.g. Rational Rose (for the UML), ROOM, and SDT for SDL. CASE tools have often been criticized as drawing tools. Clearly, the functionality of a CASE tool depends on how well the syntax and semantics of the underlying modeling language are defined. In the case of an executable modeling language, CASE tools go far beyond drawing tools.

Tools for architecture description languages partly offer more sophisticated functionality than most CASE tools, in particular for those languages in which behavior may be formally specified. An overview is provided in [7], which categorizes tool functionality into active specification, multiple views, analysis, refinement, implementation generation, and dynamism. Most of these tools are research prototypes with frequently incomplete functionality.

4   Software Configuration Management

4.1   Definition

Software configuration management (SCM) is the discipline of controlling the evolution of complex software systems [8]. In an IEEE standard [9], the four main functions of SCM are defined as follows:

> Configuration management is the process of identifying and defining the items in the system, controlling the changes to these items throughout their life cycle, recording and reporting the status of these items and change requests, and verifying the completeness and correctness of items.

In addition, [10] includes software manufacture, process management, and team work into SCM. However, in the context of this paper, we will take a *product-centered view* on SCM. That is, we will focus on the management of all software objects created throughout the whole life cycle, their composition into software configurations, and the evolution of both individual objects and their configurations.

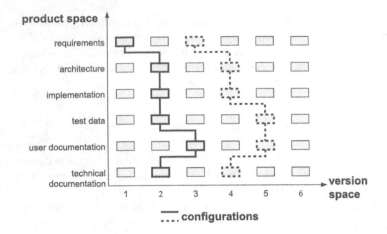

Fig. 2. Product space and version space

4.2 Concepts, Models, and Languages

SCM is concerned with the management of all *software objects* (artifacts, documents) created throughout the software life cycle. This includes requirements definitions, software architectures, implementations, test plans, test data, project plans, etc. These are arranged into *software configurations* by means of various kinds of relationships such as hierarchies and dependencies. In addition to source objects, SCM deals with derived objects such as compiled code and executables.

The evolution of software systems is addressed by version control. Generally speaking, a *version* represents some state of an evolving object. Evolution may occur along different dimensions. Versions along the time dimension are called *revisions*, where a new revision is intended to replace a previous one. In contrast, multiple *variants* may coexist at a given time, e.g., a software system required to run on multiple platforms.

Thus, SCM deals with both the *product space* and the *version space* [11]. Software objects and their relationships constitute the product space, their versions are organized in the version space. A *versioned object base* combines product space and version space. In particular, SCM has to support the consistent selection of versions across multiple software objects and their relationships. All of the above is illustrated in Figure 2.

In SCM, version control has always played an important role. Version control is based on an underlying *version model*. A version model defines the objects to be versioned, version identification and organization, as well as operations for retrieving existing versions and constructing new versions. A large variety of version models have been proposed and implemented; see [11].

Evolving software configurations can be represented in different ways, depending on the type of the respective SCM system. In a file-based system, a configuration is represented by a collection of versioned *files*. Alternatively, SCM systems may offer a (versioned) *database*. Then, the user may define types of software objects and relationships in a schema, and subsequently populate the database with instances of these types. Finally, *system modeling languages* have been developed for representing software configurations. A system model defines the system components, as well as their relationships. A system model is usually described at the level of source objects (in particular, program source code), but it may also contain rules for producing the derived objects. The system modeling language may be either specific (for design and implementation objects [12,13]), or it may deal with arbitrary software objects [14,15,16].

4.3   Tools

A great variety of tools have been developed for SCM, see e.g. the Ovum reports [17] for information about commercial tools. The services provided by SCM systems may be classified according to the functions introduced in Section 4.1 (identification, control, status accounting, verification, software manufacture, process management, and team work).The spectrum ranges from small tools for specific tasks, e.g., Make [18] for software manufacture and SCCS [19] or RCS [20] for version control), to comprehensive integrated systems such as ClearCase [21] and Continuus [22].

A driving force behind the development of SCM systems is the intent to provide general services which may be re-used in a wide range of applications. An SCM system provides a versioned object base which acts as a common repository for all of the software objects maintained by tools for requirements engineering, programming-in-the-large, programming-in-the-small, project management, quality assurance, and documentation. For the sake of generality, SCM systems make virtually no assumptions about the contents of software objects, which are usually represented by text files or binary files.

5   Interplay of Software Architecture and SCM

Based on the preceding sections, we make some initial observations concerning the relationships between software architecture and SCM. These observations will be refined in the next sections. Table 1 summarizes the relationships between software architecture and SCM as discussed so far:

Coverage. Software architecture focuses on programming-in-the-large, while SCM covers the whole life cycle.

Software objects. Software architecture deals with design objects such as components, modules, classes, etc. SCM is concerned with all kinds of software objects. While some of these may be organized according to the software architecture (e.g. module implementations), others bear no obvious relationships to design objects (e.g., requirements specifications or project plans).

Relationships. In software architectures, design objects are typically organized by means of inheritance hierarchies, import relationships, connectors, etc. SCM has to deal with all conceivable kinds of relationships between software objects.

Semantic level. Architectural languages strive for a high semantic level which allows one to analyze software architectures for syntactic and semantic consistency. On the other hand, SCM is performed at a rather low semantic level — which is both a strength and a weakness. To provide for re-usability, SCM systems abstract from the contents of software objects, which are typically treated as text or binary files.

Table 1. Comparison of software architecture and SCM

	software architecture	software configuration management
coverage	programming-in-the-large (high-level design)	whole life cycle
software objects	components, modules, classes, ...	all kinds of software objects
relationships	inheritance, import, connectors, ...	all kinds of relationships
semantic level	high (syntactic/semantic consistency)	fairly low
granularity	overall organization, but also detailed interface descriptions	overall organization (software objects as black boxes)
versions	variants	variants and revisions

Granularity. Software architecture specifically addresses the overall organization of large software systems. However, architectural languages typically cover also fine-grained descriptions of interfaces, e.g., provided and required resources. SCM also deals with the overall organization of software objects, but takes the whole software life cycle into account. Software objects are usually treated as black boxes whose internal structure is not known.

Versions. To support evolution of software systems, architectural languages typically provide concepts such as inheritance, genericity, or abstraction (distinction between interface and realization). In terms of SCM, this kind of evolution support may be used to represent variants, also called *logical versioning* in [23]. In contrast, SCM also covers *historical versioning*, i.e., revisions. In addition, SCM deals with *cooperative versioning*, i.e., versions which are created concurrently by different developers (and are merged later on).

6   Integration Approaches

In the current section, we describe different approaches which have been developed for the integration of software architecture and SCM. These approaches differ with respect to the "division of labor" between software architecture and SCM (see Figure 3 for an overview). Please note that we will discuss the interplay between software architecture and SCM not only at a conceptual level. In addition, we will address pragmatic issues of *tool integration* (inter-operation of architectural design tools and SCM tools).

6.1   Orthogonal Integration

In the case of *orthogonal integration*, software architecture and SCM are decoupled as far as possible. The versioned object base of the SCM system contains a set of ver-

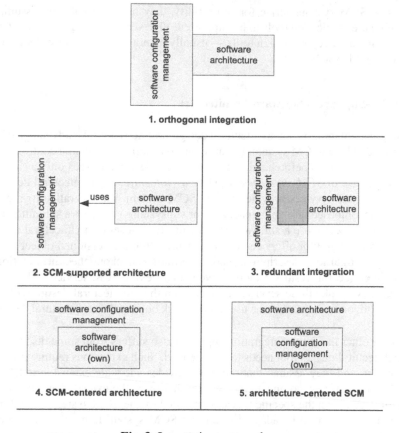

Fig. 3. Integration approaches

sioned objects (typically files). A configuration description is used to select object versions from the versioned object base. The workspace manager, a component of the SCM system, sets up a uni-version workspace which provides access to the selected object versions. Architectural design tools operate on architectural descriptions via the workspace by reading and writing the corresponding files.

Orthogonal integration is a mainstream approach to the coupling of architectural design tools and SCM systems (consider, e.g., the integration of Rational Rose [24] and ClearCase [21,25], as described in [26]). Architectural evolution is supported on two levels: *Embedded evolution* is performed <u>within</u> the software architecture, e.g., by the separation of interfaces and realizations, inheritance, or genericity (parameterization). All of these mechanisms are suitable to deal with variants, i.e., logical versioning, but they are not designed for historical versioning. In contrast, *meta-level evolution* deals with evolution of the software architecture as a whole. In this way, global evolution is supported (also with respect to other software objects).

Orthogonal integration supports *bottom-up integration* of existing tools. An architectural design tool may be combined with multiple SCM systems and vice versa. Since vendors of SCM systems strive for re-usability, they make virtually no assumptions concerning the application tools to be supported. Vice versa, the vendors of application tools — e.g., architectural design tools — usually do not want to become dependent on a specific SCM system.

6.2   SCM-Supported Software Architecture

In orthogonal integration, an architectural design tool does not take advantage of functions provided by an SCM system. In particular, this applies to version control. Version selection is performed beforehand; the architectural design tool sees only a single version. In the case of *SCM-supported software architecture*, an architectural design tool makes use of the services provided by the SCM system. The overall software architecture is decomposed into units (packages or subsystems) which are submitted to version control. To compose a software architecture from a set of architectural units, the architectural design tool offers commands for browsing the versioned object base, for supplying configuration descriptions, and for initiating checkout/checkin operations. At the user interface, this results in more convenient access to SCM services. The software architect may invoke these services directly from the architectural design tool. In the case of orthogonal integration, the user has to work outside the architectural design tool instead.

On the other hand, this integration approach also suffers from some disadvantages. The architectural design tool needs to be extended. Such extensions require implementation effort, and they assume that the tool provides adequate extension mechanisms (e.g., definition of new command menus). Furthermore, the extended architectural design tool depends on the specific services provided by the SCM system. Therefore, the extensions may have to be adapted if another SCM system is used. To a certain extent, such adaptations may be avoided by introducing an abstract interface. However, presently there is no standard interface to SCM services.

To a large extent, SCM-supported software architecture coincides with orthogonal integration. The SCM system does not make specific assumptions concerning the applications tools using it (including architectural design tools). Moreover, reusable SCM services are still implemented only once in the same way for all applications. However, in orthogonal integration the architectural design tool is not aware of the SCM system, while it depends on the SCM system and takes advantages of its services in the case of SCM-supported software architecture.

6.3   Redundant Integration

In the case of SCM-supported software architecture, the architectural design tool benefits from the services provided by the SCM system, but it does not contribute to a richer description of the software configuration. Architectural information is still contained almost exclusively only in the representation maintained by the architectural design tool (apart from the decomposition into architectural units which are maintained as versioned objects in the SCM repository). In contrast, *redundant integration* aims at providing more architectural information as part of the overall software configuration.

To this end, an abstraction of the architecture is represented in the software configuration. Please note that redundant integration and SCM-supported software architecture may complement each other, i.e., they are not mutually exclusive alternatives.

Redundant integration provides several benefits: First, it can be applied under the constraints of bottom-up integration, provided that the architectural design tool offers an interface to its architectural representation. Second, architectural information is represented in the software configuration. Therefore, the software configuration can be used as a skeleton for organizing software objects according to the architecture. Third, an abstraction of the architecture is represented in the SCM repository in an application-independent way. Therefore, it is not necessary to run the architectural design tool to access this abstraction. Moreover, if different architectural languages and tools are used for different parts of the overall software system, the software configuration (system model) acts as a neutral and integrating architectural representation.

On the other hand, a price has to be paid: redundant representations have to be kept consistent with each other. To cope with redundancy, we have to invest programming effort (to write an integration tool which maintains consistency), runtime (for executing the tool), and storage space (for storing redundant representations). Here, similar problems have to be solved as in makefile generation (where build rules are derived from the source code).

6.4   SCM-Centered Software Architecture

In this approach, software architecture is considered a part of SCM. The SCM system provides support for representing software architectures; it is assumed that there is no representation of the software architecture outside the SCM system. Software architectures are typically represented with the help of system modeling languages. As explained in Section 4, we may distinguish between system modeling languages dealing specifically with design objects, and languages for arbitrary software objects.

With respect to system modeling, it is instructive to study the evolution of the Adele system. An early version of the Adele system [13] offered a predefined module interconnection language derived from Intercol [12]. However, this made it difficult to model non-code objects; for example, even a simple textual document was required to have an interface and a body. Furthermore, the user was forced to adopt the predefined language for programming-in-the-large. Thus, more flexibility and generality is required. Therefore, the current version of Adele offers an "out of the box" system model that the user may or may not adopt. In addition, the user may define any desired system model for organizing software objects. In fact, the predefined system model is defined in terms of a database schema, i.e., on top of Adele rather than built-in [27].

SCM-centered software architecture avoids redundancy problems because it is based on the assumption that there is no representation of the software architecture outside the SCM system. This assumption may have been valid a long time ago, but it does not hold any more. Using the modeling facilities of an SCM system may be considered the "poor man's approach to software architecture": one may resort to this solution if nothing else is available. However, providing a full-fledged architectural language such as e.g. Wright [28] or Rapide [29] goes beyond the scope of an SCM system (which, on the other hand, has to deal with general software objects). Thus, we consider it more realistic to maintain abstractions of the software architecture in the SCM system, as it is done in the case of redundant integration.

6.5   Architecture-Centered SCM

Architecture-centered SCM inverts the approach described in the previous subsection. SCM is considered part of software architecture. This approach acknowledges the central role which the software architecture plays in software development and maintenance. In particular, the architecture may be used for organizing implementation and test activities, for reconfiguring deployed software systems, etc. In contrast to orthogonal integration, evolution is not handled on two levels. Rather, evolution is supported in a unified way in the underlying architectural language and the respective support tools.

In [30,31], it is argued that software architecture and SCM are highly related, and the advantages of a single, unified system model are stressed. The Mae system [32] was developed along these lines. To cope with architectural evolution, Mae provides multiple concepts such as (sequences of) revisions, variants, optionality, and inheritance. Version selection is supported at the architectural level. Several opportunities of this integrated approach are identified such as version selection based on compatibility relationships, multi-version connectors, and generation of change scripts based on architectural differences. From the user's point of view, Mae behaves in a similar way as in the case of SCM-supported software architecture. However, Mae does not use a general-purpose SCM system. The mainstream version model of SCM — version graphs — is considered inappropriate because revisions and variants are intermingled rather than separated cleanly.

Architecture-centered SCM provides several benefits. There is only a single representation of the software architecture. Furthermore, evolution is dealt with at one place (in the software architecture), while orthogonal integration and its derivatives handle evolution on two levels (meta-level and embedded evolution, respectively). Finally, many software development and maintenance activities are centered around the software architecture. For example, implementation and test activities may be planned with the help of the software architecture. Moreover, the architecture can be used to organize a large set of documents created in the software process.

However, SCM needs to be applied throughout the whole life cycle rather than only to the software architecture and the attached software objects. Therefore, the redundancy problem is not really solved from a more global perspective. That is, a general SCM system is required to manage "the rest" (requirements definitions, project plans, etc.). Taking this into account, extending an architectural design tool with SCM support works against the intent of SCM systems — namely to provide uniform, application-independent services for version control, configuration control, etc.

This goal is achieved in both orthogonal integration and SCM-supported software architecture. The latter provides similar benefits as architecture-centered SCM in that it makes SCM services available in an architectural design tool, and it avoids the disadvantages of the "SCM services in the tools" solution (re-implementation of SCM services, no global repository). On the other hand, architecture-centered SCM provides more freedom and allows e.g. to use the "favorite version model". In contrast, the conceptual world of the SCM system has to be adopted in SCM-supported software architecture.

7   Discussion

This section summarizes the discussion of the relationships between software architecture and SCM with the help of a set of theses.

7.1   Software Life Cycle

Thesis 1 (Architectural Design vs. the Whole Life Cycle). *Software architecture and SCM overlap since they both deal with the overall organization of a software system. However, while software architecture refers to programming-in-the-large, SCM addresses the whole software life cycle.*

We have stressed this point repeatedly in this paper. Architectural languages provide more high-level support for system composition and consistency. On the other hand, SCM also deals with non-design objects (requirements definitions, test plans, project plans, documentations, etc.) and offers version control, which is only partly covered by software architecture.

Thesis 2 (Limitations of an Architecture-Centered Software Process). *Even though the architecture plays a central role in the software process, an architecture-centered software process overemphasizes the importance of software architecture and neglects important parts of the software process, e.g., requirements engineering.*

Since the software architecture plays a central role in the software process, the vision of an *architecture-centered process* is quite tempting. In such a process, the software architecture is used as a "skeleton" for organizing software objects, browsing, generation of implementation frames and test plans, etc. However, the total software process can be covered only partly this way, especially for incremental development models. We may rather argue that a software process should be *requirements-centered* (or user-centered). No matter where the focus is set: An SCM system has to manage software objects created in all life cycle phases, and it also should support *traceability* from the initial or negotiated requirements to the finally delivered code.

7.2   Tool Integration

Thesis 3 (Tool Integration – Bottom-Up or Top-Down). *An SCM system has to provide general services for a wide range of applications. Therefore, it must be designed for bottom-up integration with existing tools.*

Bottom-up integration means that existing tools are integrated after the fact (toolkit approach, integration of legacy systems). Since vendors of SCM systems usually strive for re-usability, they make no assumptions concerning the tools to be integrated with the SCM system. Vice versa, the vendors of application tools usually do not want to become dependent on a specific SCM system (this independence may be achieved e.g. by a virtual workspace). In contrast, *top-down integration* means that new tools are designed and implemented as a whole, resulting in a tightly integrated software engineering environment (comprising tools for architectural design and SCM). Then, the SCM tools may be used only as a part of the integrated environment.

Thesis 4 (Different System Description Languages). *Since there are many architectural languages with different syntax and semantics, an SCM system must not prescribe a specific language for describing software architectures. In contrast, the software architecture description has to be handled like any other document.*

This thesis is underpinned by the Adele system, which evolved from an SCM system with a built-in module interconnection language to a fairly general object-oriented database system. A language for architectural design which is built into an SCM system clashes with the architectural languages being in use today. For example, if a company adopts the UML, there is not a free choice of the architectural language any more. Therefore, an SCM system should be developed under the assumption that the architecture is modeled in an application-dependent way using some architectural language, many of which are available today. A system modeling language offered by an SCM system should be considered only as a "poor man's architecture description language".

Thesis 5 (Unavoidable Redundancy in System Descriptions). *Under the constraints of bottom-up integration, there is no hope to unify software architectures and software configurations in the sense that only a single, integrated description needs to be maintained. A certain amount of redundancy is therefore inevitable.*

In [30], it is argued that multiple descriptions of the software architecture result in redundancy and increased modeling support. However, the vision of an integrated approach assumes top-down integration. That is, a new system is built where the notions of software architecture and software configuration are unified from the beginning. A user of such a system would have to commit to this conceptual world. Mostly, however, there are constraints concerning the notations and tools used throughout the software life cycle. To cope with redundancy, tools are therefore required which extract the overall organization of a software system from the software architecture into a (part of) a software configuration. With the help of such tools, we may maintain software configuration descriptions which provide more information than e.g. directory hierarchies.

7.3   Evolution

Thesis 6 (Evolution at the Architectural Level). *Architectural design deals with architectural evolution at a semantic level. In particular, variants can be represented <u>within</u> the software architecture description (as realization variants, subclasses, or instances of generic modules).*

That is, to some extent version control is supported within the software architecture description. Architectural design attempts to ensure that software architectures are reusable, and that they remain stable even under changing requirements. For example, we may define a neutral file system interface which can be mapped onto different actual file systems, confining platform changes to a single spot in the architecture.

Thesis 7 (Evolution at the SCM Level). *SCM offers general version control services for all kinds of applications. These address not only variants, but also revisions. Version control is performed at a fairly low semantic level. The SCM system deals with versioning <u>of</u> the architecture, covering temporal, logical, and cooperative versioning.*

Thus, software architecture descriptions are placed under version control, like all other software objects. If a software architecture description is composed of multiple software objects (the usual case), configuration control is also required. Version control provided by an SCM system can be used e.g. to handle change requests that imply architectural restructuring, to maintain competing architectural variants for the purpose of comparison and evaluation, to handle concurrent changes, e.g., fixes in an old release while the new release is being developed on the main branch, etc.

Thesis 8 (Evolution at Different Abstraction Levels). *Altogether, the evolution of software architectures has to be dealt with at two levels: at the architectural level and at the SCM level. These two levels complement each other and cannot be unified easily. On the other hand, the levels are not orthogonal with respect to logical versioning (variants).*

At the architectural level, we may deal with semantic changes. Interfaces, inheritance, genericity, etc. have a well-defined meaning. Therefore, evolution cannot be delegated to an SCM system which treats software objects as black boxes. In addition, we may have to use multiple variants simultaneously, while the user of an SCM system usually has to pre-select one version to work on. At the SCM level, we may handle global changes of any kind throughout the software life cycle (comprising both variants and revisions, usually at a fairly low semantic level). Handling these changes at the architectural level would defeat the very purpose of an SCM system: to relieve software tools from tasks which can be taken care of by general services.

8   Conclusion

We examined the relationships between software architecture and SCM. To this end, we delineated their roles in the software life cycle and introduced five approaches to the integration of software architecture and SCM. Finally, we summarized our conclusions with the help of eight theses. In this way, we intend to initiate further discussions; indeed, other authors take different views, see e.g. [30].

According to our view, software architecture and SCM play different roles in the software life cycle. However, they overlap both in the product space and the version space. An architectural configuration should be considered a part of an overall software configuration covering the whole life cycle. The architectural configuration constitutes an abstraction of an architectural description whose level of detail (e.g., in interface descriptions) goes beyond the fairly coarse-grained level of software configurations. Therefore, a certain amount of redundancy is inevitable, in particular under the constraints of bottom-up integration of existing tools and languages. Evolution can be handled both at the architectural level and the SCM level.

Most of the integration approaches that have been realized so far do not follow this view. In the case of orthogonal integration, coupling is reduced to an absolute minimum. SCM-centered architecture and architecture-centered SCM are unbalanced approaches which focus on one discipline at the expense of the other. Thus, the potentials for *synergy* between software architecture and SCM have to be exploited further.

Acknowledgments

This paper is an extended version of a position paper contained in the informal SCM-10 proceedings [33]. It was presented and discussed at the workshop. The authors gratefully acknowledge the contributions of the workshop participants.

References

1. Garlan, D., Shaw, M.: An introduction to software architecture. In Ambriola, V., Tortora, G., eds.: Advances in Software Engineering and Knowledge Engineering. Volume 2. World Scientific, Singapore (1993) 1–39
2. Garlan, D., Paulisch, F., Tichy, W.: Summary of the Dagstuhl workshop on software architecture. ACM Software Engineering Notes **20** (1995) 63–83
3. Software Engineering Institute Pittsburgh, Pennsylvania: How Do You Define Software Architecture? (2003)
   http://www.sei.cmu.edu/architecture/definitions.html.
4. Booch, G., Rumbaugh, J., Jacobson, I.: The Unified Modeling Language User Guide. Addison Wesley, Reading, Massachusetts (1998)
5. Prieto-Diaz, R., Neighbors, J.: Module interconnection languages. The Journal of Systems and Software **6** (1986) 307–334
6. Vestal, S.: A cursory overview and comparison of four architecture description languages. Technical report, Honeywell Systems and Research Center (1993)
7. Medvidovic, N., Taylor, R.: A classification and comparison framework for software architecture description languages. IEEE Transactions on Software Engineering **26** (2000) 70–93
8. Tichy, W.F.: Tools for software configuration management. In Winkler, J.F.H., ed.: Proceedings of the International Workshop on Software Version and Configuration Control, Grassau, Germany, Teubner Verlag (1988) 1–20
9. IEEE New York, New York: IEEE Standard for Software Configuration Management Plans: ANSI/IEEE Std 828-1983. (1983)
10. Dart, S.: Concepts in configuration management systems. In Feiler, P.H., ed.: Proceedings of the 3rd International Workshop on Software Configuration Management, Trondheim, Norway, ACM Press (1991) 1–18
11. Conradi, R., Westfechtel, B.: Version models for software configuration management. ACM Computing Surveys **30** (1998) 232–282
12. Tichy, W.F.: Software development control based on module interconnection. In: Proceedings of the IEEE 4th International Conference on Software Engineering, Pittsburgh, Pennsylvania, IEEE Computer Society Press (1979) 29–41
13. Estublier, J.: A configuration manager: The Adele data base of programs. In: Proceedings of the Workshop on Software Engineering Environments for Programming-in-the-Large, Harwichport, Massachusetts (1985) 140–147
14. Marzullo, K., Wiebe, D.: Jasmine: A software system modelling facility. In: Proceedings of the ACM SIGSOFT/SIGPLAN Software Engineering Symposium on Practical Software Development Environments. ACM SIGPLAN Notices 22-1, Palo Alto, California (1986) 121–130
15. Tryggeseth, E., Gulla, B., Conradi, R.: Modelling systems with variability using the PROTEUS configuration language. [34] 216–240
16. Leblang, D.B., McLean, G.D.: Configuration management for large-scale software development efforts. In: Proceedings of the Workshop on Software Engineering Environments for Programming-in-the-Large, Harwichport, Massachusetts (1985) 122–127

17. Burrows, C.: Ovum Evaluates: Configuration Management. Ovum Limited, London, UK. (2002) http://www.ovum.com.
18. Feldman, S.I.: Make — A program for maintaining computer programs. Software Practice and Experience **9** (1979) 255–265
19. Rochkind, M.J.: The source code control system. Transactions on Software Engineering **1** (1975) 364–370
20. Tichy, W.F.: RCS – A system for version control. Software Practice and Experience **15** (1985) 637–654
21. Leblang, D.: The CM challenge: Configuration management that works. [35] 1–38
22. Cagan, M.: Untangling configuration management. [34] 35–52
23. Estublier, J., Casallas, R.: Three dimensional versioning. [34] 118–135
24. Boggs, W., Boggs, M.: UML with Rational Rose 2002. Sybex, Alameda, California (2002)
25. White, B.A.: Software Configuration Management Strategies and Rational ClearCase. Object Technology Series. Addison-Wesley, Reading, Massachusetts (2000)
26. Rational Software Corporation Cupertino, California: Using Rational Rose and Rational ClearCase in a Team Environment. (2002) http://www.rational.com.
27. Estublier, J., Casallas, R.: The Adele configuration manager. [35] 99–134
28. Allen, R., Garlan, D.: A formal basis for architectural connection. ACM Transactions on Software Engineering and Methodology **6** (1997) 213–249
29. Luckham, D.C., Kenney, J.J., Augustin, L.M., Vera, J., Bryan, D., Mann, W.: Specification and analysis of system architecture using Rapide. IEEE Transactions on Software Engineering **21** (1995) 336–354
30. van der Hoek, A., Heimbigner, D., Wolf, A.L.: Software architecture, configuration management, and configurable distributed systems: A menage a trois. Technical Report CU-CS-849-98, University of Boulder, Colorado (1998)
31. van der Hoek, A., Heimbigner, D., Wolf, A.L.: Capturing architectural configurability: Variants, options, and evolution. Technical Report CU-CS-895-99, University of Boulder, Colorado (1999)
32. van der Hoek, A., Mikic-Rakic, M., Roshandel, R., Medvidovic, N.: Taming architectural evolution. In: Proceedings of the Joint 8th European Software Engineering Conference and the 9th ACM SIGSOFT Symposium on Fundamentals of Software Engineering. ACM Software Engineering Notes 26-5, Vienna, Austria, ACM Press (2001) 1–10
33. Westfechtel, B., Conradi, R.: Software architecture and software configuration management. In van der Hoek, A., ed.: 10th International Workshop on Software Configuration Management: New Practices, New Challenges, and New Boundaries (SCM 10), Toronto, Canada (2001) 19–26
34. Estublier, J., ed.: Software Configuration Management: Selected Papers SCM-4 and SCM-5. LNCS 1005, Seattle, Washington, Springer-Verlag (1995)
35. Tichy, W.F., ed.: Configuration Management. Volume 2 of Trends in Software. John Wiley & Sons, New York, New York (1994)

Supporting Distributed Collaboration through Multidimensional Software Configuration Management

Mark C. Chu-Carroll and James Wright

IBM T. J. Watson Research Center
30 Saw Mill River Road, Hawthorne, NY 10532, USA
{mcc,jwright}@watson.ibm.com

Abstract. In recent years, new software development methodologies and styles have become popular. In particular, many applications are being developed in the open-source community by groups of loosely co-ordinated programmers scattered across the globe.

This style of widely distributed collaboration creates a suite of new problems for software development. Instead of being able to knock on the door of a collaborator, all communication between programmers working together on a system must be mediated through the computer. But at the same time, the bandwidth available for communication is dramatically more limited than those available to local collaborators.

In this paper, we present a new SCM system called Stellation which is specifically designed to address the limits of current SCM systems, particularly when those systems are applied to large projects developed in a geographically distributed environment. Stellation attempts to enhance communication and collaboration between programmers by providing a mechanism called *multidimensionality* that allows them to share viewpoints on the structure and organization of the system; by providing a hierarchical branching mechanism that allows the granularity of coordination to be varied for different purposes; and by providing a mechanism for integrating programming language knowledge into the system, allowing it to be used for organizational and coordination purposes.

1 Introduction

The key problem introduced by geographically distributed or open-source development is communication: many of the traditional channels for communication are not available in this environment. In distributed development, programmers rarely or never communicate face to face, but rather through email, on-line chats, through the coordination facilities of the SCM system, and through the code itself.

The Stellation SCM system has been designed to work in this kind of geographically distributed environment. Many of Stellation's features are designed specifically with the goal of enhancing communication between programmers. Stellation is based on combining the following key ideas:

B. Westfechtel, A. van der Hoek (Eds.): SCM 2001/2003, LNCS 2649, pp. 40–53, 2003.

1. Finer artifact granularity, with linguistic knowledge through component modules;
2. Dynamic/multidimensional project organization;
3. Coordination in terms of artifact collections; and
4. Hierarchical change isolation and repository replication.

We believe that a software configuration management system with these capabilities, integrated with a supporting programming environment, provides significant benefits to programmers working cooperatively in a distributed environment, well beyond those provided by a conventional SCM system.

We divide the features of Stellation into three main categories: multidimensionality; repository replication; and distributed coordination. In the following sections, we will briefly describe the features of Stellation, and how they enhance communication, coordination and collaboration in a distributed environment. Due to the limits of this format, we will not be able to go into great depth; more details of the Stellation SCM system can be found in [6,5,8].

2 Multidimensionality

Multidimensionality is a way of separating code storage from code organization in a manner that enhances a programmer's ability to describe or demonstrate a viewpoint on the semantic or organizational structure of the code. This is closely related to the notion of multidimensional separation of concerns [23] and aspect-oriented software development [22]. More details of our approach to multidimensionality can be found in [7].

The key observation of multidimensionality is that in a conventional SCM system, source files are used for two distinct purposes: storage, and organization. Storage is an obvious notion: code must be placed in a source file to be stored by a file-based system. But the placement of code into a particular source file is not just for the purpose of storage: it communicates information about the system to other programmers. The layout of code into and within source files creates an organizational decomposition of the system into discrete units which demonstrates a viewpoint on the structure or meaning of the system.

In Stellation, we separate these two purposes. Stellation performs storage and versioning of relatively fine-grained artifacts, and allow those artifacts to be composed into viewable aggregates that resemble structures source files. We call these *virtual source files (VSFs)*. For example, the granularity of storage used for Java programs is shown in figure 1. Virtual source files do not play a role in program storage, but exist solely for the purpose of communicating organizational meaning. This separation of storage from organization allows programmers to create multiple, orthogonal code organizations in terms of VSFs, each of which describes a distinct viewpoint of the structure of the system. In addition to storing and versioning the individual programs, Stellation stores and versions descriptions of the programmer-defined organizations.

Through this mechanism, programmers familiar with particular parts of the system can store views that serve as an illustration or explanation of that part

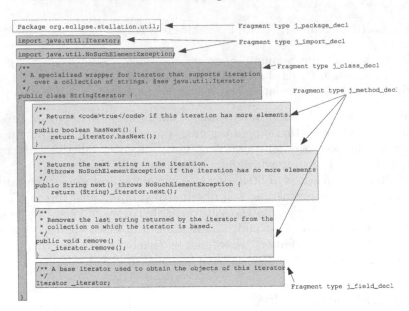

Fig. 1. Java fragments

of the system.In addition to this service for code understanding, it allows programmers to store code in structures well suited to different tasks: to perform a particular task, the programmers can choose the organization best suited to that task. We believe that this facility is generally useful for helping programmers understand large systems, but in the realm of distributed development, where communication is more limited, such a facility is particularly important.

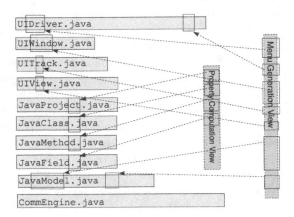

Fig. 2. Orthogonal program views in an actual system

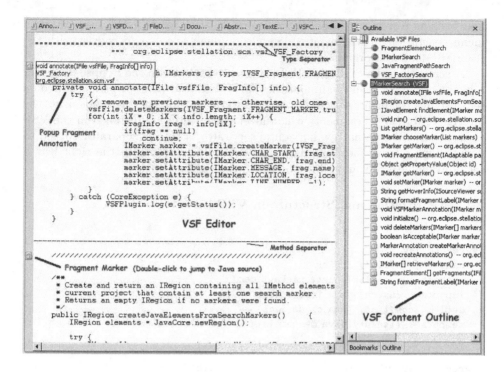

Fig. 3. A Stellation VSF editor

As an example of different organizations, in figure 2, we illustrate some uses of virtual source files for generating alternate organizational views of a real system. The horizontal boxes illustrate source code in the conventional Java source organization for the basic programming environment underlying a predecessor of the Stellation IDE.

The data model for this system is implemented using the interpreter pattern discussed in [11]. Each major property or operation on source code is implemented using identically named methods in each of the model classes. A very useful view would assemble the methods corresponding to a given operation from all of the model classes together. This is illustrated by the vertical PropertyComputation view in the figure, which gathers together the relevant methods. The value of this view is understated in the figure; the actual model package contained approximately 30 source files; to debug a single operation could mean opening editor windows on 30 different source files in a conventional system!

A more difficult example of this is the menu generation process. In this system, understanding how menus are dynamically assembled by the various components of the system can be extremely difficult to understand, because it is scattered through many files in the dominant organization of the program. There is no uniform method name for all of the code elements that should be part of this view, and it cuts across the dominant organization in a highly irregular fashion. But in Stellation, the code organization which gathers together the menu generation/management code and documentation could coexist with the standard dominant organization.

A screenshot of a Stellation VSF editor integrated into the Eclipse programming environment is shown in figure3. The VSF Editor (left) presents views on a set of source fragments selected by some criteria (in this case, methods using the interface *IMarker*). Fragments which meet the criteria are included in the VSF view, separated by a narrow horizontal separator; a thicker separator is used to denote type (source file) boundaries. The Content Outline on the right lists a set of available VSFs and all fragments in the current VSF.

2.1   Aggregation and Structure in VSFs

```
aggregate java_class {                        (a)
    name : [conflict] String
    package : [conflict] java_package_decl
    imports : [union] java_import_decl
    decl : [conflict] java_class_decl
    members : [linear] java_member List
}

aggregate java_viewpoint {                    (b)
    name : [conflict] String
    description : [linear] Text
    members : [dynamic] java_member List
}

aggregate test_case { ... }                   (c)

aggregate bug_report {                        (d)
    title : [conflict] String
    severity : [largest] Integer
    description : [conflict] Text
    subject_code : [dynamic] java_member_decl Set
    test_data : [union] test_case Set
}

aggregate specifies_relationship {            (e)
    specification : [union]Z_fragment Set
    implementation : [union]java_member_decl Set
}
```

Fig. 4. Sample aggregate declarations

Aggregates formed from collections of fine-grained artifacts can be used for a variety of different purposes, from capturing simple views, to capturing heterogeneous views containing artifacts of different types (e.g., code and rich text documentation), to representing relationships between different structures (e.g., connecting a UML diagram to the code that it models), to representing metadata. In order to support these diverse purposes, aggregates must provide more structure than a conventional source file. We have defined a mechanism which allows administrators and users to define types of aggregates for different purposes. A full discussion of the aggregate system is beyond the scope of this paper, and can be found in [8].

Briefly, the aggregate system provides a mechanism for specifying structured types for repository artifacts containing references to other repository artifacts. The aggregate type system is similar to the type systems used for defining data structures in programming languages such as ML. The aggregate types are additionally annotated with information describing how merges should be implemented for their instances.

Some sample aggregate types are illustrated in figure 4. The first example illustrates how a compilable Java class can be implemented as a Stellation aggregate; the second illustrates an aggregate structure for a simple Java view; the next two suggest how Stellation could capture bug reports using aggregates; and the final illustrates how aggregates could represent the relationship between parts of a specification and the code that implements the specified behavior.

2.2   Queries and Program Organization

A crucial key to our form of multidimensionality is the method used for generation of VSFs, aggregates, and program organizations. For this purpose, we have designed a query language that allows programmers to specify how artifacts are selected for inclusion in a VSF. It also provides higher order constructs that allow groups of related VSFs to be gathered into virtual directories and complete program organizations.

Queries specify predicates that a program artifact must satisfy for inclusion in a VSF. These predicates can be based on syntactic structure, on semantic information generated by simple program analysis, on contextual information provided by the programming environment (such as compilation context information), or from annotations attached to an artifact by the programmer. Due to space constraints, we will not describe Stellation's query language in detail here; we plan to specify it completely in a future publication. Figure 5 illustrates a query to generate the menu management VSF shown in figure 2. The syntax illustrated is based on a set theoretic query mechanism; the queries can be read as set comprehensions.

In our programming environment, programmers can build queries incrementally, by viewing the results of an approximate query, and then gradually refining it, both by changing the predicate specified in the query and by explicitly adding or removing program artifacts.

```
Menu_mgmt = new java_vsf {
    name = "menu management"
    description = "Menu management component"
    members = all m : java_method |
                m calls subscribe("menu.contribution.request", *, *)
                OR m.name = contributeMenu
                OR m calls sendMessage("menu.contribution", *, *)
                OR m.name = UIDriver.populateMenus
}
```

Fig. 5. Query to extract the menu management VSF illustrated in figure 2

2.3   Linguistic Knowledge

The query system described in the previous section requires linguistic and semantic knowledge about the system under development. In a conventional SCM system, no semantic knowledge is available: program artifacts are managed as opaque atomic entities. In Stellation, this knowledge is generated through dynamically registered extension components. Each program artifact is tagged with information about its language, and that tag is used to identify a collection of components which should be used for analysis of that artifact.

Stellation supports two kinds of extension components: analysis extensions, and query extensions. An analysis extension is executed on an artifact whenever a new version is stored in the repository, and generates a summary string which is stored with the artifact version. A query extension provides a set of predicates that can be used in a query expression. A common idiom for the use of these extensions is to provide paired analysis and query extensions, where the analysis extension provides summary information which is used by the query extension to rapidly determine if a candidate artifact belongs in a VSF.

2.4   Locks and Coordination

The query system is also used for coordination. Stellation uses an advisory lock based coordination mechanism. When a programmer wants to make a change to the system,they issue a query specifying a collection of artifacts to lock. To actually acquire the lock, they are required to give a description of the change that they are making, which is recorded by the system: this description is first associated with the lock (while it exists) and then with the change (when it is completed and the lock is released). There are two significant advantages to this approach. First, the programmer can lock exactly the set of artifacts associated with a change. Instead of locking an entire source file (as in most file-based SCM systems), or locking individual fine-grained artifacts (as in most fine-grained SCM systems), the programmer can precisely specify the scope of the change, and lock exactly the relevant artifacts.

Second, this mechanism enhances team communication and awareness of other programmers. While the change is in process, a programmer who tries to create a conflicting lock will be informed of the conflict, and will see the description of the conflicting change. If they want to break the lock, they are free to do so, but the programmer holding the lock will be notified of the break, and the description of the change that required the break.

3 Hierarchical Replication

As we mentioned earlier, one of the critical problems in widely distributed development is the limited communication bandwidth available between the programmers working on a project. In addition to this bandwidth gap, there is also a time gap: when programmers are scattered in different time zones, their active work times may not overlap at all. In order to address bandwidth limitations, the Stellation repository functions as a collection of loosely coupled repository replicas. In order to address the issues of time synchronization and the lack of direct communication available to co-located programmers, communication facilities related to coordination are integrated into the repository, so that programmers who cannot interact directly can still stay in close touch and coordinate their work.

The Stellation repository is implemented as a family of related repository replicas, which are coordinated through a low-bandwidth subscription based messaging system. The use of a repository hierarchy allows individual programmers and project sub-teams to work closely together, without having to pay the bandwidth cost of global coordination and consistency. In addition, the use of repository replicas provides a style of disciplined implicit branching that allows project sub-teams to isolate their changes in progress,but still maintain contact and coordination with the rest of the project. It enables programmers working in diverse locations to closely coordinate with an SCM program repository without requiring continual network contact with the central root server. We will present the Stellation hierarchical repository in two parts: first, we describe how repository replication and the hierarchy work to provide safe change isolation, and then we will describe how changes made in isolation are propagated outward through the system by programmer initiated releases.

3.1 Replication and Change Isolation

The Stellation repository is implemented as a hierarchy of linked repository replicas. The system provides a central master program repository, which manages the master copy of the system. Anything which has been checked in to the master repository is available to all programmers working on the project. This master repository is replicated by each project sub-team, to provide a private sub repository. The sub-repository may be further replicated to produce sub-repositories for smaller sub-teams until each programmer (or each small team of programmers) has a private sub-repository where they can place their own changes. Changes can be checked into these sub-repositories without those changes becoming visible to the rest of the project team. (We call this ability to

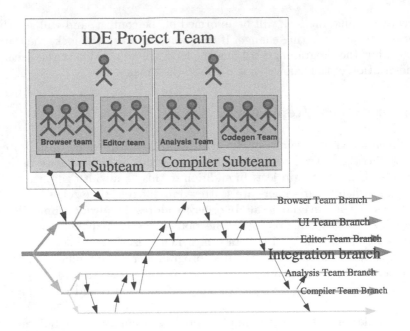

Fig. 6. Team structure and repository replication

create frequent isolated project versions *temporal fine granularity*.) We illustrate an example of a project team divided into sub-teams, and the corresponding repository replica structure in figure 6.

The sub-repositories are linked to their parent using a subscription based notification facility. When relevant events occur, notifications are transmitted between the levels of the tree. For instance, when a unit of code is changed, information about the change is transmitted from the repository where the change occurred to its parent. If appropriate, the parent transmits information about that change to its parent and to its other children. When a replica is disconnected from the network, relevant events are queued and transmitted en masse when connection is reestablished.

3.2   Change Integration

As discussed in the previous section, in Stellation, changes are initially isolated to a private repository replica. When the programmers responsible for that replica reach stable point, they need to be able to make their changes accessible to other members of the project. In Stellation, this process is called *releasing* a set of changes. Change releases are integrated into the repository hierarchy. When a programmer releases a set of changes from her replica, the entire set of changes is copied to her replicas parent. After a release, the parent repository reflects a different head version of artifacts than any other sub-repositories not involved in the release. The parent then sends out a notification to any other child replicas, informing them that they need to re-synchronize their sub-repository. Upon receiving this notification, the replicas will alert the associated users of the availability of changes. When the users of the replica are ready, they can resynchronize with the parent replica, integrating the newly released changes into their replica. This resynchronization is initiated by the user of the replica, rather than automatically, in order to prevent abrupt, unexpected changes from interfering with programmers in the middle of some task, and to ensure that programmers are always aware of updates.

For example, in figure 6, suppose that a member of project sub-team A2 makes a change to the system, affecting artifacts "j", "h", and "k" (illustrated in the figure by marking the changed artifacts with dotted lines). This change is immediately visible to other members of sub-team A2; but to members of sub-team a1 or any other sub-team, the changes are not visible. When the members of sub-team A2 become confident in the stability of the changes, these changes are integrated into repository replica "A", making them visible to all members of sub-team A, including sub-team A1, but not yet making them available to members of sub-team B.

Because of the locking mechanisms, users rarely make concurrent changes to a single fragment. But under some circumstances, concurrent changes are unavoidable. In such a situation, Stellation will perform an optimistic merge of the concurrent changes, and if any errors are detected, it will notify the programmers responsible for the conflicting changes, and they will then be responsible for resolving the conflicts.

3.3   Hierarchical Coordination

Stellation tightly integrates support for repository replication hierarchy and lock based coordination. Programmers can request that locks be placed at any point in the replication hierarchy; and a lock can be placed by a replica owner in a manner that allows changes to a collection of artifacts to all programmers accessing a given sub-hierarchy of replicas, while all programmers accessing replicas outside of the selected region view the artifacts as locked. Inside the lock-holding sub-hierarchy, the artifacts are viewed as unlocked, and further locks can be placed which affect only that sub-hierarchy.

For example, in the programming environment project shown in figure 6, we illustrate a typical scenario of how locks integrate with the replica/branch hierarchy in figure 7. In this diagram, shaded areas represent locks.

The UI sub-team places a lock on the menu management code, consisting of the set of artifacts $\{J, H, K, I, L\}$. The lock is assigned to the UI team's shared branch, resulting in the situation as shown where the artifacts are locked in the main branch and all of the child branches outside of the UI team hierarchy; within the UI team branch and its children, the artifacts remain unlocked. Thus, to all programmers outside of the UI sub-team, the menu management subsystem is locked. But for the UI team, the subsystem is unlocked.

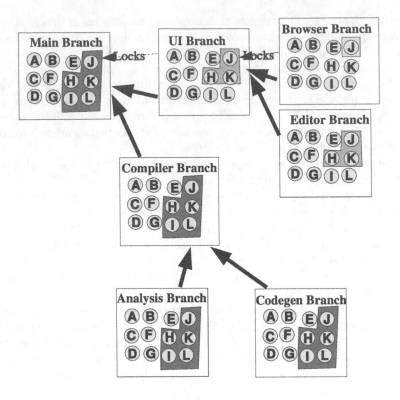

Fig. 7. Hierarchical locking

Next, a member of the browser team locks the browsers menu management code in the UI branch/replica. This lock covers artifacts $\{J, H, K\}$. Now the lock is assigned to the Browser team branch, and the artifacts are locked in the rest of the UI branch hierarchy. Finally, the programmers in the browser team could then edit that code, placing locks that affect other members of the browser sub-team as appropriate (as illustrated by the lock on artifact J in the figure.. When all of the subsystem changes were complete, then the global lock could be released, and the changes integrated into the global repository.

This hierarchical coordination mechanism allows programmers to use locks at different granularities to reflect different degrees of closeness in collaboration. The closer the collaboration, the finer the granularity of locks. This mechanism also minimizes communication bandwidth required for coordination by eliminating the need to communicate information about fine-grained locks to all of the repository replicas.

4 Related Work

For the most part, the individual features that make up Stellation are not novel; it is our combination of them in a distributed collaborative setting that provides new capabilities that better address the problems of distributed team-based programming better than any of its predecessors.

Replication has appeared in TeamWare [21], Infuse [17], and Adele [10,2]. Branching facilities that provide semantically similar functionality are provided by Vesta [13] and Clearcase [18,28]. Finally, another family of systems including Adele and Infuse allow the use of sub-repositories.

Distributed support for SCM has been provided by several systems. CVS [4], while generally a weak system, provides excellent support for remote repository access. NUCM [26,27] and ENVY [16] each provide support for remote repository access and repository replication. Bitkeeper [3] provides a mechanism for allowing programmers to work in private repositories without any inter-repository coordination, and to integrate changes through email using patch packages. The W3C has released the WebDAV [12,9] extensions to HTTP that provide a network based access mechanism to SCM repositories. The WebDAV protocol will likely be supported by a future version of Stellation.

Locks as a coordination mechanism date back at least to RCS [25] and SCCS. Optimistic coordination has been provided by a large number of systems, including the popular open-source SCM system CVS [4].

Fine-grained versioning as a mechanism for inter-programmer coordination was explored by the COOP/Orm project [1]. COOP/Orm used an even finer grained form than than Stellation. However, COOP/Orm assumed that programmers were geographically local, and had high-bandwidth network connections between the programmers.

Many systems, including Adele [10], Vesta [13], Infuse [17] and DSEE [15], have focused attention on software building as a different aspect of the collaborative programming problem. Stellation does not yet make any attempt to address this problem; we hope to make this a focus for the future.

The idea of multidimensionality used by Stellation originated in the separation of concerns community, and the ideas were developed in discussions with IBM's HyperSpaces [24] team. The basic abstractions of Stellation and HyperJ are another mechanism for achieving the same goals as aspect oriented programming [14]. This notion is closely related to the dynamic view mechanisms of the Gwydion Sheets environment [20], and Desert [19], and the dynamic hierarchical configurations in ICE [29], Adele, and Infuse [17].

5 Conclusion

In this paper, we have briefly discussed the Stellation software configuration management system. Stellation is designed to simplify the task of developing large scale software systems, particularly when that development occurs in a geographically distributed environment. Stellation provides a set of features, including multidimensionality, repository replication and hierarchical coordination, that enhance the ability of programmers separated by distance and time to communicate, collaborate, and coordinate their work.

Stellation is an open-source sub-project of the Eclipse Technologies project. The full source code of the current system is available from Eclipse at `http://www.eclipse.org/stellation`.

References

1. B. Magnusson and U. Asklund. Fine grained version control of configurations in COOP/Orm. In *ICSE'96 SCM-6 Workshop*, pages 31–48, 1996.
2. N. Belkhatir, J. Estublier, and W. Melo. Adele 2: A support to large software development process. In *Proceedings of the 1st International Conference on the Software Process*, 1991.
3. Inc. Bitkeeper. BitKeeper source management: Details of operation. Webpage: `http://www.bitkeeper.com/bk05.html`.
4. P. Cederqvist. *CVS Reference Manual*, 1998. Available online at `http://www.loria.fr/~molli/cvs/doc/cvs_toc.html`.
5. M. Chu-Carroll and S. Sprenkle. Coven: Brewing better collaboration through software configuration management. In *Proceedings of FSE 2000*, 2000.
6. M. C. Chu-Carroll. Supporting distributed collaboration through multidimensional software configuration management. In *Proceedings of the 10th ICSE Workshop on Software Configuration Management*, 2001.
7. M. C. Chu-Carroll, J. Wright, and A. T. T. Ying. Aspects and multidimensionality in software configuration management. In *Proceedings of the 2nd Conference on Aspect-Oriented Software Development*, pages 188–197, 2003.
8. Mark C. Chu-Carroll, James Wright, and David Shields. Supporting aggregation in fine grained software configuration management. In *Proceedings of SIGSOFT FSE 10*, 2002. To appear.
9. G. Clemm, J. Amsden, T. Ellison, C. Kaler, and J. Whitehead. Versioning extensions to WebDAV: Internet draft, draft-ietf-webdav-versioning-20-final. Technical Report RFC3253, The Internet Society, March 2002.
10. J. Estublier and R. Casallas. *Configuration Management*, chapter The Adele Configuration Manager. Wiley and Sons, Ltd., 1994.
11. E. Gamma, R. Helm, R. Johnson, and J. Vlissides. *Design Patterns : Elements of Reusable Object-Oriented Software*. Addison Wesley, 1994.
12. Y. Goland, E. Whitehead, A. Faizi, S. Carter, and D. Jensen. HTTP extensions for distributed authoring – WebDAV. proposed standard - request for comments (rfc) 2518. Technical report, The Internet Society, February 1999.
13. A. Heydon, R. Levin, T. Mann, and Y. Yu. The vesta approach to software configuration management. Technical Report 1999-01, Compaq SRC, 1999.
14. G. Kiczales, J. Lamping, A. Mendhekar, C. Maeda, C. Videira Lopes, J. Loingtier, and J. Irwin. Aspect-Oriented Programming. In *Proceedings of ECOOP*, June 1997.
15. D. Lubkin. Heterogeneous configuration management with DSEE. In *Proceedings of the 3rd Workshop on Software Configuration Management*, pages 153–160, 1991.
16. OTI. ENVY/Developer: The collaborative component development environment for IBM visualage and objectshare, inc. visualworks. Webpage: available online at: `http://www.oti.com/briefs/ed/edbrief5i.htm`.

17. D. Perry and G. Kaiser. Infuse: a tool for automatically managing and coordinating source changes in large systems. In *Proceedings of the ACM Computer Science Conference*, 1987.
18. Rational ClearCase. Pamphlet at `http://www.rational.com`, 2000.
19. S. Reiss. Simplifying data integration: the design of the Desert software development environment. In *Proceedings of ICSE 18*, pages 398–407, 1996.
20. R. Stockton and N. Kramer. The Sheets hypercode editor. Technical Report 0820, CMU Department of Computer Science, 1997.
21. Sun Microsystems, Inc. TeamWare user's guides, 1994.
22. R.E. Filman T. Elrad and A. Bader (editors). Special section on Aspect Oriented Programming. *Communications of the ACM*, 44(10):28–97, October 2001.
23. P. Tarr, W. Harrison, H. Ossher, A. Finkelstein, B. Nuseibeh, and D. Perry, editors. *Proceedings of the ICSE 2000 Workshop on Multi-Dimensional Separation of Concerns in Software Engineering*, 2000.
24. P. Tarr, H. Ossher, W. Harrison, and Jr. S. Sutton. N degrees of separation: Multi-dimensional separation of concerns. In *Proceedings of the 21st International Conference on Software Engineering*, pages 107–119, 1999.
25. W. Tichy. RCS - a system for version control. *Software: Practice and Experience*, 7(15), 1985.
26. A. van der Hoek, A. Carzaniga, D. Heimbigner, and A.Wolf. A reusable, distributed repository for configuration management policy programming. Technical Report CU-CS-864-98, University of Colorado Department of Computer Science, 1998.
27. A. van der Hoek, D. Heimbigner, and A. Wolf. A generic, peer-to-peer repository for distributed configuration management. In *Proceedings of ICSE 18*, March 1996.
28. Brian A. White. *Software Configuration Management Strategies and Rational ClearCase: A Practical Introduction*. Pearson Education, 2000.
29. A. Zeller. Smooth operations with square operators: the version set model in ICE. In *ICSE'96 SCM-6 Workshop*, pages 8–30, 1996.

Software Configuration Management Related to the Management of Distributed Systems and Service-Oriented Architectures

Vladimir Tosic, David Mennie, and Bernard Pagurek

Network Management and Artificial Intelligence Lab
Department of Systems and Computer Engineering, Carleton University
1125 Colonel By Drive, Ottawa, Ontario, K1S 5B6, Canada
{vladimir,bernie}@sce.carleton.ca

Abstract. We summarize our three research projects related to software configuration management and discuss three challenges for the future research in software configuration management. The three projects that we discuss are dynamic service composition from service components, extending service components with multiple classes of service and mechanisms for their manipulation, and dynamic evolution of network management software. The three challenges to software configuration management research that we are interested in are: 1) managing dynamism and run-time change, 2) integration of software configuration management with other management areas and domains, and 3) management of Web Service compositions.

1 Introduction

In the past, our research group focussed on researching the domain of network management including network configuration management. This included investigating the use of mobile agent technologies and artificial intelligence techniques to enhance how a network is controlled and managed. However, in recent years our focus has shifted more towards management of distributed systems and service-oriented architectures. Many of our recent research projects have uncovered issues related to software configuration management (SCM).

We view software configuration management as a part of the broader work on the management of distributed systems, networks, applications, and services. In particular, we are interested in managing dynamism and run-time change in distributed systems. Since this is a very complex problem with many open issues, we have broken it into sub-problems and our different research projects investigate one or more of these sub-problems from different perspectives and in different environments. The environment that is increasingly in the focus of our attention is a service-oriented architecture (SOA), particularly a Web Service composition. We view the management of dynamism and run-time change, the integration of software configuration management with

B.Westfechtel, A. van der Hoek (Eds.): SCM 2001/2003, LNCS 2649, pp. 54–69, 2003.

other management areas and domains, and the management of Web Services and Web Service compositions as three important challenges for the future research on software configuration management. While our research projects have uncovered some issues and provided some results, future work is necessary.

In this paper, we summarize some of our projects, experiences, and results related to software configuration management and discuss the three challenges to software configuration management mentioned above. In this section, we gave an introduction into the relationship between our research and software configuration management. In the next section, we define terminology used in this paper. In particular, we define the terms 'service-oriented architecture' and 'service component'. In the following three sections we summarize our three projects most related to software configuration management. Firstly, we present an architecture supporting dynamic (i.e., run-time) composition of service components. Secondly, we summarize our work on service components with multiple classes of service and dynamic adaptation mechanisms based on the manipulation of classes of service. Thirdly, we discuss our results on software hot-swapping – an approach to dynamic evolution of software with minimal disruption of its operation. After the summary of these three research projects, we discuss three challenges to software configuration management. Section 6 discusses management of dynamism and run-time change. Section 7 examines the need of integrating software configuration management and other management areas and domains. Section 8 outlines some issues related to the management of Web Service compositions. In the final section of the paper, we summarize conclusions.

2 Software Components as Service Components

The concepts such as a service-oriented architecture, the "software is a service" business model, service component, and particularly a Web Service have become common in software literature. Since our research uses these concepts and since we argue that service-oriented architectures rise new challenges to software configuration management, we briefly define these terms here.

Unfortunately, an unambiguous definition of these concepts is not possible because the term 'service' has many different meanings. These meanings vary between different areas and even between works of different authors discussing the same area. For the topic of this paper, we emphasize two of dictionary definitions of the term service: 1) useful labor that does not produce a tangible commodity; and 2) a facility supplying some public demand. These meanings are reflected in the 'software is a service' business model. In the traditional 'shrink-wrap' software business model, software is a product that is delivered on some external memory medium (e.g., a Compact Disk – CD), sold in stores, and has to be installed on the computer(s) of end users. In the 'software is a service' business model, software is no longer a product, but a service available over a network (e.g., a virtual private network – VPN or the Internet). Some of the advertised benefits of this software business model are faster and easier distribution of software updates, easier management of dependencies between software modules, and more optimal utilization of computing resources. A number of application service providers (ASPs) use this business model to provide network access to software applications. In addition, component service providers (CSPs) started to appear. They offer network access not to monolithic applications, but to libraries of composable service components.

In this paper, by a 'service component' we mean 'a self-contained, network-accessible unit of service provisioning and management that encapsulates some service functionality and data, has a well-defined interface, and can be composed with other service components'. A service component is relatively independent from other service components in a particular composition – it can be relatively easily detached and replaced with another appropriate service component. Also, it can be reused in many different service compositions. Many authors use the term 'service' with the same meaning we use for 'service component'. The two terms can be used interchangeably, but we prefer the term 'service component' because the term 'service' has far too many different meanings and does not reflect composability. In addition, when we speak about 'service management', 'service' means 'customer view of the functionality provided by the system'. Note that services and service components can provide not only software functionality and data, but also access to some hardware resources, such as memory, printing, and network bandwidth[1]. However, in this paper we are predominantly interested in software-based service components. A service component is a higher-level abstraction than a software component or a distributed object. It can be implemented with one or more software components and/or distributed objects and/or other software entities. Despite the differences, there are also many similarities between service components and software components. Consequently, we find important relationships between the creation and management of service components and the work on component configuration management [1].

A service-oriented architecture (SOA) [2] is a software architecture where monolithic applications are decomposed into distributed network-accessible service components, potentially provided by different business entities. The relationships and interactions between service components are not determined during design-time or deployment-time, but during run-time. When a new provider (supplier) service component becomes available during run-time, its description is published in a registry (directory or repository). When some requester (consumer) service component needs new functionality during run-time, it searches the repository to find an appropriate provider service component. When it finds such a provider, it retrieves its network address from the repository and invokes the provider directly. This is known as the 'publish-find-bind' model of dynamic interaction between service components.

Several industrial initiatives and standardization efforts of several industrial forums are based on the concept of a Web service. A Web service[2] is a service component (in our definition) that is identified by a set of Uniform Resource Identifiers (URIs) and can be described, published, found, composed, and invoked using Extensible Markup Language (XML) based technologies. The three most widely used Web Service technologies are the Web Service Description Language (WSDL), the SOAP XML messag-

---

[1] A recent example of a service component that can encapsulate both software and hardware functionality is a Grid Service, a special case of a Web Service.

[2] A recent definition of a Web Service can be found in [3].

ing protocol, and the Universal Description, Discovery, and Integration (UDDI) directory [2]. Web Services are currently the most widely used service-oriented architecture.

3 An Architecture Supporting Dynamic Service Composition

Dynamic service composition is the process of creating new services at run-time from
a set of service components. This process includes activities that must take place
before the actual composition such as locating and selecting service components that
will take part in the composition, and activities that must take place after the composition such as registering the new service with a service registry. Dynamic service composition can also be used for adapting running applications and changing their existing functionality by adding or removing features. Ideally, dynamic service composition
is an automated process with minimal human involvement. An example of dynamic
service composition is when a user requires an Internet search engine that will filter
out advertising from the results returned for a particular query, but this service was
not designed ahead of time. The user could ask some dynamic composition architecture to assemble such service at run-time from an Internet search engine and adver-
tisement filtering software, implemented as service components.

There are several benefits to dynamic service composition, but we emphasize increased flexibility, adaptability, agility, and availability. Firstly, support for dynamic
service composition enhances flexibility and adaptability of software systems. To
address new problems or needs, many new services can be assembled from a set of
basic service components. These services may not have been designed or even con-
ceived during design or deployment time. The composition can be performed on demand of the application or a user. While dynamic service composition has limits because not every new service can be realized as a combination of existing service components, it can be a useful mechanism for dynamic system evolution. Secondly, dynamic composition of service components increases agility of software systems. It
happens during run-time, in limited time, and with minimal human involvement. Consequently, it enables faster adaptation to new circumstances or demands than off-line
system redesign. Thirdly, dynamic service composition enhances the overall system
availability. It minimizes interruptions of services provided to users during upgrades or
the addition of new functionality into the system.

Composing service components at run-time is a challenging undertaking because of
all the subtleties of the procedure involved, the many exceptions to the compositional
rules that can occur, and the possibility of error and unexpected problems [4, 5]. One
of the main challenges is in dealing with many unexpected issues in a relatively short
time. All decisions must be made relatively quickly or dynamic composition becomes
impractical. Further, since the composition is performed at run-time, it is not possible
to predict or test everything during design time. In dynamic composition, as we have
defined it, it is extremely difficult to predict beforehand the exact environmental conditions that will exist in a system at the time the composition is performed. We call this
unanticipated dynamic composition [6], meaning that all potential compositions are

not known and neither the service components nor the supporting composition infrastructure are aware if a particular composition will be successful until it is actually carried out. While some steps can be taken to decrease the chance of a failed composition, it cannot always be avoided. Further, unexpected interactions between the composed service components can occur, but they cannot be easily and rapidly discovered and recovered from. Human input can be used for alleviating such problems, but human involvement can also significantly slow the composition process. Locating components at run-time for composition requires a component library or code repository that is integrated with the software infrastructure performing the composition.

One of the fundamental challenges in composing services at run-time is the design and implementation of an infrastructure that will support the process. There is a lack of support for dynamic techniques in programming languages and other development tools, so specialized tools are needed. We have designed and implemented a general-purpose dynamic service composition architecture called the Infrastructure for Composability At Run-time of Internet Services (ICARIS) [4, 5]. The architecture provides all of the required functionality to form composite services from two or more service components that have been designed for composability. While this architecture was developed before Web Service technologies appeared, some of its results can be beneficial for the study of Web Service compositions.

One of the measures we have taken to minimize problems with service compositions in ICARIS was to bundle each service component with a comprehensive specification that describes all known dependencies, constraints, and potential incompatibilities. This specification also contains a list of the operations contained within the service component that can be reused in a composite component. These methods are referred to as composable methods. By looking at the specification for each component of interest before attempting to aggregate them in a composite service, failed attempts can be minimized or recovered from. The general rule is that the composition is aborted if a conflict is detected by the supporting infrastructure.

The ICARIS architecture supports three primary composition techniques [4, 5]:

1. composite service interface,
2. stand-alone composite service using a pipe-and-filter architecture, and
3. stand-alone composite service with a single body of code.

The creation of a composite service interface for several service components is achieved by extracting and combining signatures of their composable methods. Service components involved in the composition remain distinct, while communicating with consumers (clients) through the common composite service interface. The composite service interface redirects all incoming calls to the appropriate service component for execution.

The creation of a new stand-alone composite service from multiple service components is achieved by interconnecting service components using a pipe-and-filter architecture. In essence, the pipe-and-filter architecture chains the output of one service component to the input of the next. While this is a fairly primitive connection scheme, some complex constructions are also possible. One example is when the outputs of one component are looped back into its inputs. Other connection schemes, such as service components processing the same input in parallel, are not supported in the

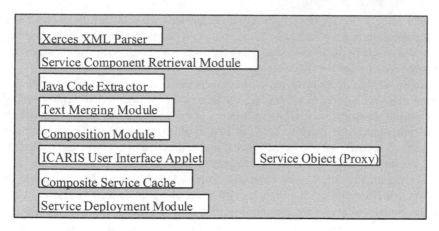

Fig. 1. Architecture of the ICARIS Configuration Manger

ICARIS architecture because they introduce a number of potential problems for dynamic service composition. While this is a limitation of ICARIS, the pipe-and-filter architecture can be enough for many applications.

The creation of a new stand-alone composite service with a single body of code is achieved by extracting and assembling the composable methods from software-based service components involved in the composition. The corresponding method signatures are also merged into a new composite service specification. This is the most challenging type of service composition and one motivation for its undertaking can be performance. In theory, a composite service with a single body of code may take longer to create than the other types of composite services, but it should also execute much faster.

To illustrate a justifiable use of dynamic service composition techniques and the viability of the ICARIS architecture, we have developed an ICARIS prototype based on Java, Jini, JavaBeans, and XML. These base technologies were not altered, but the Jini Lookup Service (LS) was extended to support the semantically rich comprehensive specification of XML service components and their "fuzzy" matching. Component composition is achieved at runtime by using an application of JavaBeans and the Extensible Runtime Containment and Services Protocol (ERCSP). The ICARIS prototype consists of the Jini infrastructure, the Registration Manager, and the Composition Manager. The Registration Manager is the entity that is responsible for managing registration and access rights. This includes registration of clients, servers, and service brokers. The Composition Manager is the entity that is responsible for the actual dynamic service composition in the system. Its architecture is given in Figure 1 [4]. Two other elements called the Service Broker and the Service Provider are also required, but they are not considered parts of the ICARIS infrastructure and can be provided by third parties. The Service Broker is used to store and retrieve Service Items. Service components are provided by a Service Provider and are stored with a Service Broker within a structure called a Service Item. A Service Item is made up of two major parts: a Service Object (Proxy) implemented as a valid JavaBean and a Service Specification written in XML. To support composition of new stand-alone services with a single body of code, a separate repository in the Service Broker stores the raw source code for the Service Object.

Based on this ICARIS prototype, we have developed the Composable Security Application (CSA). CSA enables dynamic, on-demand construction and deployment of point-to-point security associations between a client and a server in the network. It enables introduction of security services into applications that were not originally designed with security mechanisms. Since the specification of security associations is carried out at run-time, the composite client and server security services are constructed dynamically. CSA is an accessible, robust infrastructure that is capable of establishing many types of security associations for any application. Additionally, it is both fast enough to assemble and deploy these associations at run-time and flexible enough to add or remove secure services to meet the needs of the applications it serves. Our application of ICARIS to dynamic composition of security associations showed the viability and feasibility of our concepts and demonstrated the applicability of dynamic service composition.

4   Service Components with Multiple Service Offerings

Another project in our research group investigates the concept of classes of service for service components and management applications of dynamic manipulation of classes of service. Classes of service can be used for customization of service components to various consumers. Manipulation of classes of service enables dynamic adaptation of service components and their compositions without breaking these compositions. In this project, we are particularly interested in service components that are loosely coupled, i.e., distributed and not very dependent. Further, we study cases where one service component can be a part of many different compositions and serve many different consumers. Web Services are such service components, so they are in the focus of this research project. This research is compatible with Web Service industrial initiatives and explores issues that they currently do not address. It can also be viewed as complementary to the work on dynamic service composition and to the work on adaptable software using re-composition [7].

For a service component used in a variety of different service compositions, it can be useful to offer several different classes of service to its consumers. A class of service is a discrete variation of the complete service and quality of service (QoS) provided by one service component. Classes of service can differ in usage privileges, service priorities, response times guaranteed to consumers, verbosity of response information, etc. The concept of classes of service also supports different capabilities, rights, and needs of potential consumers of the service component, including power and type of devices they execute on. Further, different classes of service may imply different utilization of the underlying hardware and software resources and, consequently, have different prices. Additionally, different classes of service can be used for different payment models, like pay-per-use or subscription-based. Differentiation of classes of services gives consumers a wider choice of delivered functionality and QoS. On the other hand, it gives the provider service component an opportunity to better balance its limited hardware and software resources and to address the needs of a bigger set of consumers. Note that for software components the benefits of differentiating classes of service are not as strong as for service comp onents.

Classes of service are not the only possible mechanism for differentiation of function-tionality and QoS. We have also examined relevant alternatives, including parameteri-zation, multiple interfaces, multiple service components, and personalization tech-niques like user profiling. The main advantages of having a relatively limited number of classes of service over other approaches to service customization are limited complex-ity of required management and relatively low overhead incurred.

In the ICARIS project, we have concluded that formal and comprehensive descrip-tion of service components is needed for more precise run-time selection of service components and for minimization of unexpected side effects of dynamic service com-position. On the other hand, the benefits of the formal specification of constraints in component-based software engineering are widely recognized [8]. In this project, we have examined what are the crucial parts of classes of service for service comp onents. The formal specification of QoS (non-functional) constraints—describing issues such as performance, availability, and reliability—and prices is probably most important. As the number of service components in the market offering similar functionality in-creases, the QoS, price/performance ratio, and adaptability will become the major dif-ferentiation criteria. Formal specification of QoS constraints is also important for appli-cation and service management. It specifies what QoS metrics to monitor and what conditions to check to know whether the guaranteed QoS were obeyed. Another im-portant category of constraint is an authorization right (policy). Authorization rights can be used for differentiation of service and for security management purposes. Fu r-ther, the formal specification of constraints can be used for choosing between service components implementing operations with the same signature. In addition, the formal specification of supported coordination protocols and design patterns, as well as of known composition incompatibilities can be very useful in the dynamic composition process.

In our work, a service component can have not only mult iple interfaces (units of service functionality), but also multiple service offerings. We define a service offering as the formal representation of one class of service for a service component. Service offerings relate to the same functionality (i.e., operations of the service comp onent), but differ in QoS constraints, authorization rights, and cost. Occasionally, differences in functional constraints (preconditions, postconditions, and invariants) may exist between service offerings, but this is generally not the case. By separating the con-cepts of an interfa ce and a service offering, we provide additional support for dynamic flexibility and adaptability within a service component.

For the formal specification of service offerings for Web Services, we are develop-ing a novel XML-based language – the Web Service Offerings Language (WSOL)[3]. A comprehensive description of service components would contain description of all

---

[3] Actually, WSOL is now almost completely developed. More information about WSOL can be found in [9, 10, 11].

operations, interfaces, functional constraints, QoS constraints, access rights, prices, compatibilities and incompatibilities, service offerings, and other appropriate information. However, since operations and interfaces (ports) of Web Services are already specified in WSDL, WSOL is made compatible with WSDL and specifies only additional information. WSOL enables the formal specification of functional constraints, QoS constraints, access rights for differentiation of services, price, and some other management statements for Web Services. The specification of security information is currently outside the scope of WSOL, while the specification of supported coordination protocols, design patterns, and known composition incompatibilities is left for future work.

Apart from the formal specification of classes of service, we are also researching manipulation of classes of service as mechanisms for dynamic adaptation of service compositions. We are developing algorithms and infrastructure support for switching between service offerings, deactivation/reactivation of existing service offerings, and (to some limited extent) creation of new appropriate service offerings. By 'creation of new service offerings' we mean the creation of new sets of constraints for the existing functionality, not the creation of new functionality or new functional interfaces. While these dynamic adaptation mechanisms have limited power compared to re-composition, we find them suitable for several different situations. For example, if a service offering has to be dynamically deactivated while it is used by at least one consumer, maybe the consumer would be satisfied with another service offering from the same service component. Another example is using dynamic creation of service offerings after dynamic evolution of a service component. Some of the issues that we try to address in our research of these dynamic adaptation mechanisms are: how to relate service offerings to better support automatic switching between them, how to integrate into service components the support for deactivation/reactivation of service offerings, how to support rules governing creation of new service offerings, etc. We are developing[4] prototype architecture implementing support for service offering and their dynamic manipulation for Web Service.

5   Dynamic Evolution of Network Management Software

Our research group is also investigating the issue of the dynamic evolution of software with minimal disruption of its operation. This is an important issue for high-availability and real-time systems. The evolution required can be [12]:

1. corrective – fixing bugs or problems,
2. perfective – improving performance,
3. extensive – adding new functionality, and/or
4. adaptive – adaptation to new operation environments.

As noted in [7], a number of different approaches have been taken by research institutions trying to address this issue. The major efforts are based on the design of a

---

[4] A discussion of our recent results in this area and some recent related works is given in [11].

software architecture, a new programming language, a data-flow architecture, a distributed system, a distributed object technology such as CORBA and COM, a compiler, an operating system, or a real-time system that will support software evolution. Some of the issues that pertain to dynamic software evolution are described in [13]. These include developing the appropriate infrastructure support, developing dynamically upgradable software modules, defining the module granularity, defining the scenarios where software upgrading is allowed or not allowed, obeying the limits on the allowed duration of the upgrading process, transferring the state between module versions, and transactional issues.

We are particularly interested in the problem of dynamic software evolution as it pertains to network management software. A network management system is a relevant case study that can be used to capture general software evolution issues. Shutting down the entire network management system to perform an upgrade is not an appropriate solution for large mission critical networks. We have developed our own infrastructure and experimentally applied it to a modular Simple Network Management Protocol, version 3 (SNMPv3) system implemented in Java [12, 14].

Our approach to dynamic software evolution, called software hot-swapping [12, 13, 14], is based on the concept of swappable modules (S-modules) and corresponding non-swappable proxies (S-proxies). Only S-modules can be hot-swapped in our architecture. It must be decided during design time to make a software module a hot-swappable S-module. Currently, all application modules that are expected to be hot-swapped have to be manually converted to S-modules before a swap. We have attempted to automate the process of converting arbitrary application modules to S-modules and achieved some limited results. Each S-module has an S-proxy that is permanently associated with it. Only the S-proxy has a reference to the S-module. S-proxies are generated automatically when the application starts and are not changed during run-time. The S-module and the S-proxy together constitute an S-component. Apart from S-components, there can be a number of other non-swappable modules in the application. An application supporting hot-swapping must contain a Swap Manager that controls all swapping transactions. The Swap Manager has access to all S-modules and provides services listed in Table 1 [12].

Tab. 1. Swap Manager Services

Service	Explanation
Listening	Waits for new S-modules and instantiates them
Security	Performs authentication of incoming S-modules
Transaction	Provides control of hot-swapping transactions
Timing	Ensures timely completion of hot-swapping transactions
Event	Notification of hot-swap events to observers
Repository	Caches S-module states during transaction

When a new S-module version is transferred to the desired location using mobile code, its currently executing version has to be put into a swappable state before a hot-swap can take place. The S-proxy gets the state of the currently executing version, initializes the new S-module version with this state, and redirects all references from the current version to the new version. If during this process, the given swapping time limit is exceeded, the process is terminated and rolled-back. Otherwise, the new S-module version is started and the old S-module version is removed from the system. For the hot swap to succeed, the appropriate support for hot-swapping has to be integrated into S-modules. This includes the ability to extract the state of a running S-module and to initialize an S-module with the state extracted from the previous version. The mapping rules between different versions have to be defined for every S-module and can be implemented in S-module initialization methods.

This proxy-based approach was chosen after a study of the advantages and disadvantages of several possible solutions. Further details on this study are given in [13]. While we found the proxy-based technique to be suitable and efficient enough for the dynamic evolution of SNMPv3 modules [12], it is not applicable to all software architectures. For some real-time systems that require even higher availability, other approaches to dynamic software evolution may be more appropriate. One of the issues of this proxy approach is that it accommodates hot-swapping of S-modules that provide different operation implementations, but not S-modules with different operation signatures. Another issue is that every S-module is accompanied by one S-proxy and when the number of S-modules is high, the overhead of creating and managing the same number of S-proxies cannot be ignored. Further, our implementation uses Java reflection, which can affect system performance significantly. There is a tradeoff between the flexibility of the architecture and its performance. For network management, the flexibility likely outweighs performance issues, but this need not be the case with other applications.

6   The Challenge of Managing Dynamism and Run-Time Change

Managing dynamism and run-time change is the most important challenge for software configuration management that we have focussed on in our research. The archetypal problem we are addressing is how to dynamically and autonomously (i.e., without explicit human intervention) reconfigure and, if necessary, upgrade software to minimize the effects of a fault or a performance problem on an end user. This problem is a very complex one with many open issues.

An important aspect in all our research efforts is the modular nature of software – we investigate dynamism and run-time change issues on the level of software components or modules. Consequently, our work has relevance to the domain of component configuration management. As discussed in [1] and as we have experienced, the emphasis in software configuration management has moved:

1. from development time to run time,
2. from the source code management to the integration and version management of the components,
3. from the management of implementation libraries to the management of interfaces.

The possibility of run-time change supports valuable system agility, flexibility, and adaptability, but it also gives rise to a number of problems, some of which can be alleviated by applying software configuration management. Important examples are dependency management and ensuring consistency. The software configuration management work on dependency management is a good starting point for future research, but it should be re-evaluated in the context of very frequent change and the crucial requirement of timely reaction. Similarly, the software configuration management mechanisms for version tracking and management have to be re-evaluated. With frequent run-time changes, it becomes also harder to achieve consistency. Software configuration management should research not only methods that try to ensure consistency before the change occurs, but also methods that enable successful system operation when the change causes an inconsistency. It is not possible to always precisely predict or test the effects of run-time changes. Therefore, the run-time software configuration management infrastructure should have mechanisms to discover inconsistencies and recover (e.g., rollback) from unsuccessful changes. However, to achieve a consistent state, a system might have to pass through intermediary inconsistent states and therefore mechanisms for transactional changes are also needed. The importance of flexibility, availability, scalability, and performance of management solutions (including software configuration management) will increase further. While our research is focused on increasing flexibility and availability, we also examine scalability and performance issues in our research projects.

7 The Challenge of Integrating Software Configuration Management with Othe r Management Areas and Domains

The International Organization for Standardization (ISO) identifies configuration management as one of five management functional areas, which also include fault management, performance management, accounting management, and security management. Further, software configuration management is a subset of application management, which covers distribution, installation, configuration, monitoring, maintenance, versioning, and removal of application software. Also, the management of software (i.e., applications) is becoming more tightly connected with the management of computer systems (both stand-alone and distributed), peripheral devices, networking infrastructure, databases, and other resources. Integrated network and system management – also known as enterprise management – strives to unify these management domains within the overall computing/communication system. A further unification is achieved with service management, which focuses on monitoring and controlling service level agreements (SLAs) between service providers and users. Service management adopts business- and customer- centric point of view, instead of the technology-centered point of view. This requires mapping technology-centered management activities and data into appropriate business issues and data directly showing how the value provided to end users and service providers' responsibilities stated in service level agreements are affected.

Service components can encapsulate not only software, but also hardware functionality. In this context, the issues like balancing limited underlying hardware and software resources during run-time and managing QoS become more important. Such issues are traditionally beyond the scope of software configuration management solutions. We believe that one of the main challenges for software configuration management in the future will be its integration with other management areas (fault, accounting, performance, and security management) and domains (device, desktop, network, system, data, application, enterprise, service management). Note that enterprise management software suites like Hewlett-Packard OpenView, IBM Tivoli, and Computer Associates Unicenter TNG already include some software configuration management functionality and integrate it with other management applications in the suite. Also, the Common Information Model (CIM) standard for description of network, system, and application management data can be used for describing software configurations. However, we see the need for further work and research, at least on three tightly interrelated topics:

1. Integration of configuration management and other management areas, particularly with other areas of application management.
2. Integration of software configuration management with system and network configuration management.
3. Mapping software configuration management solutions to service management, i.e., to business-related issues and data. To better support this mapping, the price/performance ratio, uninterrupted service availability, and other issues (both technical and non-technical) relevant to end users must be addressed.

The archetypal problem of dynamic reconfiguration given in the previous section also illustrates these issues. First, this dynamic reconfiguration problem requires integration of configuration management and fault or performance management. Further, the fault or performance problem in question can be software-based, but it can also be caused by an underlying computer hardware or network infrastructure, so the integration of application management with systems and network management is needed. Finally, as the ultimate goal of management is to minimize impacts on end users, this is also a service management problem.

We have explored such integration in our projects. For example, we have used the ICARIS architecture for dynamic composition of security services and the software hot-swapping for SNMPv3 security modules. In this way, we have used software configuration management to support application and network security management.

The research of mappings between software configuration management and service management can be extended with the research of relationships between software configuration management and business process management (BPM) systems. When activities in business processes are software modules or service components (e.g., Web Services), the description of the business process can be viewed as a software configuration description. Dynamic optimization, adaptation, or re-engineering of such business processes can use extended software configuration management data and techniques. Again, we see the challenge in relating technical and business data to be able to assess business impacts of software configuration modifications.

8 The Challenge of Web Service Composition Management

We make a difference between Web Service management (WSM) and Web Service composition management (WSCM). We define Web Service management as the management of a particular Web Service or a group of Web Services within the same domain of management responsibility. For example, Web Services provided with one application server can be managed as a group. Similarly, Web Services provided by the same business entity can be managed in a unified manner as a group, either completely or only in some respects. A large number of companies already claim that their products perform some kind of Web Service management, predominantly in performance management. Many of these products are platform-specific application management products, often based on Java Management Extensions (JMX). Another frequent Web Service management approach is to use Web Service gateways, hubs, or proxies that serve as a single point of control, metering, and management.

On the other hand, we define Web Service composition management as the management of Web Service compositions. In a general case, the composed Web Services are distributed over the Internet and provided by different business entities. Some of these business entities might not want to relinquish or outsource control over their Web Services. They often have mutually incompatible and even conflicting management goals. In addition, management of the Internet infrastructure is a very challenging task. Consequently, Web Service composition management will usually not be able to involve full Web Service management of the composed Web Services and management of the Internet communication infrastructure. Therefore, the emphasis in Web Service composition management must be on decisions related to which Web Services are composed and how they interact. Contrary to Web Service management, there are relatively few results on Web Service composition management.

Note that Web Service compositions can have very different characteristics. In some cases, there will be an explicit description of the composition[5]. However, in some cases there will be no such description. A Web Service composition can emerge spontaneously, from a series of (primarily) bilateral contracts. In such case, there is no 'master plan' and no common goal; all participants have their own interests, mutually conflicting. Consequently, the Web Service composition management becomes harder, albeit possible.

Software configuration management is certainly an important part of Web Service management. A Web Service implementation can use many different software products, possibly from different vendors. Some examples are a Web Server, an application server, SOAP packaging/unpackaging software, a software component container, a number of implementation software components, performance management instrumentation, load balancing software, and security management software. It can also happen that some of these products execute on different platforms. The existing software configuration management techniques and tools can be very useful to manage such a diverse set of software entities.

---

[5] Several languages, including the Business Process Execution Language for Web Services (BPEL4WS), have appeared in this area.

On the other hand, there is a need to research further the relationships between software configuration management and Web Service composition management. The Web Service composition management is positioned between the traditional application management (including software configuration management) on one side and the business process management on the other. Significant analogies can be made between the Web Service composition management and both of these related areas. While significant body of existing knowledge can be exercised for the Web Service composition management, there are also important differences. One of the differences from the traditional application management tools is that the composed Web Services are under full control of their vendors, with different management goals. An important difference from the traditional business process management tools is that a Web Service composition is not only a representation of a business process, but also a business service and a distributed software system and component for further composition. Neither the traditional application management nor the business process management solutions completely address the complexity of multi-party, multi-goal, multi-level, and multi-aspect management.

9 Conclusions

With service-oriented architectures, such as Web Services, the distribution, dynamism, and complexity of software systems increases. Service components can abstract both software and hardware functionality, and they are increasingly viewed from the business, instead of technology, perspective. This all raises a number of new challenges that software configuration management has to address.

Many of these challenges are related to the management of dynamism and run-time change. Dynamism and run-time change improve system flexibility, adaptability, agility, and availability. However, their management is inherently complex and has a possibility error. Dynamic service composition and software hot-swapping are good examples. This possibility of error can be minimized, but not completely avoided. Since success cannot be guaranteed a priori, mechanisms for error discovery and handling are needed. Additional hardening circumstances are that such management actions have to be performed in limited time, with minimal human involvement, and with minimal disruption of the overall system and its users.

Another challenge is the integration of software configuration management with other management areas and domain, particularly the association of technical management information and business data. Software is a part of a larger computing and business system. The end users are ultimately interested in the overall functionality and QoS that they get and in business impacts of software operation and problems.

While software configuration management plays a very important role in Web Service management, it has even bigger role in Web Service composition management. The latter requires not only management of dynamism and run-time change, but also handling multiple business entities with conflicting goals.

References

1. Larsson, M., and Crnkovic, I.: New Challenges for Configuration Management. In Proc. of System Configuration Management - Software Configuration Management-9 (Toulouse, France, Aug. 1999), Springer
2. Gisolfi, D.: An Introduction to Dynamic e-Business. IBM developerWorks (April 2001), IBM. On-line at: http://www-106.ibm.com/developerworks/webservices/library/ws-arc1/
3. World Wide Web Consortium (W3C): Web Services Description Requirements. W3C Working Draft 28, October 2002. On-line at:
   http://www.w3.org/TR/2002/WD-ws-desc-reqs-20021028/
4. Mennie, D.W.: An Architecture to Support Dynamic Composition of Service Components and Its Applicability to Internet Security. M.Eng. thesis, Carleton University, Ottawa, Canada (2000). On-line at: http://www.sce.carleton.ca/netmanage/papers/MennieThesis.pdf
5. Mennie, D., and Pagurek, B.: A Runtime Composite Service Creation and Deployment and Its Applications in Internet Security, E-commerce, and Software Provisioning. In Proc. of the 25th Annual International Computer Software and Applications Conference - COMPSAC 2001 (Chicago, USA, Oct. 2001) IEEE Computer Society Press. 371-376
6. Kniesel, G.: Type-Safe Delegation for Run-Time Component Adaptation. In Proc. of ECOOP '99 (LNCS 1628), Springer-Verlag (Lisbon, Portugal, June 1999). 351-366
7. Oreizy, P., Medvidovic, N., and Taylor, R.N.: Architecture-Based Software Runtime Evolution. In Proc. of the International Conference on Software Engineering 1998 - ICSE'98 (Kyoto, Japan, April 1998) ACM Press 177-186
8. Beugnard, A., Jezequel, J.-M., Plouzeau, N., and Watkins, D.: Making Components Contract Aware. Computer, Vol. 32, No. 7. IEEE. (July 1999). 38-45
9. Tosic, V., Patel, K., and Pagurek, B.: WSOL – Web Service Offerings Language. In Proc. of the Workshop on Web Services, e-Business, and the Semantic Web at CaiSE'02 (Toronto, Canada, May 2002). Lecture Notes in Computer Science (LNCS), Springer-Verlag (2002) No. 2512, 57-67
10. Patel, K.: XML Grammar and Parser for the Web Service Offerings Language. M.A.Sc.. thesis, Carleton University, Ottawa, Canada (2003). On-line at:
    http://www.sce.carleton.ca/netmanage/papers/KrutiPatelThesisFinal.pdf
11. Tosic, V., Pagurek, B., Patel, B. Esfandiari, B., and Ma, W.: Management Applications of the Web Service Offerings Language (WSOL). To be published in Proc. of the 15th Conference On Advanced Information Systems Engineering - CAiSE'03 (Klagenfurt/ Velden, Austria, June 2003), Lecture Notes in Computer Science (LNCS), Springer-Verlag.
12. Feng, N., Ao, G., White, T., and Pagurek, B.: Dynamic Evolution of Network Management Software by Software Hot-Swapping. In Proc. of IM 2001, IEEE Publications   (Seattle, USA, May 2001) 63-76
13. Feng N.: S-Module Design for Software Hot-Swapping. M.Eng. thesis, Carleton University, Ottawa, Canada (1999). On-line at:
    http://www.sce.carleton.ca/netmanage/papers/FengThesis.pdf
14. Ao, G.: Software Hot-swapping Techniques for Upgrading Mission Critical Applications on the Fly. M.Eng. thesis, Carleton University, Ottawa, Canada (2000). On-line at:
    http://www.sce.carleton.ca/netmanage/papers/AoThesis.pdf

Uniform Comparison of Configuration Management Data Models

E. James Whitehead, Jr. and Dorrit Gordon

Dept. of Computer Science
University of California, Santa Cruz
Santa Cruz, CA 95064, USA
{ejw,dgordon}@cs.ucsc.edu

Abstract. The data models of a series of 11 configuration management systems—of varying type and complexity—are represented using containment data models. Containment data models are a specialized form of entity-relationship model in which entities may be containers or atoms, and the only permitted form of relationship is inclusion or referential containment. By using entities to represent the native abstractions of each system, and containment relationships to model inclusion and identifier references, systems can be modeled uniformly, permitting consistent cross-comparison of systems.

1 Introduction

The past 27 years of research and commercial development have witnessed the creation of scores of configuration management systems, with Conradi and Westfechtel's survey listing 21 systems [3], and the CM Yellow Pages listing an additional 43 in the commercial sector [2]. Despite the existence of solid comprehensive survey work on configuration management systems [3], it is still the case today that developing a detailed understanding of the data model of a particular system requires labor-intensive study of the papers and documentation describing it. Worse, once developed, there is no modeling mechanism that allows this understanding to be represented in a way that both aids communication about the model, and permits cross-comparison with other system models. As a result, many of the data modeling lessons embedded in configuration management systems remain difficult to access for people outside the field.

Ideally, we would like to represent the data models of configuration management systems with a mechanism that has the following properties:

- *Uniformity:* model systems using a minimal and uniform set of abstractions. Instead of providing a normative definition of versioning and configuration management concepts, and then mapping system abstractions into these concepts, ideally we want to use atomic entities to build up models of each system's abstractions.

- *Utility:* easily answer basic version data model questions such as, "how are version histories represented (if they are explicitly represented at all)", "are

B.Westfechtel, A. van der Hoek (Eds.): SCM 2001/2003, LNCS 2649, pp. 70-85, 2003.

directories and other collection-type objects versioned", and "is there some notion of workspace, activity, or configuration?"

- *Support Analysis:* be able to examine systems to tease out different design spaces employed in each system's data model.

- *Graphic formalism:* communicate to a wide range of parties, inside and outside of the configuration management community, requiring minimal time to learn the graphic language, and with most people having an intuitive understanding of the formalism. Allow commonality among systems to be visually evident.

- *Concise format:* be able to fit the containment models of multiple systems onto a single page or screen, allowing rapid comparison of system data models.

- *Cross-discipline:* model the containment properties of multiple kinds of information systems, such as document management and hypertext versioning systems, and compare them to configuration management systems.

Previous work by the authors introduced the concept of containment data modeling, using it to describe a wide range of data models for hypertext, and hypertext versioning systems [21]. Other work began a preliminary examination of using containment modeling to represent configuration management systems, but modeled only a small number of systems [6]. Though this previous work suggested that containment modeling could successfully be applied to a wide range of configuration management systems, a larger set of systems must be modeled to provide full confidence that containment modeling is applicable in this domain. The present paper provides ten additional containment data models of configuration management systems, across a range of system types. Common features visible in the data models of each class of systems are then discussed.

In the remainder of this paper, we provide a brief introduction to containment modeling, and then apply it to the well known SCCS [12] and RCS [14] systems. Next, we model systems that provide an infrastructural data model, intended for use in creating more complex data models for specific uses or environments. Since these systems provide fundamental data model building blocks, they are a good test of the uniformity of containment data modeling. As a scalability test, the models of DSEE [9], ClearCase [8], and DeltaV [1] are presented, and aspects of the evolution of these complex models are discussed. The last set of models contrast the data models of two different system types, the version graph system CoMa [18], and the change-based system PIE [5], and demonstrate that containment models make system type differences much easier to identify and analyze. Related work and conclusions complete the paper.

2   Containment Modeling

Containment modeling is a specialized form of entity-relationship modeling wherein the model is composed of two primitives: entities and containment relationships. Each primitive has a number of properties associated with it. A complete containment model identifies a value for each property of each primitive. Unlike general entity-relationship models, the type of relationships is not open-ended, but is instead restricted only to varying types of referential and inclusion containment.

2.1   Entity Properties

Entities represent significant abstractions in the data models of configuration management systems, such as source code revisions, directories, workspaces and configurations. The properties of entities are:

Entity Type. Entities may be either containers or atomic objects. Any entity that can contain other entities is a container. Any entity that cannot contain other entities is an atomic entity. Any entity contained by a container may be referred to as a containee of that container.

Container Type. There are two sub-types of container: 'and' and 'xor'. Unless otherwise specified, a container is generic. 'And' containers must contain two or more possible containee types and must contain at least one representative of each; 'xor' containers must have two or more possible containee types and may contain representatives of no more than one of them. While superficially similar to Tichy's notion of AND/OR graphs [13], the 'and' and 'xor' types herein describe constraints that apply to container classes, while AND/OR graphs are instance-level constraints. There is typically no precomputable mapping between the two sets of relationships.

Total Containees. A range describing the total number of containees that may belong to a container. A lower bound of zero indicates that this container may be empty.

Total Containers. Indicates the total number of containers to which this entity may belong. A lower bound of zero indicates that the entity is not required to belong to any of the containers defined in the model. Note that for the models in this paper, it is assumed that all elements reside in some type of file system, database, or other structure external to the system being modeled.

Cycles. Many systems allow containers to contain other containers of the same type. For example, in a standard UNIX file system, directories can contain other directories. This property indicates whether a container can contain itself (either directly or by a sequence of relationships). Unless otherwise specified this paper assumes that cycles are allowed, where possible.

Constraints, Ordering. The constraints property allows us to express other restrictions on the containment properties of an entity, such as mutual exclusion and mutual inclusion. The ordering property indicates whether there is an order between different containee types (i.e., class-level ordering; ordering of multiple containees of the same type is captured as a relationship property). In previous work [6] we used constraints and ordering in modeling characteristics of hypertext systems; in this paper we have not needed these properties.

2.2   Relationship Properties

Containment Type. Containment may be either inclusive or referential. Where inclusive containment exists, the containee is physically stored within the space allocated for the container. This often occurs when an abstraction is used to represent actual content in the system. Referential containment indicates that the containee is stored independently of the container.

Reference Location. The references that connect containers and their containees are usually stored on the container; but on some occasions they are stored on the containee, or even on both container and containee. This property indicates where the references are stored.

Membership. The membership property indicates how many instances of a particular container type an entity may belong to. If the lower bound on the value is zero, then the entity is permitted, but not required, to belong to the container indicated by the relationship.

Cardinality. The cardinality property indicates how many instances of a particular containee a container may contain. If the lower bound on the value is zero, then the container is permitted, but not required, to contain instances of the containee indicated by the relationship.

Ordering. The ordering property indicates whether there is an ordering between instances of a particular entity type within the container indicated by the relationship.

2.3   Graphical Notation

Entities are represented as nodes of the containment model graph, and relationships are the arcs. Fig. 1 below describes the graphic notation used to represent containment data models. Relationships are indicated by directed edges between pairs of entity nodes in the containment model graph. In Fig. 1, visual elements that represent the source end of an edge are shown on the left ends of lines. Visual elements that represent the sink end of an edge appear at the right ends of lines.

To readers familiar with the Unified Modeling Language (UML), a natural question is why we did not use this better-known modeling notation instead. There are several reasons. First, by definition all UML classes may potentially have attributes.

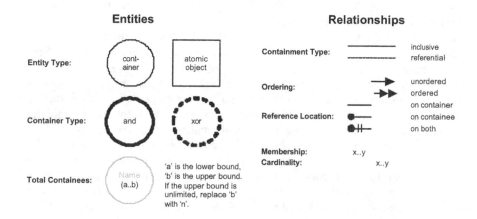

Fig. 1. Graphical notation used to represent containment data models

In our modeling of hypertext systems in [21] we found several systems with content objects that, by definition, could not have associated attributes. UML makes no visual distinction between container and non-container objects, and since containment is central to our approach, we wished to make this more explicit by representing containers as circles, and atoms as squares.

UML contains many features that are not needed for containment modeling, such as the visibility of attributes, and operations available on data. While the core of UML is simple to understand, it certainly takes more time to learn than our notation. UML also permits the expression of inheritance relationships, which we do not permit. In previous work we used inheritance in a limited way within containment diagrams [21]. In later work, we moved away from this, since we found it difficult to comprehend that all relationships that apply to the parent also apply to the child [6]. Our experience has been that not using inheritance leads to minor duplication of entities and containment relationships within diagrams, and these diagrams are much easier (for us) to understand.

It is possible to represent containment data models using UML notation, and in previous work we have found that the equivalent UML model takes up more paper space than the equivalent containment diagram [6]. A system designer familiar with UML could use UML for containment modeling with minimal loss of fidelity, and the advantages of compatibility with UML might outweigh the advantages of the notation presented herein.

3   Modeling Version Control Systems

In previous work, we have created containment models of hypertext systems [21], as well as a small set of hypertext versioning and configuration management systems [6]. Due to the complexity and variety of existing configuration management systems, we want to model a larger number of these systems, both to validate that containment modeling is sufficiently expressive to represent their data models, as well as to support an initial cross-comparison of data modeling approaches. To begin with, we present containment data models of RCS [14] and SCCS [12], two well-known version control systems, in Fig. 2 below.

Examining Fig. 2 highlights several aspects of containment modeling. First, notice that individual revisions are modeled as containers, rather than atomic entities. Since revisions have associated with them a number of attributes, as well as the textual content of the revision, this is modeled using inclusion containment relationships. That is, a revision is viewed as a container of a number of predefined attributes and the revision text. The relationship between the revision history and individual revisions is also modeled using inclusion containment, since it is not possible to delete the revision history without also deleting all revisions. Each revision also has one or more identifiers that point to the next revision, and emanating branches, and this use of identifiers to point at other entities is the characteristic quality of referential containment. Hence, even though RCS inclusively contains revisions within a revision history, there is still referential containment within its data model.

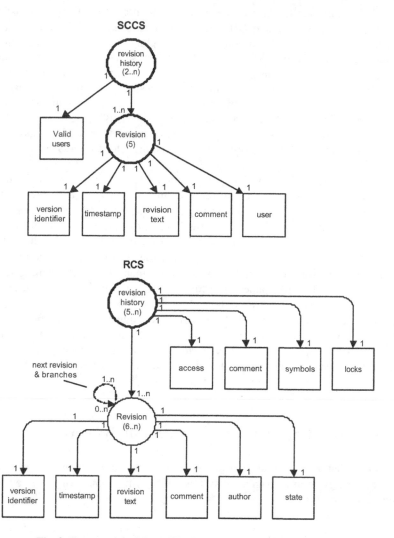

Fig. 2. Data model of the SCCS [12] and RCS [14] systems

Finally, neither model explicitly represents deltas. This is consistent with the user interface of both tools, which allow users to operate on revisions but not deltas, and agrees with Conradi and Westfechtel's characterization of these systems as state-based [3]. That revision histories and revisions are stored in files, and revisions are stored as deltas, can be viewed as *concrete representation* issues. While these concrete representation issues have an important impact on the performance of the tools (e.g., reverse deltas vs. forward deltas [14]), they are a concern that can be abstracted away when examining data models.

With implementation representation issues abstracted away, it is easy to identify differences and similarities between these two systems. The most significant difference is the referential containment arc in RCS, which points to branches and the next revision. This permits RCS to have a much richer set of branch operations than

SCCS. The other significant difference lies in the attributes of revision histories and revisions. In RCS, the revision history contains a set of symbols that are used to label specific revisions; SCCS lacks this capability. Only RCS revisions contain a state attribute, thus permitting RCS to associate revisions with specific states in a (externally defined) state-transition workflow. RCS stores information about locks as an attribute of the version history, while SCCS does not save any lock information.

Both systems share many similarities. Each has a revision history inclusively containing revisions, and the revisions in both systems share many of the same attributes (identifier, timestamp, revision text, comment, author). In both systems, access control information is stored on the revision history (SCCS: valid users, RCS: access).

Equally important, by examining Fig. 2 one can clearly see what features these systems lack. Neither has an entity representing workspaces, a first-class notion of configuration, logical change tracking (e.g., activities or change sets), or an ability to record the revision history of directories. Additionally, both systems only allow predefined attributes, and do not allow arbitrarily named attributes. While these facts are well known, what is unusual is how quickly they can be determined by examining the containment data model. Instead of spending many minutes scanning though the documentation and system papers, the containment data model allows these questions to be answered quickly. Similarly, while it is possible to provide a detailed comparison of these data models by laboriously studying the documentation of the SCCS and RCS file formats, it is much faster to just contrast two containment diagrams. Additionally, when many systems are to be compared, it is extremely difficult to remember every detail of each system's data model. A consistent, common notation is crucial.

4   Models of Configuration Management Systems

In order to demonstrate that it is possible to create containment models of a wide range of configuration management systems of varying complexity, we now present a series of such models.

4.1   Data Models of Infrastructure Systems

A major goal of containment modeling is uniformity, that is, representing data models while bringing as few biases into the modeling activity as possible. By using a simple model with limited prejudices, it permits expression of a wide range of data models using a uniform set of modeling primitives. One way to validate this quality of uniformity is to model existing systems whose goal is to provide a simple, infrastructural data model used as a basic building block for creating more complex data models for a specific application or programming environment. If it is possible to create uniform containment models of infrastructural data models, then cross comparison of these models will be possible, permitting an examination of the model-

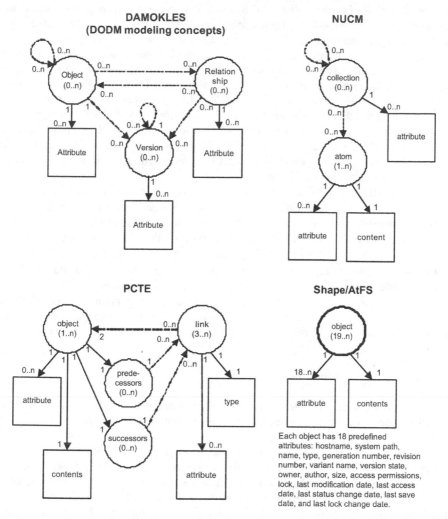

Fig. 3. Data models of DAMOKLES [4], NUCM [16], PCTE [11,17], and Shape/AtFS [10]

ing tradeoffs made by each. Examples of such systems are DAMOKLES [4], PCTE [11,17], NUCM[16], and Shape/AtFS [10], modeled in Fig. 3.

What immediately jumps out from the figure is the relative simplicity of the data models of these systems, ranging from 1 to 4 container entities. This is due to their explicit desire to have small set of entities that can then be used to build up more complex capabilities. All systems have the ability to represent version histories, however each system does so differently. DAMOKLES and NUCM can both use containment to represent version histories, though DAMOKLES has a compound object containing a series of versions (and versions containing versions), while NUCM makes it possible to use an explicit collection entity. In PCTE, every object maintains lists of links that point to predecessor and successor objects, and NUCM collections cou ld also be used to represent predecessor/successor relationships.

Neither DAMOKLES nor Shape/AtFS explicitly represent predecessor/successor relationships, with Shape/AtFS representing version histories implicitly via version identifier conventions (e.g., version 1.2 defined to be the successor of 1.1).

While the systems in Fig. 3 are generally capable of representing the data models of the others, they do so with varying degrees of mismatch. For example, DAMOKLES objects and relationships map to NUCM collections, and DAMOKLES versions map somewhat to NUCM atoms. However, DAMOKLES requires versions to belong to only one object; NUCM doesn't have this restriction. DAMOKLES objects and versions store all non-containment state in attributes, while NUCM atoms have a distinguished content chunk. Since PCTE uses links to represent containment relationships, and NUCM uses collections to represent links, it is possible to map between NUCM and PCTE by performing appropriate link/collection conversions. While Shape/AtFS could mimic collections and relationships by defining attributes on Shape/AtFS objects, these would not have any special properties, such as the referential integrity constraints enforced by PCTE on containment links.

As with RCS and SCCS, the containment data models in Fig. 3 permit a rapid examination of facilities not provided by these systems. None of the systems provide explicit support for workspaces, activities/change sets, or configurations, though these facilities could be provided by building on the existing data models.

Since all models can be represented and compared using containment modeling, it highlights the ability of containment modeling to allow cross comparison of even basic, foundational models, permitting the assumptions of each to be compared.

4.2   Tracing the Evolution of Data Models

Since all of the systems modeled so far have been relatively simple, it is reasonable to be curious about how well containment modeling handles more complex systems. We address this issue by examining the DSEE [9], ClearCase [8,19], and DeltaV [1] systems, modeled in Fig. 4-Fig. 6. Together they form a direct intellectual lineage, with DSEE and ClearCase having the same initial system architect, David Leblang, and with ClearCase influencing DeltaV via the direct involvement of Geoff Clemm, who was simultaneously an architect of both ClearCase and DeltaV from 1999-2002. Since these systems all have complex data models, ranging from 9 to 14 collection entities, the models validate that containment modeling can represent large systems. By concisely representing the data models of these systems in three pages, we can view the evolution of system concepts in this lineage more easily than by reading over 150 pages of primary source text.

All three systems have objects that represent an entire revision history, and though all systems supporting branching, only ClearCase has an entity that explicitly represents branches. While DSEE and ClearCase both use delta compression, in the DSEE data model element revisions are inclusively contained by the element history, while ClearCase uses referential containment between elements, branches, and versions.

DSEE

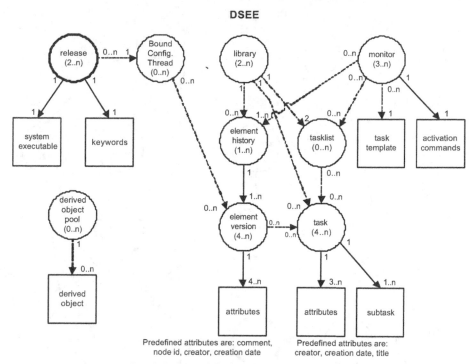

Fig. 4. Data model of the DSEE system [9]

The DSEE notion of task and tasklist evolved into the ClearCase and DeltaV notion of activity, though in DSEE a revision points at an activity, while in ClearCase and DeltaV the activity points at revisions. In ClearCase and DeltaV, activities are more integrated into version selection and workspaces than in DSEE, with ClearCase streams pointing to both activities and views, and DeltaV activities pointing directly to workspaces (and vice-versa). The dynamic version selection provided by DSEE bound configuration threads (BCTs) and ClearCase streams, views, and configuration specifications are similar, though ClearCase gains additional flexibility for handling large projects by introducing the stream entity. DeltaV supports only version selection using baselines and activities, with no equivalent concept to BCTs or views.

Both DSEE and ClearCase provide abstractions for representing groupings of multiple source objects and directories. DSEE has the notion of a library, containing a set of elements and tasklists, appropriate for modeling subsystems of a large project. ClearCase offers greater flexibility, with a distinction between Project Versioned Object Base (PVOB) and regular VOBs. PVOBs hold project and component entities, while VOBs hold source objects and their inter-relationships. A large project might have multiple VOBs, and a single PVOB, thus proving scalability advantages over DSEE. The implicit notion of a "server" in DeltaV is similar to a combined PVOB/VOB.

ClearCase 4

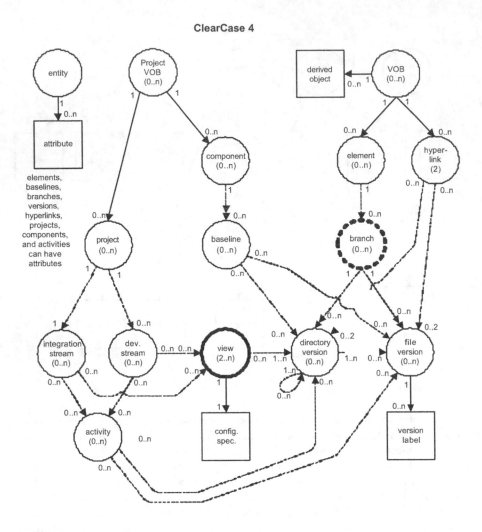

Fig. 5. Data model of the ClearCase system, version 4 [19]

All three systems have the ability to explicitly record configurations of versioned objects. In DSEE, an unversioned "release" entity performs this function, while ClearCase and DeltaV use a versionable "baseline" to record configurations. ClearCase and DeltaV also provide stronger support than DSEE for creating baselines from changes associated with tasks.

Finally, we note that while it is possible to model these systems, the exercise exposes some limitations in the visual representation of containment models. As diagrams get larger, it becomes more difficult to layout the entities and relationships to avoid diagrammatic clutter. In the DeltaV model in Fig. 6, we used a convention that omitted properties to keep the diagram on a single page, deviating from strict adherence to our graphical notation to save concision and clarity. Additionally, as

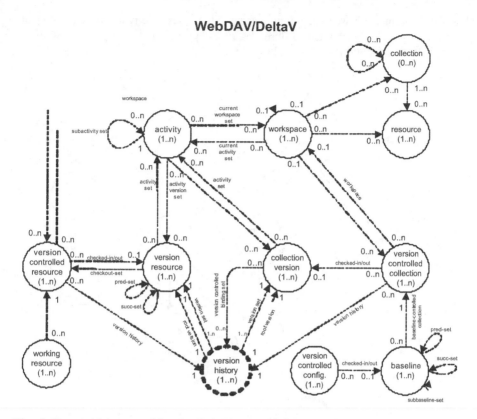

Fig. 6. Data model exposed by the DeltaV protocol [1]. To reduce figure clutter, resource properties (attributes) are not shown. For many DeltaV entities their properties contain lists of identifiers, and hence strict modeling would show these properties as container entities. Due to the complexity of the model, we use a convention of annotating containment arcs with the name of the property that contains the identifiers for that arc. Plain arcs represent containment by the entity proper (i.e., not by a property)

models grow larger, our choice to label entities with the same terminology used in the description of the system makes it more difficult to understand each diagram. While using each system's native terminology avoids modeling bias and saves us from a thorny definitional thicket, it also requires the reader to have greater knowledge of each system to understand the diagram. This was not as great a problem for the systems in Fig. 3, since their data models are less complex. In future work, we hope to distill out design spaces for such issues as representing workspaces and configurations, thereby focusing on smaller, more manageable aspects of complex systems.

4.3   Comparing Different Types of Configuration Management System

In our last set of figures, we present the data models of CoMa [18] and PIE [5] in Fig. 7. Using the taxonomy of systems provided in [3], CoMa is a version graph system, while PIE is a change-based versioning system. Since these are two different styles of system, we would expect these differences to be visible in a comparison of their containment models, and this is indeed the case.

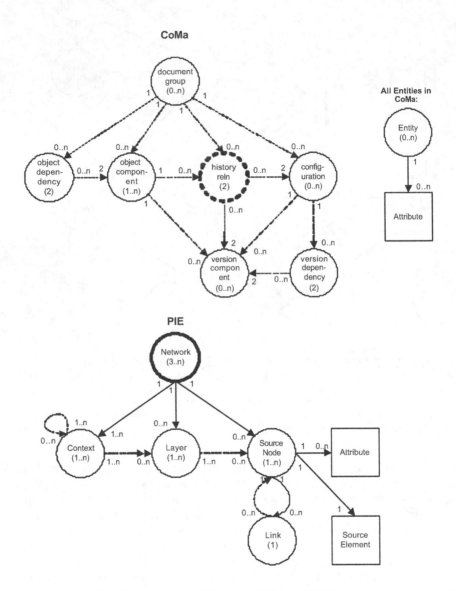

Fig. 7. Data models of the CoMa [18] and PIE [5] systems

The CoMa system represents a version history using a versioned object container that holds all revisions, as well as links for the predecessor/successor relationships. In Fig. 7 this pattern is visible twice, first as the object component (the versioned object) containing version components (individual revisions of objects) and history relationships (representing predecessor/successor relationships), next as document groups (versioned object) containing configurations (revisions) and history relationships. PIE uses a different scheme altogether, with individual source nodes organized into layers representing versions or variants, and contexts grouping layers, with occlusion among layers depending on their relative ordering.

5   Related Work

Several prior research efforts are similar to the work presented herein. Conradi and Westfechtel's survey of configuration management systems examines many issues of data modeling across a broad set of systems [3]. Our work differs in that it focuses on data modeling, and provides a modeling mechanism that permits uniform cross-comparison of data models. Conradi and Westfechtel's description of data modeling issues was primarily textual, as contrasted with the graphical technique presented here. However, their work also surveyed version selection techniques, which are not covered by containment modeling.

The schema languages in CoMa [18] and DAMOKLES [4] bear some similarity to the containment modeling approach, having notions of containment, and a separation between the schema and its concrete representation. However, neither of these schemas have been used to model existing CM systems. The data model of NUCM [15,16] is also similar to the basic set of primitives in containment modeling, since it too has containers and atoms. Since the intended use of NUCM is to construct more sophisticated configuration management capability on top of these basic entities, there is no separation between model and concrete representation, with NUCM directly representing containers and atoms in its repository. Containment modeling is intended to be more abstract, and hence doesn't have a default concrete representation. Another difference is that NUCM collections and atoms have hardwired attributes, while there are no predetermined inclusion containment relationships among entities in a containment data model. However, given that the vast preponderance of collection entities in configuration management systems have attributes, it is arguable whether the ability to explicitly model the inclusion of attributes is a significant benefit. We have primarily found this flexibility to be useful in modeling hypertext systems, where the use of attributes is not quite so universal.

6   Contributions

Containment modeling is a modeling mechanism that permits uniform representation of the data models of a wide range of configuration management systems. Containment modeling has been validated by presenting the models of 11 existing configuration management systems. In the case of ClearCase and DeltaV, these are very complicated data models, perhaps the most complex in existence. Additionally, in previous work we have created containment models of an additional 16 hypertext systems [6,21], highlighting how the uniformity of the modeling technique permits data modeling across multiple system domains.

Containment modeling provides a new technique that is useful for performing detailed comparisons of configuration management data models. Since containment data models are visual and compact, it is much easier to cross-examine data models, making it possible to quickly identify similarities and differences. In previous work we have used insights derived from containment models of hypertext versioning systems to develop design spaces for link and structure versioning [20], and in future work we wish to similarly leverage configuration management containment models to develop design spaces for features such as workspaces, change sets, and configurations.

The compact, visual notation of containment models is good for capturing the current best understanding of a system's data model. This permits iterative improvement of containment data models over time, as understanding improves. This is not possible without an explicit model. Additionally, the process of creating models is error-prone, indicative of the fact that trying to understand a data model from a textual description is also error-prone. While we have worked to remove errors from the containment models presented herein, there is no mechanical way to validate their correctness, and hence it is possible some errors may still persist. The explicit nature of containment models allows errors to be exposed, and then corrected.

Lastly, the visual notation makes it easier to communicate results across disciplinary boundaries. The existence of 27 data models of configuration management and hypertext systems makes it easier to compare/contrast across these two domains, and learn from each other. In future work we hope to extend the containment data modeling technique into other domains, including Document Management, and VLSI CAD [7], as well as to model more CM systems, to complete our data model survey of CM systems.

Acknowledgements

This research was supported by the National Science Foundation, by grant NSF CAREER CCR-0133991.

References

1. G. Clemm, J. Amsden, T. Ellison, C. Kaler, and J. Whitehead, "Versioning Extensions to WebDAV," Rational, IBM, Microsoft, U.C. Santa Cruz. Internet Proposed Standard Request for Comments (RFC) 3253, March, 2002
2. CM Today, "CM Yellow Pages," (2002). Accessed December 21, 2002. http://www.cmtoday.com/yp/configuration_management.html
3. R. Conradi and B. Westfechtel, "Version Models for Software Configuration Management," *ACM Computing Surveys*, vol. 30, no. 2 (1998), pp. 232-282
4. K.R. Dittrich, W. Gotthard, and P.C. Lockemann, "DAMOKLES - A Database System for Software Engineering Environments," *Proc. Advanced Programming Environments*, Trondheim, Norway, June, 1986, pp. 353-371
5. I.P. Goldstein and D.P. Bobrow, "A Layered Approach to Software Design," in *Interactive Programming Environments*, New York, NY: McGraw-Hill, 1984, pp. 387-413

6. D. Gordon and E.J. Whitehead, Jr., "Containment Modeling of Content Management Systems," *Proc. Metainformatics Symposium 2002 (MIS'02)*, Esbjerg, Denmark, Aug 7-10, 2002
7. R.H. Katz, "Toward a Unified Framework for Version Modeling in Engineering Databases," *Computing Surveys*, vol. 22, no. 4 (1990), pp. 375-408
8. D. Leblang, "The CM Challenge: Configuration Management that Works," in *Configuration Management*, New York: Wiley, 1994, pp. 1-38
9. D.B. Leblang and J.R.P. Chase, "Computer-Aided Software Engineering in a Distributed Workstation Environment," *Proc. ACM SIGSOFT/SIGPLAN Software Engineering Symposium on Practical Software Development Environments*, Pittsburgh, PA, April, 1984, pp. 104-112
10. A. Mahler and A. Lampen, "An Integrated Toolset for Engineering Software Configurations," *Proc. ACM SIGSOFT/SIGPLAN Software Engineering Symp. on Practical Software Development Environments*, Boston, MA, Nov. 28-30, 1988, pp. 191-200
11. F. Oquendo, K. Berrada, F. Gallo, R. Minot, and I. Thomas, "Version Management in the PACT Integrated Software Engineering Environment," *Proc. ESEC'89*, Coventry, UK, Sept. 11-15, 1989, pp. 222-242
12. M.J. Rochkind, "The Source Code Control System," *IEEE Transactions on Software Engineering*, vol. 1, no. 4 (1975), pp. 364-370
13. W.F. Tichy, "A Data Model for Programming Support Environments and its Application," *Proc. IFIP WG 8.1 Working Conf. on Automated Tools for Info. Systems Design and Dev.*, New Orleans, LA, Jan 26-28, 1982, pp. 31-48
14. W.F. Tichy, "RCS - A System for Version Control," *Software-Practice and Experience*, vol. 15, no. 7 (1985), pp. 637-654
15. A. van der Hoek, "A Generic Peer-to-Peer Repository for Distributed Configuration Management," *Proc. ICSE-18*, Berlin, 1996, pp. 308-317
16. A. van der Hoek, "A Testbed for Configuration Management Policy Programming," *IEEE Trans. Software Eng.*, vol. 28, no. 1 (2002), pp. 79-99
17. L. Wakeman and J. Jowett, *PCTE: The Standard for Open Repositories*. New York: Prentice Hall, 1993
18. B. Westfechtel, "Using Programmed Graph Rewriting for the Formal Specification of a Configuration Management System," *Proc. 20th Int'l Workshop on Graph-Theoretic Concepts in Computer Science (WG'94)*, Herrsching, Germany, June 16-18, 1994, pp. 164-179
19. B. A. White, *Software Configuration Management Strategies and Rational ClearCase: A Practical Introduction*. Boston, MA: Addison-Wesley, 2000
20. E. J. Whitehead, Jr., "Design Spaces for Link and Structure Versioning," *Proc. Hypertext 2001*, Århus, Denmark, August 14-18, 2001, pp. 195-205
21. E.J. Whitehead, Jr., "Uniform Comparison of Data Models Using Containment Modeling," *Proc. Hypertext 2002*, College Park, MD, June 11-15, 2002

Towards Intelligent Support
for Managing Evolution
of Configurable Software Product Families

Tero Kojo, Tomi Männistö, and Timo Soininen

Software Business and Engineering Institute (SoberIT)
Helsinki University of Technology
P.O. Box 9600, FIN-02015 HUT, Finland
{Tero.Kojo,Tomi.Mannisto,Timo.Soininen}@hut.fi

Abstract. Software product families are a means for increasing the efficiency of software development. We propose a conceptualisation for modelling the evolution and variability of configurable software product families. We describe a first prototype of an intelligent tool that allows modelling a software product family on the basis of the conceptualisation and supports the user in interactively producing correct configurations with respect to the model. The implementation is based on an existing general purpose configurator and thus is not application domain specific. We use the Debian Familiar Linux package configuration task over many releases and package versions as an example. Preliminary results show that the conceptualisation can be used to model evolution of such a software product family relatively easily and the implementation performs acceptably.

1 Introduction

Software product families (SPF) (or lines, as they are also known) have been proposed as a means for increasing the efficiency of software development and to control complexity and variability of products [1,2]. A SPF can be defined to consist of a common architecture, a set of reusable assets used in systematically producing, i.e. *deploying*, products, and the set of products thus produced.

Software product families are subject to evolution, similarly as other software [3]. This leads to a need for practical solutions for controlling evolution. Configuration management tools keep evolving software products under control during their development [4]. However, the configuration management of large and complex software and the post installation evolution of software products present challenges [5,6].

In this paper we propose an approach to the modelling of evolving software product families based on viewing them as *configurable software product families*. A *configurable product* is such that each product individual is adapted to the requirements of a particular customer order on the basis of a predefined *configuration model* [7]. Such a model explicitly and declaratively describes the

B. Westfechtel, A. van der Hoek (Eds.): SCM 2001/2003, LNCS 2649, pp. 86–101, 2003.

set of legal product individuals by defining the components out of which an individual can be constructed and the dependencies of components to each other. A specification of a product individual, i.e., a *configuration*, is produced based on the configuration model and particular customer requirements in a *configuration task*. Efficient knowledge based systems for configuration tasks, *product configurators*, have recently become an important application of artificial intelligence techniques for companies selling products adapted to customer needs [8,9]. They are based on declarative, unambiguous knowledge representation methods and sound inference algorithms. A configuration model traditionally captures the versioning of an SPF in space, i.e., it describes all the different configurations the SPF consists of. Evolution, i.e., versioning in time, is typically not supported.

The main contribution of this paper is a conceptual foundation for modelling evolution of configurable SPFs with the main concern being the deployment phase and generation of valid configurations. The conceptual foundation is based on a subset of a de-facto standard ontology of product configuration knowledge [10] and extended with concepts for modelling evolution.

We describe a prototype implementation of an intelligent tool for modelling configurable SPFs on the basis of the conceptualisation and supports the user in interactively producing a correct configuration with respect to the model. In this we use a state-of-the-art prototype product configurator [11] as an implementation platform. Our implementation is not product or application domain specific. It is enough to change the model to use it for another SPF.

To show the feasibility of both the modelling method and its implementation, we use the Debian Familiar Linux package configuration as an example. It is an appropriate software product family for the purposes of this work as it has a component structure consisting of hundreds of packages, resulting to well over 2^{100} potential configurations. Furthermore, there are multiple subsequent releases of the same package.

The remainder of this paper is structured as follows. Section 2 describes Debian Familiar Linux, its package model and how evolution is currently handled. Section 3 defines the conceptual foundation for representing the evolution of configurable SPFs. In Section 4 the implementation is described and some preliminary results on its feasibility are given. After that the modelling method and implementation are discussed and compared to related work in Section 5. Finally, some conclusions and topics for further research are presented in Section 6.

2 Debian Familiar Linux Case

Debian Linux Familiar is an open source operating system distribution developed for the Hewlett-Packard iPAQ handheld computer. Familiar is distributed as packages, each of which provides a piece of software, such as an application or device driver. A Familiar release is a collection of packages, which make up a complete Linux environment for the iPAQ. Therefore a release always includes a Linux kernel, device drivers and essential user software such as a shell and editor. The packages of a Familiar release are described in a package description file distributed with the release. Each release has a release date, on which that release becomes the official current Familiar distribution. The releases are stored in separate folders on the ftp.handhelds.org FTP server. Figure 1 shows an example of a single package description.

```
Package: ash
Essential: yes
Priority: required
Section: shells
Installed-Size: 152
Maintainer: Carl Worth <cworth@handhelds.org>
Architecture: arm
Version: 0.3.7-16-fam1
Pre-Depends: libc6 (>= 2.2.1-2)
Filename: ./ash_0.3.7-16-fam1_arm.ipk
Description: NetBSD /bin/sh
```

Fig. 1. Example Debian Familiar Linux package description

The package description provides information on the different properties of the package it represents. The description provides the package name, essentiality, version information and dependencies. The version information contains the revision information and the status of the package. If a revision number is followed by "a" or "alpha" or "pre", the package is an alpha or pre-release version. The possible dependencies of a package are Depends, Pre-depends, Conflicts, Provides, Replaces, Recommends and Suggests. The meanings of these are:

- Depends - the package requires another package to be installed to function correctly.
- Pre-depends - installation of the package requires another package to be installed before itself.
- Conflicts - the package should not be present in the same configuration some other package.
- Provides - the package provides the functionality of some other package.
- Replaces - the installation of the package removes or overwrites files of another package.
- Recommends - another package is recommended when it is presumable that the users would like to have it in the configuration to with the package.
- Suggests - another package is suggested to get better use of the package.

Of these dependencies Depends, Pre-depends and Conflicts directly indicate the need for an another package or conflict with another package. Provides, Recommends and Suggests can be seen as a method of providing help at installation time in the form of features. Replaces is directly associated with the installation of the package. The dependencies are used by the Familiar package management tool when installing a package. Most packages have a different maintainer, as the packages are maintained by volunteer hackers. This brings inconsistencies, for example, in the usage of dependencies and to the version naming scheme.

The Linux Familiar distribution has had four major releases, 0.3, 0.4, 0.5 and 0.6, and several minor releases between the major releases during the two years the project has been active. The releases 0.4, 0.5, 0.5.1 and 0.5.2 were chosen for this study. Release 0.6 was not included as it has just recently come out.

The total number of packages in the four releases is 1088, making the average number of packages per release 272. Of these packages 148 have their priority set as required. The number of dependencies between packages is 1221.

Installation instructions for each release of Familiar can be found on the Familiar WWW pages [12]. Each release has separate installation instructions, even though the process is similar for each release. This is a configuration problem related to the versioning in space. Problems related to evolution are the focus of this paper and include the representation of configuration knowledge over time and (re)configuration tasks that span time. For example, updating from an older release to a newer one requires that the user installs everything from scratch onto her/his HP iPAQ, which wipes the handheld clean removing all the user data. Installing packages from multiple releases is not supported. This means that once a user has installed a certain release on her/his iPAQ she/he must use packages only from that particular release. There clearly is need for a package management utility that supports (re)configuration over several releases. To achieve this one needs to incorporate the versioning in space and versioning in time. Constructing such a solution is the topic of this paper.

3   A Conceptualisation for Modelling Evolution

This section describes a conceptualisation for evolution of configurable software product families. This work is based on a de-facto configuration ontology [10], which does not contain concepts for evolution. The conceptualisation uses concepts, such as components, their properties, compositional structure and constraints, which are introduced in the following and illustrated in Figure 2. We first introduce the main concepts for modelling configurable SPFs, i.e., for capturing versioning in space, and thereafter add the concepts for modelling evolution—more detailed discussion is postponed to Section 5.

A configurable SPF fundamentally consists of a large set of potential product individuals, called *configurations*. In the conceptualisation, a configuration is represented by *component individuals*, their *properties* and *has-part* relations between component individuals. A *configuration model* is defined to describe which configurations are legal members of a configurable SPF. A configuration is related to a configuration model by a *is-configuration-of* relation.

A configuration model contains *component types*, their *part definitions* and *property definitions* and *constraints*. Component types define the characteristics (such as parts) of component individuals that can appear in a configuration. A component type is either *abstract* or *concrete* (represented by the *concreteness*

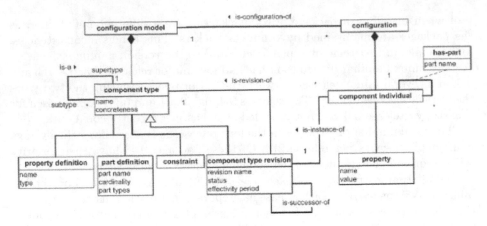

Fig. 2. Meta-model of concepts for modelling evolution of configurable SPFs

of the component type). Only an individual directly of a concrete type is specific enough to be used in an unambiguous configuration.

A component type defines its direct parts through a set of part definitions. A part definition specifies a *part name*, a non-empty set of possible *part types* and a *cardinality*. A component type may also define properties that parameterise or otherwise characterise the type.

Component types are organised in a taxonomy or class hierarchy by means of a *is-a* relation where a *subtype* inherits the property and part definitions of its *supertypes* in the usual manner. Multiple inheritance is not supported.

These concepts provide the basic variation mechanisms, i.e., means for capturing the versioning in space:

1. Alternative parts are modelled by *part type* of part definitions, which defines the component types whose individuals are allowed as parts in a has-part relation with a particular (part) *name*.
2. A *cardinality* defines a range for the allowed number of component individuals for a has-part relation. Zero minimal cardinality represents an optional part and minimal cardinality of 1 a mandatory part.
3. A property definition with an enumeration type defines a set of variation choices, e.g., "UNIX", "win2000", "MacOs".
4. Subtyping of component types can also be used for representing variation; the subtypes of a component type being the variants of the component type.

Constraints associated with component types define additional conditions that a *correct configuration* must satisfy. A constraint is a boolean expression with references to access the parts and properties of component individuals.

To model the evolution in configurable SPFs, additional concepts are introduced, namely *component type revision*, *status*, and *effectivity period*.

A component type has a set of revisions, called component type revisions, which are related to the component type by *is-revision-of* relation, and ordered by *is-successor-of* relation. These relations provide a simplified conceptualisation for revisioning and elaboration on them goes beyond the scope of this paper. Revisions capture the evolution of a component type in time. However, separating the versioning in time from versioning in space in this manner is a simplification we make in this paper. Ultimately, such versioning dimensions of a component type should be represented uniformly [13].

Status tells the life-cycle status of a component type revision [14]. The status is a measure of the maturity of a component type revision, e.g., "unstable", "stable" and "end of life", and can be used as additional information in configuration task. The status is a useful concept, e.g., for expressing the user requirements, but has no relevance in determining the correctness of a configuration.

Effectivity period is a time interval stating when an component type revision may legally appear in a configuration. Effectivity period is thus a new additional concept needed in determining the correctness of a configuration.

In the meta-model, component type revision is a subtype of component type to indicate that component type revisions have the same properties as component types plus the additional concepts for representing evolution. Each component individual is directly an instance of a component type revision, represented by *is-instance-of* relation. This basically means that component individuals are component type instances with additional revision information.

The is-a relation between component types is constrained more than what is visible in Figure 2. The relation is only allowed between component types, not component type revisions. Similarly, the is-version-of relation can only be from a component type revision to component type.

4   Implementation

This section describes a prototype implementation of the modelling method and the intelligent support system, presented in Figure 3, for managing and configuring SPFs based on the models. We first describe an existing configurator prototype, called WeCoTin[1], that is used as the implementation platform. We then show how the Debian Familiar Linux package descriptions are modelled using the conceptualisation presented in the previous section. After this we show how a model based on the conceptualisation is represented using the modelling language of the prototype configurator. Finally the functionality of the modelling and support tool is presented, and some preliminary results on the feasibility of the method and implementation are provided.

The implementation consists of two new pieces of software, software that mapped the individual Familiar package description files to the conceptualisation, software that mapped the conceptualisation to a product configuration modelling language (PCML) and the existing WeCoTin configurator.

---

[1] Acronym from Web Configuration Technology.

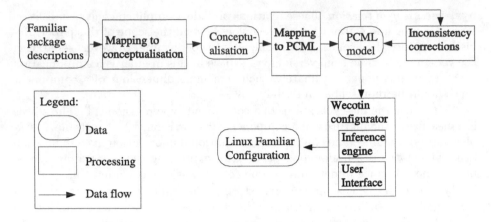

Fig. 3. The architecture of the implementation

4.1 Existing Work

An existing product configurator, WeCoTin, which is currently under development at Helsinki University of Technology, is used as the implementation platform for the conceptualisation presented in the previous section [11].

WeCoTin enables configuration over WWW and centralised configuration model management. The implementation semi-automatically generates a web-based user-interface. WeCoTin supports the user by preventing combinations of incompatible components or their versions, by making sure that all the necessary components are included, and by deducing the consequences of all selections. WeCoTin is also capable of automatically generating an entire correct configuration based on requirements. A state-of-the-art logic-based artificial intelligence knowledge representation and reasoning language and a system implementing it provide the inference mechanism for WeCoTin [15]. WeCoTin translates the configuration model presented in PCML to weight constraint rules and uses a state-of-the-art general implementation of such rules, Smodels [16], for efficiently computing configurations satisfying given requirements. PCML is based on a practically important subset of a de-facto standard ontology of configuration knowledge [10] that unifies most of the existing approaches to configuration modelling.

4.2 Mapping the Evolution of the Familiar Linux Releases

The package descriptions from the different releases of Familiar were mapped to the conceptualisation as follows (Table 1).

A root component type, the root of all configuration models was defined.

For each package a component type was defined, and made a part of the root component type by a part definition. If the package is essential the cardinality of of the part definition corresponding to it is 1, otherwise it is 0..1. The part

Table 1. The mapping of Familiar package descriptions to the conceptualisation

Familiar term	Conceptualisation
Package	Component type
	Part definition in the root component type
Name of the package	Component type name
Essentiality	Part definition cardinality
Version	Component type revision
	Component type revision status
Release date information	Component type revision effectivity period
Depends	Constraint
Pre-depends	Constraint
Conflicts	Constraint
Provides	Installation time activity (Not mapped)
Replaces	Installation time activity (Not mapped)
Recommends	Semantics unclear and installation time activity (Not mapped)
Suggests	Semantics unclear and installation time activity (Not mapped)

types of the part definition contains the component type that was mapped. The name of the component type and the name of the package were the same.

A component type has the revision of the package it represents as a property. The version identifier was taken directly from the package information. If the package had multiple versions, the is-successor-of relation was defined by the chronological order of the package versions.

Status information of a package is a property of the component type revision. The status information was derived from the package version information, if a version was marked with "a" or "alpha" or "pre", the status property of the component type revision was given the value unstable, otherwise a stable value was given.

The component type revisions have an effectivity period based on the releases the package is in. If a version of a package is present in only one release the component type revision has an effectivity period starting with the release date of that release and ending with the release date of the next release. If a version of a package is present in consecutive releases the effectivity period of the component type revision is a combination of the effectivity periods as if the package version were present in all the releases separately.

The package dependencies were mapped to constraints. Depends and pre-depends were mapped both to a requirement constraint that states, that the package requires another package. The additional information provided by pre-depends is used only in the instantiation phase, which was outside the scope of this case. Conflicts was mapped to a constraint that states, that the two packages may not exist together in the same configuration. Provides, replaces, recommends and suggests were not mapped, as they are seen as a method of providing help at installation time and thereby fall outside the scope of this work.

4.3   Mapping the Conceptualisation to PCML

The conceptualisation needed to be mapped to PCML so that WeCoTin could be used to generate configurations of the Familiar system (Table 2).

Table 2. The mapping of the conceptualisation to PCML

Conceptualisation	PCML mapping
Component type	Component type
Property definition	Property definition
Part definition	Part definition
Constraints	Constraints
Component type revision	Property of component type as a temporally ordered list of strings
Component type revision status	Property of component type as a temporally ordered list of strings
Component type revision effectivity period	Properties of component type as integers stating end and start time of effectivity period Constraints expressing which version is effective at which part of the effectivity period

PCML provides modelling concepts for component types, their compositional structure, properties of components, and constraints. The mapping from the evolution concepts to PCML concepts was simple for these concepts. PCML also provides value types and structures such as lists, strings and integers, which were used in the mapping of the other evolution terms [11].

Component type revisions were mapped to a property of component type as a temporally ordered list of strings, i.e., ordered by the is-successor-of relation. Strings were used as the version identifiers in the Familiar package descriptions contain alphanumerical characters.

Component type revision status was mapped to a property of component type as a list of strings that was ordered in the same way as the list of revisions.

Component type revision effectivity periods were combined and mapped as two integers stating the start and end of the component type effectivity period. Constraints were used to specify which component type revision can be used in a configuration at specific parts of the effectivity period. This was used in cases where a package was present in many Familiar releases and it was necessary to identify when each revision can be used in a configuration.

Due to the fact that the inference engine in WeCoTin does not at this time support reasoning over large integer domains well, time used for effectivity periods was discretised. The times selected were those at which the Familiar releases were made and single points of time in between the release times.

4.4   Implementation of the Conceptualisation

The software for mapping the Familiar package descriptions reads the package description file for a single Familiar release and maps the package descriptions to the conceptualisation as described in Section 4.2. The software performs the mapping for each Familiar release. The software was implemented with Perl and it's output is files containing the evolution models of each Familiar release that was mapped.

The software for mapping the conceptualisation to PCML reads the evolution models created by the component for mapping the Familiar package descriptions, combines them and simultaneously maps them to a PCML model as described in Section 4.3. The software searches the evolution model files for component types and collects the different component type revisions under a single component type. The constraints expressing which revision is effective at which part of the effectivity period are created as the component type revisions are collected. Identical part definitions and constraints are removed. The output from the software is a PCML model, which can be given as input to WeCoTin. The software was implemented with Perl.

Figure 4 shows the final PCML presentation of the previously shown Familiar package description (Figure 1 in Section 2).

The PCML model was then input into WeCoTin which translated it into weight constraint rules. Internal inconsistencies in the model were identified and removed. The inconsistencies come from missing or erroneous package definitions, such as requirements on packages that are not in the model and inconsistent requirements, where a package at the same time depends on another package and conflicts with it. Requirements on packages that are not in the release are an implication that the package has been ported from somewhere else, like the main Debian Linux PC distribution, and the maintainer has not updated the package dependencies. After the inconsistencies were removed the PCML model was ready for use. The final PCML model file was an ASCII text file of 781 kiloBytes.

WeCoTin can semi-automatically generate a web-based user-interface for the end user based on the PCML model, presented in Figure 5. WeCoTin provides the possibility of defining default property sets, which in this implementation were used to set the default component type revisions according to the current time set by the user. WeCoTin supports the user by preventing combinations of incompatible component types or their versions, by making sure that all the necessary component types are included, and by deducing the consequences of already made selections. The implementation is also capable of automatically generating entire correct and complete configurations from the model based on user requirements. The inference engine makes inferences on the basis of the model in a sound and complete manner, meaning that e.g. the order in which

```
component type ash
subtype of concrete
property revision value type string constrained by $ in
list("0.3.7-16-fam1","0.3.7-16")
property status value type string constrained by $ in
list("stable","unstable","eol")
property refinement effectivity_start value type integer always 20010606
property refinement effectivity_end value type integer always 20020621

part ashpart
allowed types ash
cardinality 0 to 1

constraint ash_0_3_7_16_fam1_time
ashpart.ash:revision = "0.3.7-16-fam1" implies current_time > 20020514
and current_time < 20020621

constraint ash_0_3_7_16_time
ashpart.ash:revision = "0.3.7-16" implies current_time > 20010606
and current_time < 20020621

constraint ash_DEP_libc6_2_2_1_2
present(ashpart) implies present (libc6part) and
libc6part.libc6:revision >= "2.2.1-2"
```

Fig. 4. Example Debian Familiar Linux package description

the package descriptions appear in a model do not affect the set of correct configurations. The inference engine does not need to be changed if the model changes.

It took about one minute to map the individual Familiar package description files to the conceptualisation and a similar amount of time to map the conceptualisation to PCML. The translation of the configuration model by WeCoTin took 20 minutes. The removal of inconsistencies took about an hour of work, but had to be performed only once to the package descriptions. After that the model can be used to generate a correct Familiar configuration in seconds. No programming is necessary at any step of the configuration process. The configurations generated by WeCoTin are according to our initial experiences correct with respect to the package descriptions used in configuration and based on manual inspection could be loaded into an iPAQ to provide a bootable working Familiar installation.

5 Discussion and Related Work

5.1 Modelling Method

The concepts provided by PCML for configuration were used in the conceptualisation presented in this paper. In addition to these concepts PCML offers other

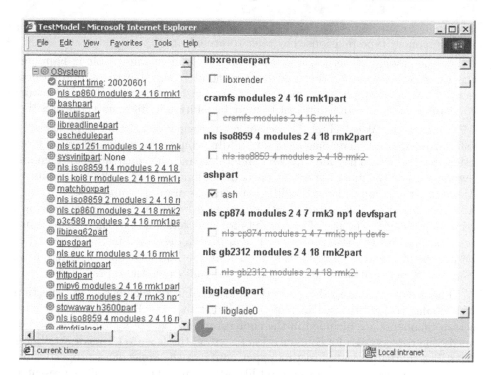

Fig. 5. WeCoTin user-interface

modelling primitives, that are not discussed here. We chose to use PCML since it
provides a means for modelling the component types and their dependencies and
there is a prototype configurator supporting PCML on top of which we could
build the implementation of the modelling method.

The method presented in this paper was sufficient for modelling the evolution and structure of Linux Familiar package descriptions over multiple releases.
However the modelling method has limitations. The separation of the versioning
in time from versioning in space performed in the conceptualisation is a simplification. Ultimately, such versioning dimensions of a component type should
be represented uniformly [13,?]. However for the prototype implementation the
limited version concept was sufficient. The modelling method supports variation,
e.g., through the use of alternative and optional parts of a component type. This
is not a optimal method for representing component type variants, but more a
way of presenting the variation in the product family structure. The relationships
between versions should perhaps be modelled with a richer set of relations.

In the mapping of the Familiar package descriptions to PCML some com-
promises were made. Versions of a package were mapped as properties of the
component type. Constraints did not have explicit effectivity periods, but were
effective throughout the model, when the effectivity should be the same as the
component type revisions' that they refer to. The global effectivity period of con-

straints does not impact the configuration results, as they only have meaning if the component type revisions they refer to are effective.

As the modelling method was tested on one product family, Linux Familiar, the question of whether the modelling method is suitable to other products is open. More example implementations are needed to verify that the model concepts are suitable and sufficient to model evolution in different types of SPFs.

Conradi and Westfechtel [5] present an overview of existing approaches in software configuration management for building consistent configurations of large software products. They identify version models and the constraints for combining versions as the most important parts in configuring large software products. Managing the complexity of the different versions of objects under SCM control and the close ties of the configuration rule base with the version database are seen as problems. The use of constraints for and versioning of the rule base are seen as solutions to these problems. The approach described in this paper relies on an object-oriented configuration modelling method that allows representing constraints between components types to partially solve these problems.

The use of attribute value pairs [14,6] or attribution schemes in the selection of a configuration are used in many SCM systems [18]. By selecting attribute sets components are included in the configuration. Feature logic can be used to verify the correctness of a configuration based on the feature terms or attributes [18]. The model presented in this paper contains the concept of properties for component types, which can be used like attributes. The constraints presented in this work can be used in selecting the component types as in SCM systems using an attribution scheme or feature logic. In addition this work also provides formal semantics for the model giving a more powerful language which can be used to generate a correct configuration.

Configuration management techniques are applied for presenting the variability, optionality and evolution of software architecture in [19]. The tool Menage can be used to graphically specify software architectures. The work of Menage has been continued in Mae [20], which added an environment for architecture based analysis and development. Their works bridges the gap between the areas of software architecture and configuration management by introducing a system model combining architectural and configuration management concepts in a way which is similar to the model presented here, with the exception that our model does not include concepts for modelling connections of components types. These were not required for Linux configuration but may well be appropriate for other SPF configuration problems.

Software release management is the process of making a working piece of software available to users [21]. Software release management provides the notion of dependency between components. The tool SRM (Software Release Manager) [21] supports the release management process. It provides developers with a tool to track and control dependencies between components and users with a single source of software. The approach described in this paper differs from SRM in that it uses formal semantics in describing the configuration model and relies on artificial intelligence methods to generate a correct configuration. However SRM provides installation help and hides the physical distribution of of software from users.

The Koala component model provides a method for describing the product configuration through components and interfaces [22]. The Koala model does not provide a method for modelling evolution in itself, but a separate process which handles evolution is needed. The process includes rules for making changes in the interfaces and components. The approach in this paper provides support for modelling evolution on the concept level rather than on the process level, giving more freedom in choosing a development process.

5.2 Implementation

Based on the modelling method a prototype implementation of the evolution of Linux Familiar package descriptions was presented. The implementation showed that it is possible to model the evolution of a large software product using product configuration techniques. The model made from four releases of Familiar Linux can be used to configure a valid Linux environment for the HP iPAQ. Even reconfiguration of the system over time is possible. The model provides a way for creating a configuration containing any packages which have an effectivity at the current time. This overcomes the problem of needing to make a clean install when the user wishes to have packages from different Familiar releases on her/his HP iPAQ. The model supports having packages from multiple releases in a single configuration and the system checks that the generated configuration is correct based on the declarative semantics of the model. These are clear benefits compared to the current release system of Familiar Linux.

WeCoTin also support structuring the Familiar packages into categories and provides an intuitive web interface, with intelligent support for the user, such as graying out packages that may not be selected. None of these are possible with the current package management tools of Familiar. However this is only a prototype implementation and not yet capable of replacing the current package management tools of Familiar. For example the installation tools of Familiar have not been integrated to the current implementation.

Configuration problems are typically at least NP-complete [11]. However, it is not clear that the worst-case exponential computation for generating a configuration occurs in practise, since many physical products seem to be loosely constrained and can be configured efficiently [11]. This same potential for expensive computation holds for WeCoTin [15] and the implementation presented in this paper. This should be studied further by extensively testing the current implementation as well as with other software product families.

The Debian Linux PC distribution has been successfully modelled with a similar approach as presented in this paper [23]. Also a release of Familiar has been modelled as a configurable software product with PCML [24]. The two works proved that the modelling of software products with configuration modelling languages is feasible. This paper brings the addition of evolution concepts to the configuration of SPFs.

6   Conclusions and Further Work

In this paper we proposed an approach to modelling the evolution and variability of software product families based on viewing them as configurable products. We presented a conceptualisation for modelling evolution of such product families that is based on a subset of a de-facto standard ontology of product configuration. This subset was extended with concepts for modelling evolution: revision, effectivity and status. With these concepts the compositional structure and evolution of a software product family can be modelled. We further described a first prototype implementation of an intelligent tool that allows modelling a configurable software product family on the basis of the conceptualisation, and, supports the user in interactively producing a correct configuration with respect to the model. The implementation is based on an existing general purpose configurator prototype and thus it is not product or application domain specific.

To show the feasibility of both the modelling method and its implementation, we use a Debian Familiar Linux package configuration task over many releases as an example. Preliminary results from the implementation show that the modelling language can be used to model evolution of such a product family relatively easily and that the implementation performs acceptably. However, several topics for further research remain. It is not clear that the modelling method is applicable for all software product families. In particular, the concepts for modelling evolution were relatively simple and may need to be strengthened to incorporate more complex semantics for example generic objects and the evolution of the entire model. Furthermore, it may be that some dependencies between components of a product family were easier to model if concepts for modelling interfaces and connections between components were included. In addition, as the configuration problem solving can be computationally very expensive, more thorough testing of the efficiency of the implementation should be carried out. These issues should be investigated by more empirical research into modelling different types of software product families and testing the implementation more thoroughly on those and also on the Linux distribution discussed in this paper. This would probably require and result in further developments to the conceptual foundation and improving the usability and efficiency of the prototype implementation.

Acknowledgements

We gratefully acknowledge the financial support of Technology Development Centre of Finland. We also thank Andreas Anderson and Juha Tiihonen for providing the configurator used in this research and for their help in using it.

References

1. Bosch, J., Evolution and Composition of Reusable Assets in Product Line Architectures: a Case Study, Proc. 1.st Working IFIP Conf. on SW Architecture, (1999)
2. Clements, P., Northrop, L., Software Product Lines: Practices and Patterns, Addison-Wesley, (2001)

3. Svahnberg, M., Bosch, J., Evolution in Software Product Lines: Two Cases, Journal of Software Maintenance - Research and Practise 11(6), (1999) 391–422
4. Estublier, J., Software Configuration Management: A Roadmap, ICSE - Future of SE Track, Ireland,(2000) 279–289
5. Conradi, R., Westfechtel, B., Configuring Versioned Software Products, in: ICSE'96, Proc., LNCS, Vol. 1167, Springer, (1996) 88–109
6. Belkhatir, N., Cunin, P.Y., Lestideau V., Sali, H., An OO framework for Configuration of Deployable Large Component based Software Products, OOPSLA 2001
7. Soininen, T., An Approach to Knowledge Representation and Reasoning for Product Configuration Tasks, PhD thesis, Acta Polytechnical Scandinavica, No. 111, (2000)
8. Faltings B, Freuder EC, editors., Special Issue on Configuration. IEEE intelligent systems & their applications; 13(4), (1998) 29–85
9. Darr T, McGuinness D, Klein M, editors., Special Issue on Configuration Design. AI EDAM; 12(4), (1998)
10. Soininen, T., Tiihonen, J., Männistö, M., Sulonen, R., Towards a General Ontology of Configuration, AI EDAM 12(4), (1998) 357–372
11. Tiihonen, J., Soininen, T., Niemelä, I., Sulonen, R., Empirical Testing of a Weight Constraint Rule Based Configurator, ECAI 2002 Configuration Workshop, (2002)
12. Hicks, J., Nelson, R., Familiar v0.6 Installation Instructions http://handhelds.org/familiar/releases/v0.6/install/install.html
13. Männistö, T., Soininen, T. and Sulonen, R., Product Configuration View to Software Product Families, SCM-10 held at ICSE 2001, Canada, (2001)
14. Mahler, A., Lampen, A., An integrated toolset for engineering software configurations, SIGPLAN Software Engineering Notes, 13(5), USA, (1988)
15. Soininen, T., Niemelä, I., Tiihonen, J., Sulonen, R., Representing Configuration Knowledge With Weight Constraint Rules, AAAI Spring 2001 Symposium, USA, (2001)
16. Simons, P., Niemelä, I., and Soininen, T., Extending and implementing the stable model semantics, Artificial Intelligence, 138(1-2), (2002) 181-234
17. Männistö, T., A Conceptual modelling Approach to Product Families and their Evolution, PhD thesis, Acta Polytechnical Scandinavica, No. 106, (2000)
18. Zeller, A., Configuration Management with Version Sets, PhD thesis, Technical University of Braunschweig, (1997)
19. van der Hoek, A., Heimbigner, D., Wolf, A.L., Capturing Architectural Configurability: Variants, Options and Evolution, CU-CS-895-99, Univ of Colorado, (1999)
20. van der Hoek, A., Mikic-Rakic, M., Roshandel, R., Medvidovic, N., Taming Architectural Evolution, ESEC/FSE 2001, (2001) 1–10
21. van der Hoek, A., Hall, R., S., Heimbigner, D., Wolf, A., L., Software Release Management, ESEC/FSE 1997, (1997) 159–175
22. van Ommering, R., van der Linden, F., Kramer, J., Magee, J., The Koala Component Model for Consumer Electronics Software, IEEE Computer 33(3), (2000)
23. Syrjänen, T., A rule-based formal model for software configuration, Master's thesis, Helsinki University of Technology, (2000)
24. Ylinen, K., Männistö, T. and Soininen, T., Configuring Software with Traditional Methods - Case Linux Familiar, ECAI 2002 Configuration Workshop, (2002)

Integrating Software Construction
and Software Deployment

Eelco Dolstra

Utrecht University, P.O. Box 80089
3508 TB Utrecht, The Netherlands
eelco@cs.uu.nl

Abstract. Classically, software deployment is a process consisting of building the software, packaging it for distribution, and installing it at the target site. This approach has two problems. First, a package must be annotated with dependency information and other meta-data. This to some extent overlaps with component dependencies used in the build process. Second, the same source system can often be built into an often very large number of *variants*. The distributor must decide which element(s) of the variant space will be packaged, reducing the flexibility for the receiver of the package. In this paper we show how building and deployment can be integrated into a single formalism. We describe a build manager called *Maak* that can handle deployment through a sufficiently general module system. Through the sharing of generated files, a source distribution *transparently* turns into a binary distribution, removing the dichotomy between these two modes of deployment. In addition, the creation and deployment of variants becomes easy through the use of a simple functional language as the build formalism.

1 Introduction

Current SCM systems treat the building of software and the deployment of software as separate, orthogonal steps in the software life-cycle. Controlling the former is the domain of tools such as Make [1], while the latter is handled by, e.g., the Red Hat Package Manager [2]. In fact, they are not orthogonal. In this paper we show how building and deployment can be integrated in an elegant way. There are a number of problems in the current approaches to building and deployment.

Component Dependencies. Separating the building and deployment steps leads to a discontinuity in the formalisms used to express component dependencies. In a build manager it is necessary to express the dependencies between source components; in a package manager we express the dependencies between binary components.

Source vs. Binary Distribution. Another issue is the dichotomy between source and binary distributions. In an open-source environment software is provided as

B. Westfechtel, A. van der Hoek (Eds.): SCM 2001/2003, LNCS 2649, pp. 102–117, 2003.

source packages and sometimes as binary packages. The packaging and installation mechanisms for these are quite different. This is unfortunate; after all, a binary distribution can be considered conceptually to be a source distribution *that has been partially evaluated with respect to a target platform* using, e.g., a compiler.

Variability. Most software systems exhibit some amount of *variability*, that is, several *variants* can be instantiated from the same source system. Typical *variation points* are choosing between exclusive alternatives, whether to include optional features, and so on. Deployment in binary form makes it hard to change build time variation points.

Contribution. This paper demonstrates how build management and package management can be elegantly integrated in a single formalism. We show a build tool called *Maak* that constructs systems from descriptions in a simple functional language. By providing a sufficiently powerful module system and caching facility, the desired deployment characteristics can be obtained. In addition, the Maak language makes it easy to describe build variants.

Overview. The remainder of this paper is structured as follows. We motivate our research in section 2. We give a brief overview of the Maak system in section 3. We discuss the integration of deployment into build management in section 4. The state of the implementation is addressed in section 5, and related work in section 6. We end with concluding remarks and directions for future work in section 7.

2   Motivation

The task of a build manager is to generate *derivates* from *sources* by invoking the right *generators* (such as compilers), according to some formal specification of the system. The specification defines the actions by which derivates can be produced from sources or other derivates; that is, actions can depend on the outputs of other actions. The job of the build manager is to find a topological sort on the graph of actions that performs the actions in the right order. There are several important aspects to such a tool.

2.1   Correctness

A build manager should be *correct*: it should ensure *consistency* between the sources and the derivates, i.e., that all derivates are derived from current sources, or are equal to what they would be if they had been derived from current sources.

2.2 Efficiency

It is desirable to have a degree of *efficiency*: within the constraints of consistency redundant recompilations should be avoided. It is debatable whether this is the task of the build manager: it can be argued that this problem is properly solved in the actual generators, since only they have complete dependency information. Nevertheless, the efficiency aspect is the main purpose of classic build managers such as Make.

2.3 Variability

The system specification formalism should enable us to easily specify *variants*. That is, we want to parameterize a (partial) specification so that the various members of a *software product line* [3] (a set of systems sharing a common set of features) can be instantiated by providing different parameters.

In open-source systems in particular there tend to be many build-time variation points in order to make the system buildable in a wide variety of environments that may or may not have the characteristics necessary to implement certain features. In turn this is due to the use of fine-grained deployment strategies: many small independent packages are used to compose the system. For example, a program might have the ability to generate graphical output in JPG and PNG format, but only if the respective libraries libjpg and libpng are available.

Open-source distributors typically need to use binary packages for speed of installation. Unfortunately, binary packages tend to force a "one-size-fits-all" approach upon the distributors for those variation points that are bound at build-time. In packaging the previous example system the distributor would either have to deny the JPG/PNG feature to the users, or force it on users that don't need it, or deploy binary packages for each desired set of feature selections.

Let's look at a real-life example. The ATerm library [4] is a library for the manipulation and storage of tree-like data structures. The library is fairly small, consisting of a dozen C source files. An interesting aspect of the package is that the library has to be built in several variants: the regular library, the library with debug information enabled, the library with *maximal subterm sharing* (a domain feature) disabled, and various others.

Support for this in the package's Makefile (actually, an Automakefile) is rather *ad hoc*. To prevent the intermediate files used in building each variant from overwriting each other, the use of special filename extensions has to be arranged for:

```
SRCS = aterm.c list.c ...

libATerm_a_LIBADD     = $(SRCS:.c=.o)
libATerm_dbg_a_LIBADD = $(SRCS:.c=-dbg.o)
libATerm_ns_a_LIBADD  = $(SRCS:.c=-ns.o)
```

This fragment causes the extensions .o, -dbg.o, and -ns.o to be used for the object files used in building the aforementioned variants. To make it actually work, we have to provide pattern rules:

```
%.o: %.c
    gcc -c $< -o $@

%-dbg.o: %.c
    gcc -g -c $< -o $@

%-ns.o: %.c
    gcc -DNO_SHARING -c $< -o $@
```

Also note that this technique does not cover all variants in the variant space; for example, no library *without* maximal sharing but *with* debug information is built.

2.4   Modularity and Composability

Fourth, and most relevant to this paper, we claim that a build manager should provide support for the composition of source components. Software seldom exists in a vacuum; to build a component, it is generally necessary that certain other components are built as well. Most build managers work well when components are *statically composed*, that is, when they are part of the same source tree. For components that need to be separately deployable, this often does not hold.

Continuing the previous example, apart from the library itself, the ATerm distribution also provides a set of utility programs for manipulating terms. These utilities are linked against the ATerm library, of course. Such a dependency is easy to express when the library and utilities are part of the same package. E.g., one of the utilities, **termsize**, can be constructed as follows using Make:

```
termsize: termsize.o ../aterm/libATerm.a
    cc -o termsize termsize.o libATerm.a

termsize.o: termsize.c
    cc -o termsize.o -c termsize.c -I../aterm
```

(The references to **../aterm** are present because the library proper is built in a subdirectory **aterm** of the package, while the utilities are located in the **utils** directory.) The Makefile properly expresses the relationships between the components; e.g., if any of the sources of the library changes, the program will be rebuilt as well. That is, the build manager has access to the full dependency graph.

Suppose, however, that we want to move the utilities into a separate package, so that, e.g., it can be deployed independently. The typical procedure for installation from source in a Unix environment would be:

1. Fetch the source code for package `aterm` containing the library.
2. Configure and build it (e.g., using Make).
3. Install it. This entails copying the library and C header files to some "global" location, such as `/usr/lib` and `/usr/include`.
4. Fetch the source code for package `aterm-utils` that contains the utilities.
5. Configure and build it. Configuration includes specifying or finding the location of the `aterm` library; for example, Autoconf configuration scripts scan a number of well-known directories for library and header files.
6. Install it. This means copying the programs to, e.g., `/usr/bin`.

What is wrong with this approach? Note that we end up with two Makefiles for each package, each providing an insufficient amount of dependency information. For example, for the program package we might have the following Makefile:

```
termsize: termsize.o
    cc -o termsize termsize.o -lATerm

termsize.o: termsize.c
    cc -o termsize.o -c termsize.c
```

The dependency of the program component on the library component is no longer explicit at the Makefile level. The `aterm-utils` package depends on the `aterm` package, but this is not a formal dependency (i.e., it's not made explicit); rather, `aterm-utils` uses some artifacts (say, `libATerm.a`) that have hopefully been installed by `aterm`. This is unsafe. For instance, we link in a file such as `/usr/lib/libATerm.a` (through `-lATerm`). This file is an "uncontrolled" input: we have to hope that it is the right version, has been built with the right parameters, and so on, and in any case we have no way to rebuild it if it isn't.

We now have to express the dependency at the level of the package manager (if we express it at all; these things are often left implicit for the user to figure out from the documentation!). That is, splitting one package into several lifts dependencies to the higher level of package management, making them invisible to the lower level of build management.

In summary, splitting components in this manner leads to more work for both the developer of the package and the users of the package and is unsafe. This is very unfortunate, because the refactoring of large components into smaller ones is desirable to promote small-grained reuse [5]. What we really want is to *import* in a controlled manner the `aterm` package into `aterm-utils` package, so that the former can be build if necessary during the construction of the latter. Since these packages are not part of a single source tree and can come from separate sources, this implies that there can be a *deployment aspect* to build management. For example, we may want to fetch packages transparently from the network if they are not available locally.

3   The Maak System

Maak (from the Dutch verb for "to make") is a build manager. It allows system models to be described in a simple functional language. Maak evaluates an expression that describes a *build graph*—a structure that describes *what* to build and *how* to build it—and then *realizes* that graph by performing the actions contained in it.

In this section we give a brief overview of Maak. It is not the intent to provide a full overview of the syntax, semantics, and feature set of the system. Rather, we focus on some examples that show how the problems of modularity and variability can be solved in Maak.

A Variability Example. The variants of the ATerm library (introduced in section 2) can be built using Maak as follows. First, we consider the simple case of building just the regular variant:

```
srcs = [./aterm.c ./list.c ...];

atermLib = makeLibrary (srcs);
```

What happens here is that we define a list `srcs` of the C sources constituting the library. The variable `atermLib` is bound to the library that results from applying the function `makeLibrary` to the sources; `makeLibrary` knows that it should compile the sources before putting them in the library.

It should be noted that `atermLib` is a variable name and not a filename, unlike, e.g., `./aterm.c`; the sole difference between the two syntactical classes is that filenames have slashes in them. So what's the filename of the library? The answer is that we don't need to know; we can unambiguously refer to it through the variable `atermLib`. (The function `makeLibrary` generates a name for us).

Hence, we can now *use* the library in building an executable program:

```
test = link {in = ./test.c, libs = atermLib};
```

We see here that Maak has two calling mechanisms: *positional parameters* (e.g., `f (x, y, z)`) and by passing an *attribute set* (`f {a = x, b = y, c = z}`). The latter allows arguments to be permuted or left undefined.

Similarly, we can create the debug and no-maximal-sharing variants:

```
atermLibDbg = makeLibrary {in = srcs, cflags = "-g"};
atermLibNS = makeLibrary {in = srcs, cflags = "-DNO_SHARING"};
```

Much better, though, is to solve the variability issue comprehensively as follows. We can abstract over the definitions above by making `atermLib` into a *function* with arguments `debug` and `sharing`:

```
atermLib = {debug, sharing}:
  makeLibrary
    { in = srcs
    , cflags = if (sharing, "", "-DNO_SHARING")
             + if (debug, "-g", "")
    };
```

after which we can select the desired variant:

```
test = link
  { in = ./test.c
  , libs = atermLib {debug = true, sharing = false}
  };
```

Lazy Evaluation. Maak's input formalism is a lazy functional language, meaning that variable bindings and function arguments are evaluated only when actually needed. This has two advantages. First, it prevents unused parts of the build graph from being evaluated. Second, it allows the definition of *control structures* in the language itself. For example, an if-then-else construct can take the form of a regular function `if` taking three arguments: the conditional and the values returned on true and false, respectively; only one of the latter is evaluated.

Model. Build graphs consist of two types of nodes: *file nodes* and *action nodes.* Nodes are represented as *attribute sets*: mappings from names to values. A file node consists of an attribute **name** that denotes the name of the file, and optionally (for derivates) an attribute **partOf** whose value is the action that builds the derivate; that is, **partOf** denotes an edge in the graph.

Action nodes are also represented as attribute sets. There are several kinds of attributes involved in an action. File attributes denote either the action's sources or its derivates (i.e., they denote graph edges). A file x is a derivate of an action y if x.**partOf** == y, where == denotes pointer equality. The special attribute **build** specifies the command to be executed to perform the action.

We can therefore describe the action of generating a parser from a Yacc grammar as follows:

```
parser =
  { in = ./parser.y
  , csrc => ./parser.c
  , header => ./parser.h
  , build = exec "yacc -b {in}"
  };
```

The notation `=>` is sugar: it ensures that the **partOf** attribute of the value points back at the defining attribute set, i.e., it defines a derivate of the action. Inputs are not marked in a particular way. Given the action **parser**, the C source can be selected using the expression **parser.csrc**.

Defining Tools. Rather than write each action in the graph explicitly, we can abstract over them, that is, we can write a function (i.e., a λ-abstraction) that takes a set of attributes and returns an action. The following example defines a basic C compiler function that takes two arguments: the source file **in**, and the compiler flags **cflags**.

```
compileC = {in, cflags}:
  { in = in
  , cflags = cflags
```

```
, out => prefix (in) + '.o'
, build = exec "cc -c {in} -o {out}"
}.out;
```

The syntax {*args*}: *body* denotes a function taking the given arguments and returning the body. We select the out attribute of the action to make it easier to pass the output of one action as input into another (e.g., link (compile (./foo.c))).

Module System. Maakfiles are modular: they can import other Maakfiles. For example, the declaration import ./src/Maakfile makes the definitions in the specified Maakfile visible in the current Maakfile. The argument to the import keyword is an *expression* (rather than a filename) that evaluates to a filename. Crucially, as we shall see in section 4, this allows arbitrary module management policies to be defined by the user (rather than have them hard-coded in the language). Local definitions in a module take precedence over imported definitions. In addition, qualified imports are possible: import *e* into *x* binds the definitions in a module to the qualifier *x*, so that a definition *y* in the imported module can be referenced as *x*.*y*.

4   Deployment

As stated previously, software deployment generally proceeds as follows. First, the software is *built* using, e.g., compilers, generally under the control of a build manager such as Make. Then, the relevant artifacts are *packaged*, that is, put in some deployable unit such as a zip-file or an RPM package; depending on the mechanism meta-data can be added to describe package dependencies and so on. Finally, the package is *installed*, typically by an *installer* shipped as part of the package, or by a *package manager* present on the target system such as the Red Hat Package Manager.

Let's consider the example based on the ATerm library mentioned in section 2 where we wanted to split this distribution into two separate packages: aterm (containing the library), and aterm-utils (containing the utility programs). In this section we show a simpler approach to the deployment process. The central idea is to deploy packages in source form, i.e., along with an appropriate Maakfile. Packages can depend on each other by having the Maakfile import the Maakfiles of other packages. Since the packages are not part of the same source tree, an indirection is required.

Figure 1 shows the Maakfile for the aterm package. It exports a function atermLib that builds a variant of the ATerm library, along with a pointer to the header files. Note that no installation occurs; the source code *is* the installation.

Figure 2 shows the Maakfile for the aterm-utils package. It imports the library package through the statement import pkg ("aterm-1.6.7-2"). The function pkg maps abstract package names to Maakfiles, while ensuring that the package is present on the system.

```
import stdlibs; # for makeLibrary etc.

atermLib = {debug, sharing}:
  makeLibrary
    { in = srcs
    , cflags = if (sharing, "", "-DNO_SHARING")
             + if (debug, "-g", "")
    };

atermInclude = ./;
```

Fig. 1. Maakfile for package `aterm`

```
import stdlibs;
import pkg ("aterm-1.6.7-2");

default = progs;

progs = [termsize ...];

termsize = link' (./termsize, ./termsize.c); # and so on...

link' = {out, in}: put (out, link  # put copies a file to 'out'
  { in = in
  , libs = [atermLib {debug = false, sharing = true}]
  , includes = [atermIncl]
  });

activate = map ({p}: activateExec (p), progs);
```

Fig. 2. Maakfile for package `aterm-utils`

An Example Deployment Strategy. Now, how do we deploy this? It's a matter of defining an appropriate implementation for the function `pkg`. It must be emphasized that `pkg` is not a primitive: it is a regular function. The user can define other functions, or change the definition of `pkg`, to obtain arbitrary package management policies. A possible implementation is outlined in figure 3. Here the source code is obtained from the network; in particular, it is checked out from a *Subversion* repository[1]. The source code for package X is downloaded into `/var/pkg/`X on the local machine, and `pkg` will return `/var/pkg/`X`/Maakfile` to the `import` statement.

Of course, `pkg` needs to know how to map package names to URLs. This mapping is maintained locally: through the function `registerPkg` (*package-name*, *url*) we can associate a package name with a URL. These mappings can also be

---

[1] Subversion is a version management system intended to be "a compelling replacement for CVS in the open source community" [6]. It fixes CVS's most obvious deficiencies, such as unversioned directories and non-atomic commits.

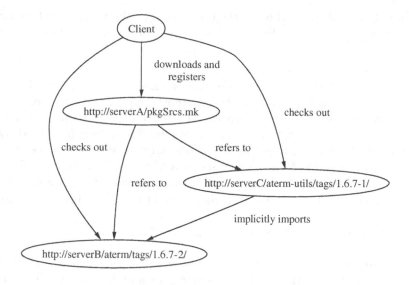

Fig. 3. A deployment strategy

obtained over the network by fetching a Maakfile containing calls to `registerPkg` from the network and executing it (clearly, security issues need to be addressed in the future!). The package `aterm-utils` can now be built by issuing the command

```
maak -f 'pkg ("aterm-utils-1.6.7-1")'
```

which will recursively obtain the source for `aterm-utils` and `aterm`, build the variant of `atermLib` required for the utilities, and finally build the utilities. (The switch `-f` obtains a Maakfile from the given expression rather than from the current directory).

Installation. The above command will build the ATerm utilities, but it will not "install" them. In the Make paradigm, it is customary to have a *phony* `install` target that copies the appropriate files to the right system directories. This is essentially a redundant step. Indeed, it's just an additional complication (for example, it is often quite troublesome to get executables using dynamically linked libraries to work both in the source and installed location).

The main point of installing is to make software available to the user; for example, copying a program to `/usr/bin` has the effect of having it appear in every user's search path. That is, the point of installing is to *activate* the software. For example, the function `activateExec` will create a symbolic link in `/usr/bin` to its argument. Hence, the command

```
maak -f 'pkg ("aterm-utils-1.6.7-1")' activate
```

will build the utilities and make them available to the user. (The function `map` used in figure 2 applies a function—here, `activateExec`—to all elements of a list).

Binary Distribution. Of course, we cannot expect the clients to build from source, so we need the ability to transparently export derivates to the client; if a client runs Maak to build derivates that have already been built, i.e., were built with the same attributes, then the pre-existing ones will be used. On the other hand, if the client attempts to build a derivate with attributes or sources such that no equivalent derivate exists in any cache, it must be built locally. This enables a graceful fallback from *binary* distribution to *source* distribution.

Maak provides a primitive implementation of this idea. The command

```
maak 'exportDerivates (/tmp/shared, foo)'
```

will copy all derivates occurring in the build graph defined by the variable `foo` to the directory `/tmp/shared`, where a mapping is maintained from build attributes to files. (Generally, we would put such a cache on the network or on distribution media). Subsequently, another user can build `foo` through the command `maak --import /tmp/shared foo`; Maak will try to rebuild missing derivates first by looking them up in the mapping, and by rebuilding them if they do not occur in `/tmp/shared`. Therefore, if any changes have been made to the sources of `foo`, or to the build attributes, the derivates will be rebuilt.

Barriers. When we share derivates, we encounter a problem: *any* change to the attributes or dependencies will invalidate a derivate. This is often too rigid. For example, recompilation will be triggered if the recipient has a different C compiler (since it's a dependency of the build process). If this behavior is not desired, we can use *update barriers* to prevent a change to the compiler from causing a rebuild, while a change to any "real" source file still triggers a rebuild.

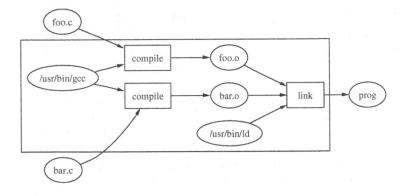

Fig. 4. An update barrier

The idea is outlined in figure 4 where we have two source files, foo.c and bar.c, to be compiled and linked into an executable. The C compiler gcc is also a dependency, but changes to it should not trigger recompilation. We ensure this by making an action node which has foo.c and bar.c as inputs, prog as output, and as its action the *building of the subgraph that builds* prog. If neither foo.c nor bar.c changes, the action (the big box in the figure) will not be executed. If either of them changes, Maak will execute the action, which consists of updating prog using the subgraph. Note that if either has changed, and the C compiler has changed as well, then both files will be recompiled! This is exactly right: we have to maintain consistency between the object files in the presence of potential changes to the Application Binary Interface (ABI) of the compiler.

5   Implementation

A prototype of Maak has been implemented and is available under the terms of the GNU Lesser General Public License at http://www.cs.uu.nl/~eelco/maak/. The implementation comes with a (currently small) standard library providing tool definitions for a number of languages and tools, include C and Java. The prototype is written in Haskell, a purely functional programming language. This is a nice language for prototyping, but ultimately a re-implementation in C or C++ would be useful to improve portability and efficiency.

Maak implements up-to-date checking by maintaining per directory a map from the derivates to the set of attributes used to build them, along with exact timestamps (or for improved safety, hashes of the contents) of input files.

A problem in building variants is that we have to prevent the derivates from each variant from overwriting each other; hence, they should not occupy the same names in the file system. We take the approach that the actions (i.e., the tool definition functions) are responsible for choosing output filenames such that variants do not overwrite each other. The usual approach is to form an output name using a *hash* of the input attributes. For example, compileC (./foo.c) might yield a filename .maak_foo_305c.o, while compileC {in = ./foo.c, cflags = "-g"} would yield .maak_foo_54db.o; in actuality, we use longer hashes to decrease the probability of a collision. If a collision does occur, a derivate may overwrite an older derivate, but since Maak registers the attributes used to build them, this will not lead to unsafe build; if the older derivate is required again, it will be rebuilt.

A useful feature of the prototype is the ability to perform *build audits* on Linux systems to verify the completeness of Maakfile dependencies. By using the strace utility Maak can trace all open() system calls, determine all actual inputs and outputs of an action, and complain if there is a mismatch between the specified and actual sets of inputs and outputs.

Another useful feature are *generic operations* on the build graph: given a build graph, we can, for example, collect all leaf nodes to *automatically* create a source distribution, or collect all nodes that are *not* inputs to actions to create a binary distribution.

6   Related Work

Build Managers. The most widely used build manager is Make [1], along with a large number of clones, not all of them source-compatible. Make's model is very simple: systems are described as a set of rules that specify a command that builds a number of derivates from a number of sources. Make rebuilds a derivate if any of the sources has a newer timestamp (a mechanism that is in itself subject to race conditions). Unfortunately, Make often causes inconsistent builds, since Makefiles tend to specify incomplete dependency information, and the up-to-date detection is unreliable; e.g., changes to compiler flags will not trigger recompilation. Make's input language is also quite simplistic, making it hard to specify variants.

The Makefile formalism is not sufficiently high-level; it does not provide scalable abstraction facilities. The abstraction mechanisms — variables and pattern rules — are all global. Hence, if we need to specify different ways of building targets, we cannot use them, unless we split the system into multiple Makefiles. This, however, creates the much greater problem of incomplete dependency graphs [7].

Can't we do the sort of deployment strategy described in section 4 using Make? Through Make's ability to invoke external tools, we can of course in principle do anything with it. However, Make lacks a serious module system. It does provide an include mechanism, but its flat namespace makes it unsuitable for component composition.

There have been attempts to fix this defect by building layers on top of Make rather than replace it, such as Automake [8], which generates Makefiles from a list of macro invocations. For example, the definition foo_SOURCES = a.c b.y will cause Automake to generate Make definitions that build the executable foo from the given C and Yacc source, install it, create a source distribution, and so on. The problem with such generation tools is that they do not shield the user from the lower layers; it is the user's job to map problems that occur in a Makefile back to the Automakefile from which it was generated. Automake does not provide a module system and so does not solve the problem of incomplete dependency graphs. It provides some basic variability mechanisms, such as the ability to build a library in several variants. However, Automake is not extensible, so this feature is somewhat *ad hoc*.

Autoconf [9] is often used in conjunction with Make and/or Automake to specialize an element of a product line automatically for the target platform. It is typically used to generate Makefiles from templates with values discovered during the configuration process substituted for variables. The heuristic approach to source configuration promoted by Autoconf is very useful in practice, but also unreliable. For example, we should not *guess* whether /usr/lib/libfoo.so is really the library we're looking for; rather, we should import the desired version of the library so that the process can never go wrong.

Autobundle [10] is a tool to simplify composition of separately deployable Autoconf-based packages. Based on descriptions of package dependencies, locations, etc., Autobundle generates a script that fetches the required source packages from the network, along with a configuration script and a Makefile for the composed package. This is similar to the package management strategy described in section 4, but it is yet another layer in the construction and deployment process.

A handful of systems go beyond Make's too-simple description language. Vesta [11] integrates version management and build management. It's *Software Description Language* is a functional language [12], similar to Maak's. An interesting aspect is the propagation of "global" settings (such as compiler flags), which happens by passing down an *environment* as a hidden argument to every function call; the environment is bound at top-level. In Maak propagation is explicit and left to the authors of tool definitions. Vesta also allows derivates to be shared among users; if a user attempts to build something that has previously been built by another user, the derivates can be obtained from a cache. This is quite reminiscent of our stated goal of allowing transparent binary deployment. However, the Vesta framework only allows building from immutable sources; that is, all sources to the build process (such as compilers) must be under version control. When deploying source systems, unfortunately, we cannot expect the recipient to have a identical environment to our own.

Odin [13] also has a somewhat functional flavor. For example, the expression `hello.c` denotes a source, while `hello.c :exe` denotes the executable obtained by compiling and linking `hello.c`; variants build can be expressed easily, e.g., `hello.c +debug :exe`. However, tool definitions in Odin are special entities, not functions.

Amake [14] is the build tool for the Amoeba distributed operating system. Like Odin, it separates the specification of build tools and system specifications. Given a set of sources Amake automatically completes the build graph, that is, it finds instances of tool definitions that build the desired targets from the given sources. This is contrary to the model of explicit tool application to values in Vesta and Maak. The obvious advantage is that specifications become shorter; the downside is that it becomes harder to specify alternative ways of building, and to see what's going on (generally, it is a good idea to be explicit in saying what you want).

Package Managers. There are many package management systems, ranging from the basic— providing just simple installation and uninstallation facilities for individual packages—to the advanced—providing the features needed for ensuring a consistent system. The popular Red Hat Package Manager (RPM) [2], used in several Linux distributions, is a reasonably solid system. By maintaining a database of all installed packages, it ensures that packages can be cleanly uninstalled and do not overwrite each other's files, allows tracibility (e.g., to what package does file X belong?), verifies that the prerequisites for installation of a package (specified by the developer in an *RPM specfile*) are met, and so on.

But RPM also clearly demonstrates the dangers of separating build and package management: RPM packages often have incomplete dependency information [15]. For example, a package may use some library `libfoo.so` without actually declaring the foo package as a prerequisite. This cannot happen in Maak because the way to access the library is by importing package foo.

Not a failing of RPM per se but of RPM package builders (and, indeed, most Unix packaging systems) is the difficulty of having several variants of the same product installed at the same time; e.g., RPMs of different versions or variants of Apache typically all want to be installed in /usr/lib/apache/. This is mostly a "cultural" problem: a better installation policy (such as described in section 4) solves this problem. For example, a very useful feature for system administrators is the ability to query to what package a file belongs. This query becomes trivial if every package X is installed in /var/pkg/X.

There also exist several *source-based* package management systems, such as the FreeBSD Ports Collection [16]. The main attraction is that the system can be optimized towards the platform and requirements of the user, e.g., by selecting specific compiler optimization flags for the user's processor, or by disabling unnecessary optional package features. The obvious downsides are slowness of installation, and that validation becomes hard: with so many possible variants, how can we be sure that the system compiles correctly, let alone runs correctly? For most ports pre-compiled *packages* exist (which do not offer build-time variability, of course). The two modes of installation are not abstracted over from the user's perspective; i.e., both present different user interfaces. With regard to the slowness of source deployment, the holy grail would of course be the transparent use of pre-built derivates described in section 4.

Of course, most users are not interested in building from source; the goal is to relieve the developer from the burden of having to deal explicitly with the build and deployment processes. As stated in the introduction, we can view binary deployment as an optimization of source deployment. Such optimization should happen transparently.

7   Conclusion

Van der Hoek [17] has argued that deployment functionality should be added to SCM tools (and vice versa). In this paper we have shown how we can integrate deployment with the build system. Also, since Maak is policy-free with regard to the deployment policy, we can integrate deployment with version management. For example, the deployment policy suggested in section 4 obtains packages from a networked version management system; this could, for instance, be used to push component updates to clients.

In the remainder of this section some issues for future work will be sketched. The most important one is that the sharing of derivates—essential for transparent binary/source distribution—is currently rather primitive. A related issue is that we need to be able to do binary-only distributions. This could be done by making Maak pretend that the source does exist (e.g., by supplying file content hashes). Security issues related to derivate sharing need to be addressed as well. For example, if the administrator has built a package, other users should use it; but not the other way around.

We need to address scalability. For example, in the case of a Java package that requires a Java compiler, the former should import the package that builds the latter, just in case it hasn't been built yet. But this would make the build graph huge. Update barriers could be used to confine up-to-date analysis to the package at hand.

Acknowledgments

This work was supported in part by the Software Engineering Research Center (SERC). I am grateful to Eelco Visser, Andres Löh, Dave Clarke, and the anonymous referees for commenting on drafts of this paper.

References

1. Feldman, S.I.: Make — a program for maintaining computer programs. Software — Practice and Experience **9** (1979) 255–65
2. Bailey, E.C.: Maximum RPM. Sams (1997)
3. Bosch, J.: Design and Use of Software Architectures: Adopting and Evolving a Product-Line Approach. Addison-Wesley (2000)
4. van den Brand, M.G.J., de Jong, H.A., Klint, P., Olivier, P.: Efficient annotated terms. Software—Practice and Experience **30** (2000) 259–291
5. de Jonge, M.: To Reuse or To Be Reused. PhD thesis, University of Amsterdam (2003)
6. CollabNet: Subversion home page. http://subversion.tigris.org (2002)
7. Miller, P.: Recursive make considered harmful (1997)
8. Free Software Foundation: Automake home page.
   http://www.gnu.org/software/automake/ (2002)
9. Free Software Foundation: Autoconf home page.
   http://www.gnu.org/software/autoconf/ (2002)
10. de Jonge, M.: Source tree composition. In: Seventh International Conference on Software Reuse. Number 2319 in Lecture Notes in Computer Science, Springer-Verlag (2002)
11. Heydon, A., Levin, R., Mann, T., Yu, Y.: The Vesta approach to software configuration management. Technical Report Research Report 168, Compaq Systems Research Center (2001)
12. Heydon, A., Levin, R., Yu, Y.: Caching function calls using precise dependencies. In: ACM SIGPLAN '00 Conference on Programming Language Design and Implementation, ACM Press (2000) 311–320
13. Clemm, G.M.: The Odin System — An Object Manager for Extensible Software Environments. PhD thesis, University of Colorado at Boulder (1986)
14. Baalbergen, E.H., Verstoep, K., Tanenbaum, A.S.: On the design of the Amoeba configuration manager. In: Proc. 2nd Int. Works. on Software Configuration Management. Volume 17 of ACM SIGSOFT Software Engineering Notes. (1989) 15–22
15. Hart, J., D'Amelia, J.: An analysis of RPM validation drift. In: LISA'02: Sixteenth Systems Administration Conference, USENIX Association (2002) 155–166
16. The FreeBSD Project: FreeBSD Ports Collection.
   http://www.freebsd.org/ports/ (2002)
17. van der Hoek, A.: Integrating configuration management and software deployment. In: Proc. Working Conference on Complex and Dynamic Systems Architecture (CDSA 2001). (2001)

Data Product Configuration Management and Versioning in Large-Scale Production of Satellite Scientific Data

Bruce R. Barkstrom

Atmospheric Sciences Data Center
NASA Langley Research Center
Hampton, VA 23681-2199 USA

Abstract. This paper describes a formal structure for keeping track of files, source code, scripts, and related material for large-scale Earth science data production. We first describe the environment and processes that govern this configuration management problem. Then, we show that a graph with typed nodes and arcs can describe the derivation of production design and of the produced files and their metadata. The graph provides three useful by-products:

- a hierarchical data file inventory structure that can help system users find particular files,
- methods for creating production graphs that govern job scheduling and provenance graphs that track all of the sources and transformations between raw data input and a particular output file,
- a systematic relationship between different elements of the structure and development documentation.

1 Introduction – On the Meaning of 'Version'

Scientific data management must deal with several configuration management issues that are more general than those that arise in tracking software versions. Indeed, it is useful to consider several possible meanings of the term version that arise in dealing with scientific data.

For archives with genomic or chemical data, the structure of the archive contents is relatively fixed, but contributors constantly add new information [1, 2]. This constant addition and revision leads to distinct annual or semi-annual versions of genomic or chemical databases that are similar to annual versions of encyclopedias. Users have a clear motivation to use the latest version, since new and improved information is likely to replace older versions of the same kind of information.

Experimental fields of science, such as high-energy physics, need to record their basic observational data. These data include the particle tracks in detectors located around the targets in accelerators. Data users interpret these observational data, sometimes using extensive simulation programs, sometimes using

B.Westfechtel, A. van der Hoek (Eds.): SCM 2001/2003, LNCS2649, pp. 118–133, 2003.

calibrations of the parameters of the original detectors [3]. While the simulations are often easy to produce anew, the original data and the calibrations become targets for longer term data preservation. For these fields, a version of the archived data is likely to keep the original observations intact, but to append new values for the calibration coefficients.

In observational sciences, such as astronomy [4], solar physics [5], and Earth science, observations are unique. Unfortunately, neither the data downlinks nor the instrument understanding is perfect. Furthermore, scientists usually need to convert the instrument data into other geophysical parameters using code that embodies complex algorithms. Data from satellite instruments cascades through layers of editing and processing. Scientists desire long time series of data with homogeneous uncertainties. To satisfy it, data producers create long series of data with the 'same' code. At the same time, reexamination of previously produced data suggests changes that should be inserted into the production system to improve data quality. Such revisions force the scientists to rerun the old data with new 'versions' of the code and coefficients. The new revisions may also force reprocessing of 'higher level,' derived data products. In contrast with software configuration management that only needs to track source code revisions, management of observational data requires careful tracking of the total configuration of computer code, input coefficients, and versions of 'lower level' data products.

In the remainder of this paper, we concentrate on data production, versioning, and configuration management of both data and source code for Earth Science data. We are particularly interested in data produced by instruments on NASA's Earth-observing satellite systems. The large volume of data and the production approach we just discussed lead to discrete, batch production. In other words, versions of Earth science data products are discrete collections of files that contain time series of related data.

2   Data Production Paradigms and CM Requirements for Earth Science Data

In general, it is reasonable to divide data production approaches into "database-like" or "batch" production. The first approach uses transactions that update individual elements of data. The second ingests files, operates on the ingested data values, and outputs new files. Database practitioners have been hopeful about the use of databases. Musick [6] suggests that scientific computing needs both computation at rates limited by CPU speed and data bandwidth as close to native I/O as possible. Unfortunately, his benchmarks suggest that current, commercial databases use so much CPU that their performance on very large data volumes is unacceptable.

NASAs Earth Observing System Data and Information System (EOSDIS) [7] illustrates a file-oriented system that provides reasonable production and data distribution throughput. EOSDIS now includes seven major data centers, with stored data volumes ranging from about 1 TB to more than 2 PB. At the authors data center at Langley Research Center, data production adds about 20 TB/month. This production will continue to add to the total data volume for most of the next decade.

Within EOSDIS, there are a number of identifiable "data production paradigms." At the simple end, Landsat data producers use a simple process to create images of the Earth. At the complex end, the CERES data production uses priority interrupt scheduling with thirteen major subsystems. In the latter case, the science team responsible for the instrument and for the data has about 650,000 source lines of code (SLOC) in the science production software. The team also has about 45,000 lines of scripts to control production, and about 450,000 SLOC of code for production of coefficient files and data validation. In addition, the data center has a similar volume of infrastructure code and Commercial Off-The-Shelf software. There is a substantial variation in the number of jobs being run each day for various instruments in EOSDIS. At the simple end are instruments that require only a few tens of jobs per day. Two of the instruments now producing data in the Langley Atmospheric Sciences Data Center (ASDC) run about 1,000 jobs per day each. At the high end of production rate is the MODerate-resolution Imaging Spectroradiometer (MODIS), for which the data producers may run more then 10,000 discrete jobs per day.

As one might expect, different instrument teams meet different production control problems. Some of these problems for Earth science data are similar to those found in other branches of industrial engineering. From a sociological standpoint, the data producers are like small to mid-sized firms with varying market sizes. Each science team devises data products and data production strategies appropriate to their market niche.

One important and universal problem for Earth science data centers is the production volatility induced by changes in algorithms and coefficients as result of validation and reprocessing. Earth scientists require data validation to quantify the data uncertainties in a scientific data product. Of course, validation entails detailed data examination that reveals correctable problems with the data. Corrections introduce unexpected delays and force the data center to perform rework that may not be present in other kinds of data management.

Other production control problems are probably unique to production of Earth science data. One key difference between this production and other industrial engineering problems is that data products produced at intermediate stages in the production process are useful in their own right. Use of these intermediate products in later steps of the production process does not destroy them. A second key difference is that scientific data production for research always involves requirements revisions. Both of these differences lead to stringent requirements for configuration management. The traceability of the production process can be the key to understanding whether data anomalies are due to changes in the Earth or are simply the result of errors in the algorithms or input parameters.

3   A Simple Example Data Production Topology

Earth science data managers usually group NASA satellite data into file collections known as Data Products. They classify each data product as falling into one of four levels:

- **Level 0 (L0)** - raw data from instrument data sources, usually consisting of time-ordered packets of data
- **Level 1 (L1)** - calibrated data with geolocation included, with the individual measurements retaining substantially the same temporal and spatial resolution as the Level 0 data
- **Level 2 (L2)** - geophysical fields derived from the calibrated data, with the fields retaining the same temporal and spatial resolution as the Level 1 data
- **Level 3 (L3)** - time and space averaged fields derived from the Level 2 data, where the same fields as Level 2 now appear at larger spatial resolutions and longer time intervals than they had in the Level 2 data products

As an example of this classification, fig. 1 shows a Data Flow Diagram for a simple, linear production system that creates one data product for each of three levels. In this figure, Data Products appear in rectangular boxes; Algorithm Collections (ACs) appear in circles. We also show various coefficient files that encapsulate key variable values for each AC. Because the coefficients are changeable (and often voluminous), most science teams do not embed them in their production code. Rather, they put the coefficients in files.

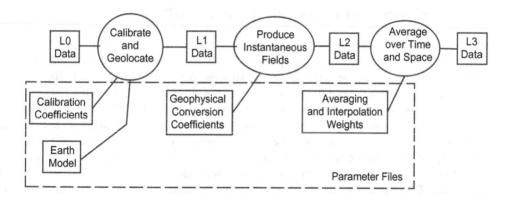

Fig. 1. Data flow diagram for simple linear data production

There are three important ideas that flow from this representation of data production. First, the basic topology is a directed graph, in which the Data Products are one kind of node and the Algorithm Collections are another. Second, the Data Products themselves form a tree. In fig. 1, for example, we can take the L0 Data node as the root of the tree. We can then count the data products (or data product levels) by distance from this root node. Distance in the graph is roughly equivalent to the number of ACs between a data product and the root node. In more complex production topologies, data product Level can be quite misleading about the number of predecessor processes. Third, including the coefficient files in the production graph improves identification of the factors that determine the possible scientific versions of the higher level data products.

Consider, the first Algorithm Collection in fig. 1. As its name implies, this collection contains two algorithms: a calibration algorithm and a geolocation algorithm. If either of these algorithms changes, then the AC will produce different numerical values in the Level 1 data than the ones found in the original version. Suppose the original geolocation algorithm located the pixels on a spherical Earth and a new version locates them on an ellipsoidal one. Data users need to be able to verify which version of the algorithm created data they are using. Likewise, we might suppose that the original calibration algorithm used a linear relation between the pixel data numbers and the calibrated radiances. Then suppose the science team introduced a revised calibration algorithm that had a small quadratic correction. The revision would produce different numerical values in the Level 1 data products – and in the subsequent Level 2 and 3 products. It is easy to devise a combinatorial expansion of the number of versions that are possible. There is no easy way to provide a linear sequence of versions, rendering the conventional approach of sequential numbering inaccurate.

4   A Deeper Exploration of a Hierarchy for Classifying Earth Science Data and File Collections

While the four data product levels we just discussed are useful, they may seriously distort the data production topology for an investigation that has multiple input sources and multiple data products. In this section, we identify a more robust hierarchy of data groupings. We start with a discussion of scientific parameters and measurement values that form the basis for placing data in files. Then we consider homogeneous groupings of files whose data has (nearly) identical structure and similar samplings in time and space. We call these homogeneous groupings of files Data Products. Within a Data Product, we then describe file collections that become more and more homogeneous.

Scientific Parameters and Measurement Values. Data lies at the heart of data production. When we think of scientific data, we invariably think of measurements and measurement values. These quantities are typically numerical - and the numerical values have units attached. If we want to use data intelligently, we care about the units – transforming to other units would require changes in numerical values. Furthermore, individual data values represent spatial and temporal averages of continuous fields. The spatial and temporal extent of the measurement values is a critical component in identifying appropriate scientific uses for data.

Files as Collections of Measurement Values. When data producers place measurement values into files, they usually make sure that each file has the same parameters as well as a particular spatial and temporal scale. They are somewhat less sensitive to the internal structure of the files. For example, a stratospheric investigator might create files that contain one-day, latitudinal averages of instantaneous ozone profiles. It is unlikely that this producer would make a strong distinction between files that organized instantaneous values into vertical profiles from files that organized the same numerical values into latitudinal arrays for each altitude level.

Data Products. The largest collection of files we discuss is the **Data Product**. We expect that all of the files in a Data Product will contain the same parameters. They will also have similar samplings of time and space, and be similar in structure. In most cases, the files contain data from regular intervals of time. In other words, we can often characterize Data Products as being 'hourly', 'daily', 'weekly', or 'monthly'.

The regularity of files within a Data Product makes it relatively easy to produce a natural enumeration of the file instances within a Data Product. Informally, we might say "This file contains data from the first time interval we sampled and this other one contains data from the second interval." More formally, we can index such regularly occuring files that contain data in the time interval $(t_i, t_i + \Delta t)$ with an index, i, computed as

$$i = \lfloor ((t - t_0)/\Delta t) \rfloor + 1 \tag{1}$$

where Δt is the time interval for data in any of the files, and t_0 is the start time of the data series in the data product files.

Data Sets. Within a Data Product, we can distinguish between large collections of files produced by different instruments or by similar instruments on different platforms. This distinction may not be important for small collections of data from a single ground site or a single, low data rate instrument. However, when similar instruments make measurements from different platforms, breaking the files within a Data Product into smaller groupings we call Data Sets is particularly important. Different Data Sets within a Data Product may have quite different properties.

For example, at the author's data center, the CERES investigators need to distinguish files from the CERES instrument on the Tropical Rainfall Measuring Mission (TRMM) from those obtained with the two instruments on Terra, the first satellite of the Earth Observing System. The data from these three instruments are similar to the data from the two instruments on Aqua, the second major satellite in that System. However, TRMM only samples the Earth within about forty degrees latitude from the Equator; Terra and Aqua obtain measurements from Pole-to-Pole. CERES data from TRMM started in January, 1999 and effectively ended about two months after the two CERES instruments on Terra started collecting data. The latter two instruments now have many more files than the TRMM instruments provided.

Each data set has a distinct start time associated with the time when its data source started collecting data. Each data set also will eventually have a distinct end time, when the source data collection stops. For the uniform time discretization shown in equation (1), a data set thus has a computable number of possible file instances.

We can state this rule more formally. The files in a Data Set particularize the instances of possible files in a Data Product. We can think of a Data Product as establishing a rule for indexing a sequence of files. A Data Set identifies a first element and a last element in a Data Product's potential sequence. A Data Set might also have rules that identify which elements of a Data Products sequence a particular data source sampled and which it did not. In other words, from a formal point of view, a Data Set establishes a *Sampling Strategy* that identifies the actual files that can exist within a Data Product's sequence.

This fundamental principle makes it relatively easy to establish which files in two Data Sets cover the same time interval. Recognition of this fact may help to improve the probability of obtaining coincident and synchronous data from two different data sources. Of course, if a Data Product enumerates its files by time and if two Data Sets in the Product do not overlap in space when they overlap in time, the files may not have spatially coincident data. We do not consider the problem of how to find spatially coincident data in this paper – our focus is on the intrinsic structure of file collections.

Data Set Versions. If scientific data production were easy, instruments would have stable calibrations and validation activities would discover no need for corrections that vary with time. Unfortunately, validation invariably shows that instrument calibrations drift and that algorithms need a better physical basis. Within a Data Set, we can think of a **Data Set Version** as a collection of files in a Data Set that have a homogeneous *Data Production Strategy*. Within a Data Set Version, we expect the code producing the files to be stable. We also expect that the algorithm input coefficients will be stable as well. The intent of data production is to produce data whose uncertainties are statistically similar under similar conditions of observation. In other words, a Data Set Version strives to be a "scientifically homogeneous" collection of files within a Data Set.

Data Set Version Variants. While scientists may not notice variations within a Data Set Version, there are a number of sources of variability that are apparent to people who have to manage data production. The compiler may change. The operating system or the programs that do scheduling may change. The data center operators may add disks or CPUs - or some of the hardware may break. The data producer may even introduce scientifically unnoticeable changes in the format of the file or in the documentation and metadata embedded within the file. Such variations in production mechanisms are apparent to the programs and scripts that control data production. They do not affect the numeric values or the uncertainty of data values. We lump these scientifically unnoticeable variations together as **Variants** within a Data Set Version.

Granules. If we now return to the environment in which a data center stores the data, we meet several complications to the presentation of the files in Data Products or Data Sets. A data center or the data producer may find it convenient to group several files together into a single inventory entry. We call such an entry a **Granule**. If a data user wants a particular file, the data center may need to find and extract the Granule and then extract the file from those in the granule.

The data center may also put data files onto tapes that break a file into pieces stored on separate tape volumes. From the standpoint of the Data Center, these pieces still belong to the same file and the same granule. A data user would have to read the tape volumes in the proper sequence to recover the original order of data within the file (or granule).

For our purposes, the distinction between files and granules is mildly academic. We will ignore it in the remainder of this paper.

A Somewhat More Formal Description. We are now at the point where we can provide a somewhat more formal description of the data file groupings. The lowest level of our grouping has files. These are the leaves in the tree representing the hierarchy in fig. 2. In most cases, we can index the files within a Data Set Version sequentially, usually by the starting time of data in a file. If we base the design of the file storage on this natural indexing principle, then we can recognize complete collections and incomplete ones. A complete (or potentially complete) collection of files in a Data Set Version forms an "Edition" of that Data Set. A Data Set Version created as part of a validation exercise may have gaps in its sequence that will never exist. By analogy with book or encyclopedia editions, we would probably label such an incomplete collection as a "Partial Edition" or an "Incomplete Collection."

Figure 2 shows a hierarchy that contains all of the file collections a project or investigation could produce. At the highest level of the hierarchy, we group a project's files into **Data Products**. At the next level, we group the files in a Data Product into **Data Sets**. We identify each Data Set with a *Sampling Strategy*. Still deeper in the hierarchy, we break each Data Set into **Data Set Versions**. A *Production Strategy* distinguishes one Version from another. The Data Set Versions are scientifically distinguishable from one another. We distinguish **Data Set Version Variants** within a Version by a *Configuration Code* that identifies sources of file-to-file variability that are not scientifically important. The configuration code is typically an integer that we increment with each new variant in a version. The leaves of this hierarchy are the individual files.

From a scientific standpoint, the most important characteristic about a Data Set Version is that the data in its files have homogeneous uncertainties. The production of a Data Set Version uses stable algorithms, stable input coefficients, and input data with homogeneous uncertainties. Users should expect that data values taken under similar conditions (e.g., daylight, over the clear Indian Ocean) will have similar uncertainties. The most important difference between one Version of a Data Set and another Version is the uncertainty of the data. We can now see that a Data Set is a collection of Data Set Versions. The difference between versions appears in the Production Strategy. That strategy specifies the collection of algorithms and parameters that change input data into output data. At a still larger collection scale, we distinguish Data Sets by their Sampling Strategy – typically the platforms or instruments creating the data. Finally, a Data Product consists of all of the Data Sets that have the "same kind" of data.

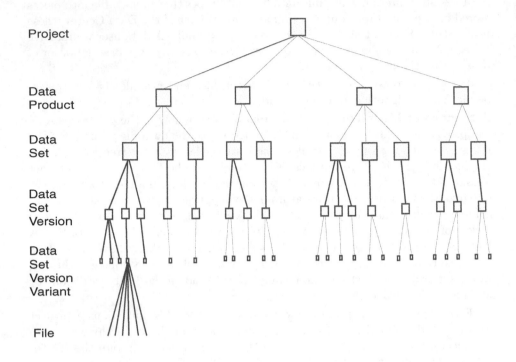

Fig. 2. Hierarchical groupings of files from data products to individual files

5   Discretized Production Processes

This paper treats data production as batch processing - not continuous or quasi-continuous transaction updates. Thus, we need a discrete entity corresponding to what computer operators used to call a "job." In those ancient times, a job was a collection of punched cards that a data producer put through a card reader to program the computer. In the modern version, the equivalent is a script that directs the computer to perform a sequence of computational activities. The script may call for one or more executable files to perform one of these sequences. The executable files contain compiled code that instantiates algorithms that transform input files into output files. In the material that follows, we consider how to organize collections of "jobs" into a hierarchy of recognizable and useful entities. The natural elements of the hierarchy are

- Algorithm Collections in Subsystems
- Subsystem Design Templates
- Subsystem Designs
- Code
- Code Versions
- Executables

Algorithms. In the nomenclature of this paper, we define an **Algorithm** as a finite procedure that transforms one kind of data into another within the context of a subsystem. Knuth [8, p4ff.] provides a more detailed definition.

We can distinguish between specific algorithms and **Algorithm Classes** or "algorithmic functionality." In the nomenclature we are using, an algorithm has all of its coefficients fixed. In contrast, an Algorithm Class provides a generic kind of functionality, but might include many different algorithms, each with its own set of fixed coefficients.

Algorithm Collections in Subsystems. In the production context, a science team typically combines several Algorithm Classes into an Algorithm Collection within a Subsystem. A **Subsystem** is then a major design element in a Project's data system that contains one or more Algorithm Classes. Simple data production systems may not need more than one algorithm for each subsystem over the life of the project. On the other hand, complex production systems may have several algorithm collections in each subsystem.

We do not prescribe the order in which the Algorithm Classes in a collection transform the input data to output data. Neither do we guarantee that the Subsystem will use exactly the same algorithm on each input file. Experience suggests that our hierarchy needs to recognize the possibility of completely replacing one algorithm with another that performs a similar function (or, more generically, that isa member of the same Algorithm Class).

One simple example of how an algorithm family works in practice comes from the CERES experience on TRMM. The first Subsystem in the CERES data production is one that geolocates and calibrates the "raw" instrument data. In the first runs of this subsystem, the algorithm for geolocation located the individual footprints on a geocentric Earth. When the data management team looked at the location of these footprints along coastlines, they decided they needed to use a geodetic Earth location. The new algorithm still fit into the first CERES subsystem and still did geolocation. However, the new algorithm did not follow the same steps as the first one did. In the terms we suggest, the geocentric and geodetic Earth location algorithms belong to the same Algorithm Class.

It is also important to note that the two algorithms in this example class do not have the same input parameters. The Earth locations they produce do not have the same uncertainty. However the input and output from the algorithms in the family is recognizably the same. In more general cases, the output may differ. The key point is that the Algorithms in an Algorithm Class perform clearly identified transformations that create output data products. We can anticipate that changes in the specific algorithms (as reflected in the algorithm source code) will produce different Data Set Versions.

Subsystem Design Templates. The data flow diagram for a large and complex science project usually does not include the Coefficient Collections and QC Summary files. Such a diagram is like an "architectural plan view" of a house within its environment. It doesn't include enough information to actually build the house. In order to do that, we need "blueprints" that provide the necessary details. In other words, we need diagrams that show how the coefficient collections and quality control files interact with the subsystems.

We call such diagrams **Subsystem Design Templates** (SSDT's). The Template for a Subsystem Design identifies the input Data Products and the output Data Products for the Subsystem. It also identifies the Algorithm Coefficient Collections that must be input and the Quality Control Summaries that must be output. Because it serves as an architectural design element, the SSDT is also an appropriate system element to use for developing an estimate of the volume of code that a science team will have to create to provide a working version of the subsystem.

Subsystem Design. At a more concrete level, a **Subsystem Design** (SSD) should provide a detailed design for the algorithmic steps that the Subsystem must perform. The SSD needs to identify input data sets (not data products) and output data sets (not data products). It also needs to identify the appropriate file collections for coefficients and quality summaries. While a SSD may inherit Algorithm Classes from a SSDT, it needs to be quite specific about whether the same algorithms will be used for the same functionality if there are different data sources.

In CERES, the instruments are similar enough that there is only one design for the Subsystem that calibrates and geolocates the Level 1 data. On the other hand, the CERES Cloud Identification Algorithm Collection provides an example of a divergence in Subsystem Designs for the same SSDT. For TRMM, the Cloud Identification Subsystem needs to ingest data from the VIRS instrument. VIRS has five spectral channels, a fairly narrow swath (600 km), and a spatial resolution of about 2 km. For Terra and Aqua, this Subsystem needs to ingest data from the MODIS instrument particular to each satellite. The MODIS instrument has about forty channels, a swath nearly as wide as CERES (about 2000 km), and a spatial resolution of about 1 km. The marked differences between VIRS and MODIS made the CERES team create two separate versions of the Cloud Subsystems design to deal with cloud property data products.

For object-oriented design, we can view Algorithm Collections, SSDTs, and SSDs as successive steps in an inheritance chain. The AC is the most abstract form; the SSDT inherits connectivity from the AC. It also provides a template that constrains the choices that the SSD can make for its connectivity. The process inheritance is similar to the inheritance chain that leads from a Data Product to the Data Sets that are its children.

Code. When the time comes to get the computer to perform the operations identified in a SSD, the science team needs to instantiate the design in Code. For our purposes, Code lies at the level of detail below Design. The difference between Code and Designs is perhaps clearer if we think of instantiating a Design in different languages. In code, the designers must specify a number of details that are not important in the subsystem algorithm description. For example, suppose the team codes an Algorithm in C that uses a multi-dimensional array. The array indexing for this implementation will have a different order than it would if the team codes the algorithm in FORTRAN. The output numerical values from the two implementations should be the same, but the code may store the data in a different order.

Code Version and Code Version Variants. Normal configuration management systems operate on Code Versions. However, there may be several Code Versions that produce output that is scientifically indistinguishable. For example, we might need to change the names of functions in the code that access OS functions when there is a new release of the OS. We call such scientifically indistinguishable collections of code, **Code Version Variants**. Code Version Variants produce Data Set Version Variants; Code Versions produce Data Set Versions. A science team would use a single Code Version to produce the sequence of files in a single Data Set Version.

Executables. Executables are the lowest level entities that implement algorithms. **Executables** consist of compiled and linked object code. When the appropriate execution invocation calls them, an executable converts input files to output files. An executable may also accept and send messages within the operational environment.

It is clear that a single executable can create many different file instances. In the next section, we consider how to catalog sequences of runs.

6   Discretized Production Flow Design

Within the framework we have described, the hierarchy of file collections and the hierarchy of processes are the static portion of production. To this framework we need to add a description of the production flow. If we adapt the industrial engineering analogy, the files contain the material being processed from a raw state to finished products. The processes are the tools that perform the conversion. To complete the analogy, we need a procedure for sequencing the tools that work on the material that is transformed by the data production process.

The atomic element in the procedure is usually a script that controls the sequence in which particular files and particular executables operate. We also need to take into account the fact that batch processes operate on large collections of files. For example, CERES needs to collect about 20 TB of data on disk in order to process a month of data efficiently. The production system will have to stage and destage large data volumes. These staging and destaging processes are collections of jobs in their own right.

In rough accord with EOSDIS nomenclature, we call a generic instance of an atomic script a **Product Generation Executable**, or PGE. However, as we needed to carefully define set of terms to describe the organization of groups of files, we need a careful description of collections of PGEs. The paragraphs that follow provide the appropriate concepts.

PGE Runs. In operating a discrete data production system, we identify the lowest level of control as a Product Generation Executable (PGE) run. A PGE is a self-contained unit that consists of a script that calls one or more executable objects into operation. A **PGE Run** accesses specific data files as well as specific executables. In our hierarchy, a PGE Run is the smallest (i.e., the atomic) element of execution control. We expect a PGE Run to have executable (object) files that come from Code Version Variants.

PGE Run Collections. We use the term **PGE Run Collection** (PGERC) to describe the PGE Runs that accept Data Set Version Variants as input and create Data Set Version Variants as output. A PGE Run Collection should also include staging and destaging processes. In scheduling terms, a PGERC is an entity that a system scheduler can send to a job dispatcher. The scheduler may separate the individual PGE Runs and dispatche them to individual CPU's for execution.

7 Implementing the Graph

The structure we have described is a particularly intricate graph with typed nodes. Perhaps surprisingly, it is relatively straightforward to instantiate its core functions with a pair of tables. The key to this implementation is to recognize that we can represent both connectivity between file collections and processes and the inheritance between different levels of abstraction as arcs between nodes that represent the entities in the description. The nodes go into one array. The arcs between the nodes go into a second.

With this representation, pointers between nodes and arcs become equivalent to array indices. This equivalence has the advantage that in-memory storage is easily converted to off-line storage (and vice versa). Furthermore, it is useful to separate the storage of the files, their metadata, and the connectivity for individual PGE Runs from the arrays that provide the graph for collections of files and the processes that produce them. Such a separation makes the collection structure quite compact and easy to search. In other words, this structure provides a way to structure the catalog and inventory of a large, Earth science data center, as we suggest in fig. 3.

The two structures in the upper left of fig. 3 represent the arrays we just discussed. At the lower center, we have the files in the data set versions. Corresponding to the file inventory structure, there is an equivalent structure of file-specific metadata, which appears on lower left. To put it in slightly different terms, this metadata associates a collection of parameters that are common for all of the files in a Data Set Version with each file. The metadata serves as a statistical summary of the file contents. The other elements in fig. 3 are arrays that provide the attributes of file or process collections.

This structural organization allows us to pull out very useful views of the file organization within the archive. In particular, the two arrays that hold the graph make it easy to create the inheritance tree that shows the data products for a particular project. We can build an inheritance tree by making a graph traversal that extracts only the Data Product nodes. By going deeper into the tree, it is easy to view the Data Sets belonging to each Product – or the Data Set Versions belonging to each Data Set. It is easy to store these structures for rapid presentation to users in the form of the familiar "Tree-View" control used to present folders and files in the Windows family of interfaces.

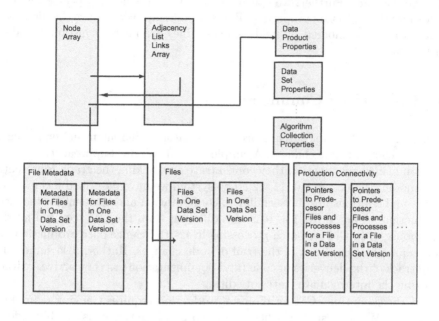

Fig. 3. Relationship of graph to other elements in an archive

A second feature of this data structure design is that it makes it easy to provide a view of the inheritance from a Production Graph Template (containing SSDTs and Data Products) to a Production Graph (containing Files and PGE Instances). Production Graphs are useful for deriving automated production plans. Furthermore, it is easy to assemble the graph that provides the full production history of a particular data product. For this purpose, we can start a graph traversal at the node that represents the file of interest. This node will have only one predecessor PGE. That PGE will, in turn, have predecessor files that were produced by previous PGE's. This approach to deriving provenance is similar to that suggested in [9], except that here we place the Provenance Graph in a systematic, top-down framework.

Fig. 3 also shows that the time ordering of files within a Data Set Version provides a theoretical justification for storage sequence of these files. As we commented earlier, one of the key attributes of a Data Product is the time interval of the data in each file. A Data Set has a start date and an end date. These two times and the data time interval allow us to use time interpolation to find the index of the file that holds data for a particular data. A file whose data comes from a time about half-way between the start date and the end date will have an index about half-way through the array.

The data structure connections in fig. 3 provide a compact representation of file collections that is natural to the properties imposed by the time ordering of data collection. With care, the auxiliary tables of collection properties will also be compact. Further, we can bring nearly constant, file-specific metadata fields into the collection properties. This summarization will leave the file-specific metadata unencumbered by fields whose values are nearly constant for all file instances.

8   Concluding Comments

Versioning for discrete, batch processing is rather different from versioning for tracking complex code changes. A simple view of standard approaches to configuration management is that they concentrate on tracking the graph representing text modifications, e.g. [10, 11, 12]. The system we have described has more elements and relationships. It is similar to configuration management for industrial production, as noted by [13]. It is also different from the CM required for data warehouses [14]. CM for batch processing in Earth Science data production does not require keeping track of the trail of code changes. Rather, it is sufficient to keep track of the deliveries of code (and documentation) as they arrive - without tracking the intermediate states of editing.

At the same time, CM for discrete production requires tracking many kinds of entities. We suggest that it helps to use a graph that is considerably different than the graph used to track changes only in the code. What we have demonstrated is that by maintaining the coefficient files, PGE's, and related entities in an explicit graph representation, we can efficiently combine information that is useful in design with information that is needed for tracking the provenance of data production for particular files.

References

1. Cavalcanti, M. C., M. L. Campos, and M. Mattoso, "Managing Scientific Models in Structural Genomic Projects," paper presented at the Workshop on Data Lineage and Provenance, Chicago, IL, Oct. 10-11, 2002, available at
   http://people.cs.uchicago.edu/~yongzh/position_papers.html
2. Pancerella, C., J. Myers, and L. Rahn, "Data Provenance in the CMCS," paper presented at the Workshop on Data Lineage and Provenance, Chicago, IL, Oct. 10-11, 2002, available at
   http://people.cs.uchicago.edu/~yongzh/position_papers.html.
3. Cavanaugh, R., G. Graham, and M. Wilde, "Satisfying the Tax Collector: Using Data Provenance as a way to audit data analyses in High Energy Physics," paper presented at the Workshop on Data Lineage and Provenance, Chicago, IL, Oct. 10-11, 2002, available at
   http://people.cs.uchicago.edu/~yongzh/position_papers.html.
4. Mann, R., "Some Data Derivation and Provenance Issues in Astronomy," paper presented at the Workshop on Data Lineage and Provenance, Chicago, IL, Oct. 10-11, 2002, available at
   http://people.cs.uchicago.edu/~yongzh/position_papers.html.

5. Fox, P., "Some Thoughts on Data Derivation and Provenance," paper presented at the Workshop on Data Lineage and Provenance, Chicago, IL, Oct. 10-11, 2002, available at
   `http://people.cs.uchicago.edu/~yongzh/position_papers.html`.

6. Musick, R., and T. Critchlow, "Practical Lessons in Supporting Large Scale Computational Science," Lawrence Livermore Report UCRL-JC-135606, 1999.

7. Baum, B., and B. R. Barkstrom, "Design and implementation of a prototype data system for Earth radiation budget, cloud, aerosol, and chemistry data," *Bull. Amer. Meteor. Soc.*, **74**, 591-598, 1993

8. Knuth, D. E., *The Art of Computer Programming, Volume 1: Fundamental Algorithms*, 2nd Ed., Addison-Wesley, Reading, MA, 1973.

9. Frew, J., and R. Bose, "Lineage Issues for Scientific Data and Information," paper presented at the Workshop on Data Lineage and Provenance, Chicago, IL, Oct. 10-11, 2002, available at
   `http://people.cs.uchicago.edu/~yongzh/position_papers.html`

10. Mahler, A., Variants: Keeping Things Together and Telling Them Apart, *Configuration Management*, W. F. Tichy, ed., 73-97, J. Wiley, 1994.

11. Zeller, A., and G. Snelting, Unified Versioning through Feature Logic, *ACM Trans. On Software Engineering and Methodology*, **6**, 398-441, 1997.

12. Conradi, R. and B. Westfechtel, Version models for software configuration management, *ACM Computing Surveys*, **30**, No. 2, 232-282, 1998.

13. Estublier, J., J-M. Favre, and P. Morat, "Toward SCM/PDM integration?," Proc. SCM8, Bruxelles, Belgium, July, 1998, Springer-Verlag, **LNCS 1439**, 75-95.

14. Cui, Y. *Lineage Tracing in Data Warehouses*, Ph.D. Dissertation, Stanford Univ., 2001.

Merging Collection Data Structures in a Content Management System

Axel Wienberg

CoreMedia AG, Ludwig-Erhard-Straße 18, Hamburg, Germany
axel.wienberg@coremedia.com
http://www.coremedia.com

Abstract. Motivated by our work on object-oriented Content Management, this paper proposes an extensible formal framework for delta and merging strategies, each applicable to a specific type of content under specific constraints. By exploiting type-specific constraints, adequate deltas can be computed even without detailed operation logs. The framework thereby allows the use of unmodified third-party editing applications. We present initial experience with conflict detection and content merging algorithms for a number of link collection types, namely sets, lists, and maps without duplicates.

1 Introduction and Motivation

As experienced in application domains such as CAD or Software Engineering, the collaborative development of complex, compound artifacts is best supported by incremental design transactions in autonomous workspaces. As a necessary consequence, concurrent, conflicting changes occur and have to be merged. Due to the volume of content, an automated analysis and resolution of conflicts is desirable. Due to the complexity of the content, however, merging in the general case requires interactive user decisions.

This experience applies directly to Content Management. In a Content Management System such as the CoreMedia Research Platform (CRP)[1], the content is represented as a network of structured objects, and is edited within workspaces. Websites or other desired products are generated continuously or on-demand from the fine-grained object repository.

The CRP is based on an object-oriented meta model, which allows the definition of application-specific object types and constraints. Such an explicit schema can contribute to merging in the following ways:

- by improving the locality of changes,
- by supporting the automated generation of merge proposals,
- by improving the user presentation of merge conflicts, and
- by detecting unsuccessful merges, which violate schema constraints.

We realized that due to the important role and rich selection of link types offered by the CRP, and in order to support an open-ended set of application-specific "binary" content types edited by third-party applications, we needed a generic framework for merge support.

B. Westfechtel, A. van der Hoek (Eds.): SCM 2001/2003, LNCS 2649, pp. 134–147, 2003.

In this paper, we therefore define an extensible formal framework for delta and merging strategies, each applicable to a specific type with specific constraints. Using this framework, we present initial experience with conflict detection and content merging algorithms for a number of link collection types.

After introducing the running example for this paper in section 2, we briefly describe the modeling language used in the CoreMedia Research Platform in section 3, then recapitulate the general concept of three-way merging in section 4, and go on to apply this concept to selected link collection data structures in section 5, which forms the body of this paper. After reporting on related work in section 6, we conclude with a summary in section 7.

2   Example Scenario

As an example scenario, let us consider two editors working on the web site for a music portal. We shall concentrate on the home page, shown in Fig. 1, since it portrays the site's functionality.

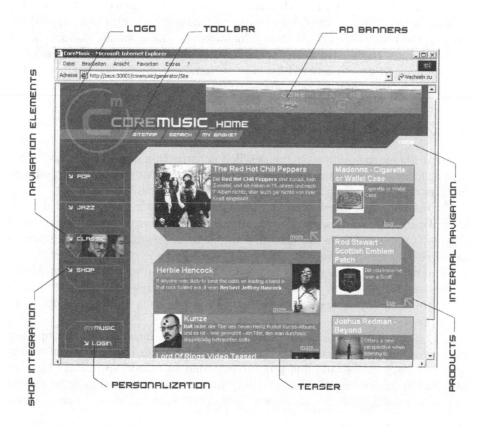

Fig. 1. Home page of a web portal

As indicated by the navigation elements on the left, the site consists of several music departments. These can again contain subdepartments etc., leading to a hierarchical navigation structure. For each node in the hierarchy there is a home page which features selected articles (in the middle) and selected products (on the right) from this area of the site.

Now assume there are two content editors, one responsible for the Classics department, the other for Jazz. The Classics editor writes a teaser for a new article, and carefully selects a location on the homepage for the teaser. The editor reviews her changes in the context of her workspace, and decides to publish it. However, in the meantime the Jazz editor has also edited the homepage, so their changes have to be reconciled.

Since the editors are using a modern Content Management System, they are not working on HTML pages directly. The actual web site is generated from a content base using templates which select and combine the content. For example, the navigation bars are computed from the current position in the navigation hierarchy. The "teasers" for the selected articles are printed in the order arranged by the site editors, and each teaser's representation is made up from its title, its body text, and an associated image.

The use of a content schema has two important consequences in this scenario: Firstly, by providing a conceptual model understood by both the users and the system, the area of changes is clearly localized. In the example, the only point where changes clash is the list of teasers. Secondly, knowing that the teasers on the homepage form an ordered list, the system can present the conflict to the user in an intelligible way, and offer sensible merge proposals.

3   Content Schema

Content Management involves the detailed construction of web pages and other output formats integrating fragments of different content objects, and therefore requires a rather fine-grained understanding of content by the system.

In the approach followed by the CoreMedia Research Platform, the schema is explicitly defined, stored in, and understood by the Content Management System. Content objects are classified by their structure, and their properties and associations are defined.

The modeling language used by the CRP is object-oriented, implementing a subset of UML. Objects are the semantic unit for reference, collaboration, and versioning. An object aggregates property bindings, each binding a property to an appropriate value.

As shown in Fig. 2, available classes of properties include atomic properties such as string and integer properties, media properties bound to application-specific binary values, and link properties bound to collections of links to other objects.[1] A declaration of a link property includes the expected type for targets of the contained links, cardinality and uniqueness constraints, and may indicate

---

[1] In this paper, we restrict our scope to explicitly modeled links, and do not consider the extraction of link information from media data.

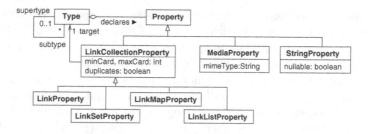

Fig. 2. UML class diagram for the content meta-model

that the link collection is *keyed* or *ordered*, turning it into a map or a list, respectively. The available link collection types therefore correspond to those in most modern programming languages: simple link, link set, link list, link map.

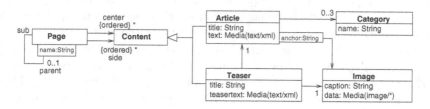

Fig. 3. A simple Content Schema, represented as UML

Figure 3 shows a partial content schema for the example from section 2, featuring all mentioned collection types:

- A Teaser has a *simple link* to an Article.
- An Article holds a *link set* of up to three Categories.
- A Page has a *link list* of Content objects appearing in the center row.
- An Article has a *link map* of Images, keyed by their anchor in the text.
- A Page further has a *link map* of named subpages, where each subpage occurs at most once.

We will refer to this content schema in subsequent examples.

4   Workspaces and Merging

In the CoreMedia Research Platform, all content is put under configuration management, and is edited within workspaces. A workspace is the place where a user or a group of users work together on advancing the web site in some direction. The workspace concept is well-known in SCM, and its applicability to content development is discussed e.g. in [2].

Merging is a necessary consequence of using workspaces. We realized that due to the important role and rich selection of link types, and in order to support different kinds of application-specific "binary" content, we need a generic framework for merge support, especially three-way merge.

A so-called "three-way merge" generally serves to combine the changes made to a versioned object in two parallel branches. It requires a common ancestor version (v_a) to be identified, and works by computing a delta from the ancestor to each derived version v_1, v_2, resulting in $\Delta_i = \mathrm{delta}(v_a, v_i)$. These deltas are then combined to produce a merge delta $\Delta_m = \mathrm{merge}(\Delta_1, \Delta_2)$, which, when applied to the common ancestor, yields the merge result: $v_m = \mathrm{apply}(v_a, \Delta_m)$.

In practice, the "merge" function cannot be completely formalized; rather, it aims to solve the obvious cases and support a human user in resolving the more difficult ones.

To separate the changes for which independent decisions are required, a delta Δ_i is split up into delta chunks δ_j^i, $\Delta_i = \{\delta_1^i, ..., \delta_n^i\}$. The delta chunks of each delta are then paired with corresponding chunks in the other delta, by observing if two delta chunks affect, or depend on, overlapping regions of the common ancestor. Such a pair of delta chunks is said to be in conflict.

How the resolution of the conflict is decided is determined by a merge policy[3], depending on the types of delta chunks: one option may be chosen automatically, or one option out of a set may be proposed to the user, giving him an opportunity to disagree and select a different option, or the choice from a set of options may be left entirely to the user.

5   Merging Content

The three-way merge framework just described is traditionally applied to line-oriented text files. So for example, if the same line was inserted in two descendant text files at the same position, the deltas agree on this delta chunk. However, if two different lines were inserted at the same position, the affected region overlaps, so a user decision will usually be requested.

In the following, we will apply the framework to collection data structures. For each kind of data structure to be merged, the types of the values and the types of the delta chunks have to be specified. Next, we can specify the algorithm for determining the delta of two values, and for applying a delta to a value; then, we examine the notion of the region of influence of a delta chunk for the respective data structure, which defines when two regions overlap. Finally, the options for resolving conflicting chunks are described.

A resolution option is described as a set of delta chunks which replace the conflicting chunks. This resolves the original conflict, and may also resolve or cause other (hopefully less severe) conflicts. The process is repeated until all conflicts have been resolved.

5.1   Sets

As a warm-up exercise, we start by considering sets of objects, $o \in \mathcal{O}, v \in \mathcal{P}(\mathcal{O})$. Link set properties are used in the content schema whenever an unordered 1:n or m:n relationship is modeled, which needs to be navigable towards the "n" side. Examples include the categories assigned to an article, or the set of products to be presented along with an article.

When a set property has been modified between two versions and is to be merged with independent changes to the same property, the delta of two values is (naturally) reconstructed as the insertions and deletions that have taken place:

$$\mathrm{delta}(v_1, v_2) = \quad \{\mathbf{ins}(o) \mid o \in v_2 \setminus v_1\}$$
$$\cup \{\mathbf{del}(o) \mid o \in v_1 \setminus v_2\} \qquad \Delta^{\mathrm{Set}} = \quad \{\mathbf{ins}(o) \mid o \in \mathcal{O}\}$$
$$\cup \{\mathbf{del}(o) \mid o \in \mathcal{O}\}$$

$$\mathrm{apply}(v, \Delta) = v \setminus \{o \in \mathcal{O} \mid \mathbf{del}(o) \in \Delta\}$$
$$\cup \{o \in \mathcal{O} \mid \mathbf{ins}(o) \in \Delta\}$$

The equations satisfy the requirement that $\mathrm{apply}(v, \mathrm{delta}(v, v_1)) = v_1$.

The region influenced by a delta chunk is simply defined to be the object inserted or deleted. An insertion and a deletion for the same object are therefore in conflict, and therefore must not both occur in a wellformed delta.

$$\mathrm{region}(\mathbf{ins}(o)) = \{o\}$$
$$\mathrm{region}(\mathbf{del}(o)) = \{o\}$$

Given any two conflicting delta chunks δ_1 and δ_2, the possible ways to resolve them can be represented as a set of options, where each option is a set of delta chunks. For a non-conflicting delta chunk δ, the options are always to take it or to leave it, i.e. the empty set $\emptyset$ and the singleton $\{\delta\}$. For conflicting delta chunks, the options always include taking none or exactly one of the two: $\emptyset, \{\delta_1\}, \{\delta_2\}$. Also note that the table of options is always symmetrical (even though a concrete policy need not be). For sets, this already describes all available options.

We observe that, when computing the difference to a common ancestor, set delta chunks are always equal or are not in conflict at all: existing elements of the ancestor value can only be removed, and elements not contained in the ancestor can only be added. So the only distinction is whether a delta chunk is contained in none, exactly one or both of Δ_1 and Δ_2. This can easily be displayed to a user, by visualizing the operation on the respective sides of the affected element.

A preliminary merge may violate additional semantic constraints, for example the minimum or maximum cardinality, or may produce links to deleted objects. The system supports this by allowing, but flagging these temporary violations[1], and blocking publication until all integrity issues have been resolved. This way, we also take inter-object constraints into account.

Example. Coming back to our example scenario, let's say we have an article assigned to two categories, "interview" and "tour". Two editors work on the article in parallel and both edit the keywords. One editor replaces "tour" by "concert", while the other replaces "tour" by "festival". For simplicity, we write the category's name to represent a link to the category object. Then, the situation is as follows:

$$v_a = \{\text{interview}, \text{tour}\}$$
$$v_1 = \{\text{interview}, \text{concert}\}$$
$$v_2 = \{\text{interview}, \text{festival}\}$$
$$\text{delta}(v_a, v_1) = \{\mathbf{del}(\text{tour}), \mathbf{ins}(\text{concert})\}$$
$$\text{delta}(v_a, v_2) = \{\mathbf{del}(\text{tour}), \mathbf{ins}(\text{festival})\}$$

$$\text{region}(\mathbf{del}(\text{tour})) = \{\text{tour}\}$$
$$\text{region}(\mathbf{ins}(\text{concert})) = \{\text{concert}\}$$
$$\text{region}(\mathbf{ins}(\text{festival})) = \{\text{festival}\}$$

The only overlapping regions are those of the (equal) delete chunks for v_1 and v_2. The framework computes the following resolution options:

$$\text{options}(\mathbf{del}(\text{tour}), \mathbf{del}(\text{tour})) = \{\emptyset, \{\mathbf{del}(\text{tour})\}\}$$
$$\text{options}(\mathbf{ins}(\text{concert}), \text{no conflict}) = \{\emptyset, \{\mathbf{ins}(\text{concert})\}\}$$
$$\text{options}(\text{no conflict}, \mathbf{ins}(\text{festival})) = \{\emptyset, \{\mathbf{ins}(\text{festival})\}\}$$

The user or a configured policy picks one option in each case. Assuming the deletion is rejected, but both inserts are accepted, we get:

$$\Delta_m = \{\mathbf{ins}(\text{festival}), \mathbf{ins}(\text{concert})\}$$
$$v_m = \text{apply}(v_a, \Delta_m)$$
$$= \{\text{interview}, \text{festival}, \text{concert}\}$$

The result is within the limits of the declared cardinality constraint. Otherwise, the constraint violation would be flagged, and some merge decisions would have to be reconsidered.

5.2   Lists

For differencing lists (sequences) of text lines, longest-common-subsequence based algorithms[4] have been used successfully for years. Since the concepts are well-known in the SCM community, we do not repeat the actual algorithm for computing an alignment of two sequences here, but only show how to fit it into the general merging framework.

Mathematically, a list of length n can be described as a function $l : \{1...n\} \to \mathcal{O}$. We denote literal lists as $\langle l_1, l_2, ..., l_n \rangle$.

$$\Delta^{\text{List}} = \{\mathbf{ins}(i, \langle o_1, ..., o_n \rangle) \mid i \geq 0 \wedge o_k \in \mathcal{O}\}$$
$$\cup \{\mathbf{del}(i, j) \mid 1 \leq i \leq j\}$$
$$\cup \{\mathbf{upd}(i, j, \langle o_1, ..., o_n \rangle) \mid 1 \leq i \leq j, o_k \in \mathcal{O}\}$$

Informally, $\mathbf{ins}$ inserts a subsequence after position i, $\mathbf{del}$ deletes and $\mathbf{upd}$ replaces the sublist in the range $i...j$, where i and j are inclusive.

$$\text{region}(\mathbf{ins}(i, l)) = \{\mathbf{after}(i)\}$$
$$\text{region}(\mathbf{del}(i, j)) = \{\mathbf{on}(k) \mid i \leq k \leq j\} \cup \{\mathbf{after}(k) \mid i \leq k < j\}$$
$$\text{region}(\mathbf{upd}(i, j, l)) = \{\mathbf{on}(k) \mid i \leq k \leq j\} \cup \{\mathbf{after}(k) \mid i \leq k < j\}$$

The regions are defined so that an insert is in conflict with an insert at the same position, and with a deletion or update that spans both its left and its right neighbor.

As always, possible conflict resolutions include taking none or exactly one of the conflicting chunks. Two overlapping delete chunks may be split into three, generating two non-conflicting delete chunks and one delete chunk common to both deltas.[2] This simplifies the user interaction.

The algorithm of diff3[5] simplifies the comparison further by joining and extending conflicting delta chunks until the regions are equal, effectively taking the symmetric, transitive closure of the "conflicts with" relation. This is achieved by converting **ins** and **del** operations to updates, and then joining the updates by adding intervening elements of the ancestor version into the substituted list. After this simplification, each chunk is in conflict with at most one other chunk, which allows a linear side-by-side output format. On the downside, some precision of the delta analysis is lost, which could be avoided if the merge is executed in an interactive process as assumed in this paper.

For conflicting insert operations, the user may decide an order of insertion, effectively inserting the concatenated sublist. Another resolution option is to compute a two-way lcs-based delta between the inserted sublists, and to replace the conflicting big insert with a sequence of smaller inserts, which are again non-conflicting or equal.[3]

Example. In the example content schema of Figure 3, a Page has a list of Content objects to be displayed in the center column. Let the center list of the home page be

$$v_a = \langle \text{ChiliPeppers}, \text{Hancock}, \text{Kunze} \rangle$$

Editor 1 moves Kunze to position one, while editor 2 adds Madonna as number 1 and removes Herbie Hancock and Heinz-Rudolf Kunze.

$$v_1 = \langle \text{Kunze}, \text{ChiliPeppers}, \text{Hancock} \rangle$$
$$v_2 = \langle \text{Madonna}, \text{ChiliPeppers} \rangle$$

The LCS algorithm computes the following deltas:

$$\text{delta}(v_a, v_1) = \{\mathbf{ins}(0, \langle \text{Kunze} \rangle), \mathbf{del}(2, 2)\}$$
$$\text{delta}(v_a, v_2) = \{\mathbf{ins}(0, \langle \text{Madonna} \rangle), \mathbf{del}(1, 2)\}$$

---

[2] The refinement of delta chunks, i.e. changing the representation of a delta to facilitate the comparison with another delta, is not formalized in this paper.

[3] To express the ordering of the smaller insert operations, the syntax of the **ins** operation needs to be extended with a sub-index: $\mathbf{ins}(i, i_{sub}, l)$.

$$\text{region}(\mathbf{ins}(0, \langle \text{Kunze} \rangle)) \quad = \{\mathbf{after}(0)\}$$
$$\text{region}(\mathbf{del}(2, 2)) \quad\quad\quad = \{\mathbf{on}(2)\}$$
$$\text{region}(\mathbf{ins}(0, \langle \text{Madonna} \rangle)) = \{\mathbf{after}(0)\}$$
$$\text{region}(\mathbf{del}(1, 2)) \quad\quad\quad = \{\mathbf{on}(1), \mathbf{after}(1), \mathbf{on}(2)\}$$

There are several options for resolving the conflicting chunks:

$$\text{options} \; (\mathbf{ins}(0, \langle \text{Madonna} \rangle), \mathbf{ins}(0, \langle \text{Kunze} \rangle))$$
$$= \{ \; \emptyset,$$
$$\{\mathbf{ins}(0, \langle \text{Madonna} \rangle)\},$$
$$\{\mathbf{ins}(0, \langle \text{Kunze} \rangle)\},$$
$$\{\mathbf{ins}(0, \langle \text{Madonna,Kunze} \rangle)\},$$
$$\{\mathbf{ins}(0, \langle \text{Kunze,Madonna} \rangle)\}\}$$
$$\text{options} \; (\mathbf{del}(1, 2), \mathbf{del}(2, 2))$$
$$= \{ \; \emptyset, \{\mathbf{del}(1, 2)\}, \{\mathbf{del}(2, 2)\}\}$$

Picking a combined insert and the larger delete, we get:

$$\Delta_m = \{\mathbf{ins}(0, \langle \text{Madonna, Kunze} \rangle), \mathbf{del}(1, 2)\}$$
$$v_m = \text{apply}(v_a, \Delta_m)$$
$$= \langle \text{Madonna, Kunze, ChiliPeppers} \rangle$$

5.3 Maps

Link map properties are often used in the CRP to express file system like structures. Link maps are also used to provide further information about the contained links, such as a link's source position, or the role of the link target.

Formally, a map is a partial function f from keys $k \in \mathcal{K}$ to values $o \in \mathcal{O}$. We identify a map with the set of its entries, $f \subset K \times O$, where each key occurs at most once. The delta is constructed as the insertions, deletions and updates that have taken place:

$$\Delta^{\text{Map}} = \quad \{\mathbf{ins}(k, o) \mid k \in \mathcal{K}, o \in \mathcal{O}\}$$
$$\cup \{\mathbf{del}(k) \mid k \in \mathcal{K}\}$$
$$\cup \{\mathbf{upd}(k, o) \mid k \in \mathcal{K}, o \in \mathcal{O}\}$$
$$\text{delta}(v_1, v_2) = \quad \{\mathbf{ins}(k, v_2(k)) \mid k \in dom(v_2) \setminus dom(v_1)\}$$
$$\cup \{\mathbf{del}(k) \mid k \in dom(v_1) \setminus dom(v_2)\}$$
$$\cup \{\mathbf{upd}(k, v_2(k)) \mid k \in dom(v_1) \cap dom(v_2)\}$$
$$\text{apply}(v, \Delta) = v \setminus \{(k, v(k)) \in \mathcal{K} \times \mathcal{O} \mid \mathbf{del}(k) \in \Delta\}$$
$$\setminus \{(k, v(k)) \in \mathcal{K} \times \mathcal{O} \mid \mathbf{upd}(k, o) \in \Delta\}$$
$$\cup \{(k, o) \in \mathcal{K} \times \mathcal{O} \mid \mathbf{ins}(k, o) \in \Delta \vee \mathbf{upd}(k, o) \in \Delta\}$$

The region affected by a map operation is defined to be its key, so different delta chunks for the same key are in conflict.

$$\text{region}(\mathbf{ins}(k, o)) = \{k\}$$
$$\text{region}(\mathbf{del}(k)) = \{k\}$$
$$\text{region}(\mathbf{upd}(k, o)) = \{k\}$$

Note that when computing the deltas to a common ancestor, insert/delete or insert/update conflicts cannot occur; the only conflicts are insert/insert with different value, delete/update and update/update with different value.

Renaming of entries is not modeled, since it cannot be distinguished from a sequence of insert and delete: There is no constraint forbidding a deletion without an insert, or an insert while rejecting the delete, so it is not appropriate to couple both into one decision presented to the user.

Example. In the example content schema of Figure 3, an Article has a link map of Images, whose positions (anchors) in the article's text are given by the map keys.

Let bigImage and smallImage be two image objects. We start in a situation where the article has the smallImage at position "#A1". Editor 1 replaces the smallImage with the bigImage, while Editor 2 removes the smallImage and adds the bigImage at position "#A2". Formally:

$$v_a = \{(\text{``#A1''}, smallImage)\}$$
$$v_1 = \{(\text{``#A1''}, bigImage)\}$$
$$v_2 = \{(\text{``#A2''}, bigImage)\}$$

$$\text{delta}(v_a, v_1) = \{\textbf{upd}(\text{``#A1''}, bigImage)\}$$
$$\text{delta}(v_a, v_2) = \{\textbf{del}(\text{``#A1''}), \textbf{ins}(\text{``#A2''}, bigImage)\}$$

$$\text{region}(\textbf{upd}(\text{``#A1''}, bigImage)) = \{\text{``#A1''}\}$$
$$\text{region}(\textbf{del}(\text{``#A1''})) \qquad = \{\text{``#A1''}\}$$
$$\text{region}(\textbf{ins}(\text{``#A2''}, bigImage)) \ \ = \{\text{``#A2''}\}$$

Obviously, the update and the delete are in conflict. The resolution options, and a possible merge obtained by rejecting both the update and the delete are shown below.

$$\text{options}(\ \textbf{upd}(\text{``#A1''}, bigImage), \textbf{del}(\text{``#A1''}))$$
$$= \{\emptyset, \{\textbf{upd}(\text{``#A1''}, bigImage)\}, \{\textbf{del}(\text{``#A1''})\}\}$$
$$\text{options}(\ \text{no conflict}, \textbf{ins}(\text{``#A2''}, bigImage))$$
$$= \{\emptyset, \{\textbf{ins}(\text{``#A2''}, bigImage)\}\}$$
$$\Delta_m = \{\textbf{ins}(\text{``#A2''}, bigImage)\}$$
$$v_m = \text{apply}(v_a, \Delta_m)$$
$$= \{(\text{``#A1''}, smallImage), (\text{``#A2''}, bigImage)\}$$

5.4   Maps without Duplicates

A map property presenting a file hierarchy will often be constrained by the content model not to contain duplicates, with a cardinality of at most 1 on the parent side of the relationship.[4] In this case, a different delta and merging

---

[4] This gives the semantics of the Windows file system, as opposed to the UNIX file system.

strategy can be applied, which detects moves, and which avoids merges that would violate the map's uniqueness constraint.

So we consider partial one-to-one functions $f : \mathcal{K} \to \mathcal{O}$, where each key as well as each object occurs at most once in the set of entries $f \subset K \times O$. Since f is injective, we can define the inverse partial function $f^{-1} : dom(f) \subset \mathcal{O} \to \mathcal{K}$.

The delta is constructed as the insertions, deletions and moves that have taken place. Delta chunks within a delta are not ordered, so moves are conceptually executed all at the same time. This allows cycles to be represented without introducing arbitrary temporary names, which would be difficult to merge.

$$
\begin{aligned}
\mathit{\Delta}\mathrm{MapUniq} = \quad & \{\mathbf{ins}(k,o) \mid k \in \mathcal{K}, o \in \mathcal{O}\} \\
& \cup \{\mathbf{del}(k) \mid k \in \mathcal{K}\} \\
& \cup \{\mathbf{mov}(k_1,k_2) \mid k_i \in \mathcal{K}\} \\
\mathrm{delta}(v_1,v_2) = \quad & \{\mathbf{ins}(v_2^{-1}(o),o) \mid o \in cod(v_2) \setminus cod(v_1)\} \\
& \cup \{\mathbf{del}(v_1^{-1}(o)) \mid o \in cod(v_1) \setminus cod(v_2)\} \\
& \cup \{\mathbf{mov}(k_1,k_2) \mid v_2(k_2) = v_1(k_1) \wedge k_1 \neq k_2\} \\
\mathrm{apply}(v,\mathit{\Delta}) = \; v \; & \setminus \{(k,v(k)) \in \mathcal{K} \times \mathcal{O} \mid \mathbf{del}(k) \in \mathit{\Delta}\} \\
& \setminus \{(k_2,v(k_2)) \in \mathcal{K} \times \mathcal{O} \mid \mathbf{mov}(k_1,k_2) \in \mathit{\Delta}\} \\
& \cup \{(k_2,v(k_1)) \in \mathcal{K} \times \mathcal{O} \mid \mathbf{mov}(k_1,k_2) \in \mathit{\Delta}\} \\
& \cup \{(k,o) \in \mathcal{K} \times \mathcal{O} \mid \mathbf{ins}(k,o) \in \mathit{\Delta}\}
\end{aligned}
$$

The region affected by a map operation is defined to be the keys removed and the keys added, so two moves to the same target are in conflict, but a move from the target of another move is not. Insertion and deletion of the same key cannot occur during merging, since both deltas are computed relative to a common ancestor, so this conflict does not have to be detected.

$$
\begin{aligned}
\mathrm{region}(\mathbf{ins}(k,o)) &= \{\mathbf{add}(k)\} \\
\mathrm{region}(\mathbf{del}(k)) &= \{\mathbf{rem}(k)\} \\
\mathrm{region}(\mathbf{mov}(k_1,k_2)) &= \{\mathbf{rem}(k_1), \mathbf{add}(k_2)\}
\end{aligned}
$$

Apart from the standard conflict resolutions, we offer the interactive entry of a new name to be used as the key.

Example. As an example, we use the subpage property from Figure 3, which is a link map without duplicates. In the ancestor version, the home page has the subpages PopRockPage and JazzPage, referenced under the name "Pop/Rock" and "Jazz". Now Editor 1 adds a new Rock Page and renames "Pop/Rock" to "Pop", while Editor 2 renames "Pop/Rock" to "Rock" and adds a new "Pop" Page.

$$
\begin{aligned}
v_a &= \{(\text{``}Pop/Rock\text{''}, PopRockPage), (\text{``}Jazz\text{''}, JazzPage)\} \\
v_1 &= \{(\text{``}Pop\text{''}, PopRockPage), (\text{``}Rock\text{''}, RockPage), (\text{``}Jazz\text{''}, JazzPage)\} \\
v_2 &= \{(\text{``}Pop\text{''}, PopPage), (\text{``}Rock\text{''}, PopRockPage), (\text{``}Jazz\text{''}, JazzPage)\}
\end{aligned}
$$

In contrast to the algorithm given in the previous subsection, this delta algorithm recognizes the move operation:

$$\text{delta}(v_a, v_1) = \{\textbf{ins}(\text{``}Rock\text{''}, RockPage), \textbf{mov}(\text{``}Pop/Rock\text{''}, \text{``}Pop\text{''})\}$$
$$\text{delta}(v_a, v_2) = \{\textbf{ins}(\text{``}Pop\text{''}, PopPage), \textbf{mov}(\text{``}Pop/Rock\text{''}, \text{``}Rock\text{''})\}$$

$$\text{region}(\textbf{ins}(\text{``}Rock\text{''}, RockPage)) \quad = \{\textbf{add}(\text{``}Rock\text{''})\}$$
$$\text{region}(\textbf{ins}(\text{``}Pop\text{''}, PopPage)) \quad\quad = \{\textbf{add}(\text{``}Pop\text{''})\}$$
$$\text{region}(\textbf{mov}(\text{``}Pop/Rock\text{''}, \text{``}Pop\text{''})) = \{\textbf{rem}(\text{``}Pop/Rock\text{''}), \textbf{add}(\text{``}Pop\text{''})\}$$
$$\text{region}(\textbf{mov}(\text{``}Pop/Rock\text{''}, \text{``}Rock\text{''})) = \{\textbf{rem}(\text{``}Pop/Rock\text{''}), \textbf{add}(\text{``}Rock\text{''})\}$$

The two moves are in conflict, as well as each move with the insert of its target name. One insert/move conflict can be resolved by entering a different name for the new PopPage object ("PopTemp"). Both remaining conflicts can be solved by accepting the move to "Pop" instead of "Rock".

$$\text{options}(\ \textbf{ins}(\text{``}Pop\text{''}, PopPage), \textbf{mov}(\text{``}Pop/Rock\text{''}, \text{``}Pop\text{''}))$$
$$= \{\ \emptyset,$$
$$\{\textbf{ins}(\text{``}Pop\text{''}, PopPage)\},$$
$$\{\textbf{mov}(\text{``}Pop/Rock\text{''}, \text{``}Pop\text{''})\},$$
$$\{\textbf{ins}(\textbf{enterName}(), PopPage), \textbf{mov}(\text{``}Pop/Rock\text{''}, \text{``}Pop\text{''})\},$$
$$\{\textbf{ins}(\text{``}Pop\text{''}, PopPage), \textbf{mov}(\text{``}Pop/Rock\text{''}, \textbf{enterName}())\}\}$$
$$\text{options}(\ \textbf{mov}(\text{``}Pop/Rock\text{''}, \text{``}Pop\text{''}), \textbf{mov}(\text{``}Pop/Rock\text{''}, \text{``}Rock\text{''}))$$
$$= \{\ \emptyset,$$
$$\{\textbf{mov}(\text{``}Pop/Rock\text{''}, \text{``}Pop\text{''})\},$$
$$\{\textbf{mov}(\text{``}Pop/Rock\text{''}, \text{``}Rock\text{''})\}\}$$
$$\Delta_m = \{\ \textbf{ins}(\text{``}Rock\text{''}, RockPage), \textbf{ins}(\text{``}PopTemp\text{''}, PopPage),$$
$$\textbf{mov}(\text{``}Pop/Rock\text{''}, \text{``}Pop\text{''})\}$$
$$\text{apply}(\ v_a, \Delta_m)$$
$$= \{\ (\text{``}Pop\text{''}, PopRockPage), (\text{``}Rock\text{''}, RockPage),$$
$$(\text{``}PopTemp\text{''}, PopPage), (\text{``}Jazz\text{''}, JazzPage)\}$$

6   Related Work

The concept of combining sequences of change operations is expressed succinctly in [6]. However, the framework presented by the authors is only applicable if atomic changes are recorded by the environment. We transfer their ideas to merging deltas computed after-the-fact, to gain some of the benefits even when operating outside a closed development environment, and without the potentially huge volume of operation logs that would have to be maintained to support pure operation-based merging.

Merging of object graphs is also addressed in [7] in the context of a UML diagram editor, but the authors only consider unordered n:m relationships, which roughly corresponds to the merging of link set properties detailed above.

A way of specifying a default policy for resolving overlapping delta chunks is described in [3], where depending on the conflicting operations, one resolution option can be fixed, a configurable merge function can be invoked, or the decision can be passed to a user. Our work is complementary in that we give type-specific resolution options for the considered link collections data structures, and define when two delta chunks are considered to be in conflict. Since our algorithm aims to generate as many sensible resolution options as possible, it actually *depends* on some semi-automatic policy in order to make large merges feasible.

Another way to determine conflicts between delta chunks is to say that two operations are in conflict if they do not commute, i.e. that the order of their application matters[6]. This criterion works best if detailed operation logs are available, and if a consolidation merge [3] is intended. With synthesized delta chunks, and to also support more critical review policies, we preferred the broader notion of the region of influence. This notion should even extend to hierarchical structures as in [8], or to cross-cutting concerns as in [9].

The context free merge algorithms for abstract syntax trees given in [10] can be seen as a specialized application of the framework presented in this paper, coupled with a default policy. The author goes on to describe context sensitive merge, which also checks identifier scoping. This is an application specific interobject constraint, which in our approach would not be implemented inside the merge framework, but as a separate tool used to verify a preliminary merge.

Algorithms for semantic merging of programs [11] can be integrated into our framework at the granularity of entire programs, yielding an additional conflict resolution option (reject, accept program A, accept program B, accept semantic merge). More research is required to facilitate partial and interactive semantic merging.

7   Summary and Concluding Remarks

Motivated by the requirements of an object-oriented Content Management System, we have presented a framework for type- and constraint-specific delta computation and merging. A strategy for a constrained type is added to the framework by defining

- the types of delta chunks,
- an algorithm for computing a delta,
- an algorithm for applying a delta,
- the type of locations that are affected by delta chunks, and
- type-specific conflict resolution options.

We presented strategies for a small selection of collection data structures, which can detect changes that would be obscured in a less constrained data structure and which avoid detecting artificial changes induced by the coincidences of representation.

By requiring a type-specific delta algorithm to be supplied, we also avoid the need to maintain detailed operation logs. The framework therefore allows the integration of unmodified third-party editing applications.

We hope to extend this framework by integrating strategies for all common combinations of type and constraints occurring in the CoreMedia Research Platform, including link collection types as well as common application data formats. We also look forward to validating the framework and strategies using a practical prototype.

References

1. Wienberg, A., Ernst, M., Gawecki, A., Kummer, O., Wienberg, F., Schmidt, J.W.: Content schema evolution in the CoreMedia content application platform CAP. In: Proceedings of the 8th International Conference on Extending Database Technology (EDBT 2002). Volume 2287 of Lecture Notes in Computer Science. (2002) 712–721
2. Frohlich, P., Nejdl, W.: WebRC: Configuration management for a cooperation tool. In Conradi, R., ed.: Software Configuration Management (SCM-7). Volume 1235 of Lecture Notes in Computer Science., Springer-Verlag, Berlin (1997) 175–185
3. Munson, J.P., Dewan, P.: A flexible object merging framework. In: Proceedings of the 1994 ACM Conference on Computer Supported Cooperative Work, ACM Press (1994) 231–242
4. Myers, E.W.: An O(ND) difference algorithm and its variations. Algorithmica **1** (1986) 251—266
5. Smith, R.: UNIX diff3 utility. http://www.gnu.org (1988)
6. Lippe, E., van Oosterom, N.: Operation-based merging. In: Proceedings of the 5th ACM SIGSOFT Symposium on Software Development Environments, ACM Press (1992) 78–87
7. Zuendorf, A., Wadsack, J., Rockel, I.: Merging graph-like object structures. Position paper in [12] (2001)
8. Asklund, U., Magnusson, B.: Support for consistent merge. Position paper in [12] (2001)
9. Chu-Carroll, M.C., Sprenkle, S.: Coven: Brewing better collaboration through software configuration management. In: Proceedings of the 8th ACM SIGSOFT International Symposium on Foundations of Software Engineering, ACM Press (2000) 88–97
10. Westfechtel, B.: Structure-oriented merging of revisions of software documents. In: Proceedings of the 3rd International Workshop on Software Configuration Management, ACM Press (1991) 68–79
11. Binkley, D., Horwitz, S., Reps, T.: Program integration for languages with procedure calls. ACM Transactions on Software Engineering and Methodology (TOSEM) **4** (1995) 3–35
12. van der Hoek, A.: International Workshop on Software Configuration Management (SCM-10): New Practices, New Challenges, and New Boundaries. ACM SIGSOFT Software Engineering Notes **26** (2001) 57–58

Compatibility of XML Language Versions⋆

Daniel Dui and Wolfgang Emmerich

Department of Computer Science
University College London
Gower Street, London WC1E 6BT, UK
{D.Dui,W.Emmerich}@cs.ucl.ac.uk

Abstract. Individual organisations as well as industry consortia are currently defining application and domain-specific languages using the eXtended Markup Language (XML) standard of the World Wide Web Consortium (W3C). The paper shows that XML languages differ in significant aspects from generic software engineering artefacts and that they therefore require a specific approach to version and configuration management. When an XML language evolves, consistency between the language and its instance documents needs to be preserved in addition to the internal consistency of the language itself. We propose a definition for compatibility between versions of XML languages that takes this additional need into account. Compatibility between XML languages in general is undecidable. We argue that the problem can become tractable using heuristic methods if the two languages are related in a version history. We propose to evaluate the method by using different versions of the Financial products Markup Language (FpML), in the definition of which we participate.

1 Introduction

The eXtensible Markup Language (XML) is a meta-language for defining markup languages. It became a recommendation of the World Wide Web Consortium (W3C) in February 1998 [5] and since then it has gained enormous popularity. An XML document is simply a text file containing tags that identify its semantical structure. The XML specification [6] precisely defines the lexical syntax, or in XML-parlance "well-formedness", of a document. The well-formedness constraints impose what characters are allowed in an document, that for all open tags there shall be a corresponding closing tag, etc.

Satisfaction of well-formedness constraints alone is sufficient for a document to be parsed and processed by a variety of libraries and tools, but for most non-trivial applications the language designer will want to define a grammar for the language explicitly and precisely. She can define a concrete syntax by means of a schema language and a static semantics by means of a constraint language.

The most common schema languages are currently Document Type Definition (DTD), XML Schema [12], and Relax NG. The DTD language is part of the

---

⋆ This work is partially funded by UBS Warburg.

B. Westfechtel, A. van der Hoek (Eds.): SCM 2001/2003, LNCS 2649, pp. 148–162, 2003.

XML 1.0 specification, it is simple, but of limited expressiveness. XML Schema and Relax NG have gained acceptance more recently; they are more expressive than DTD and support, among other things, data types and inheritance. Unlike DTD, they are themselves XML-based languages. XML Schema is a W3C recommendation as of May 2001 and Relax NG is currently an ISO draft standard.

Static semantic constraints can be specified with languages like Schematron [15] or the xlinkit [21] rule language. Schematron is a rule-based validation language that allows to define assertions on tree-patterns in a document and it is undergoing ISO standardisation at the time of writing. The xlinkit rule language is part of xlinkit, a generic technology for managing the consistency of distributed documents, that was successfully used to specify static semantic constraints for complex financial documents [10]. There is not currently a generic constraint language endorsed by the W3C.

A large number of organisations are currently using XML to define data formats. The data format can be a simple file format used by one single application or it could be a complex interchange format standardised by many organisations that constantly produce, store, and exchange innumerable instance documents. XML-based languages have been developed to represent chemical structures, gene sequences, financial products, business-to-business (B2B) transactions, and complex software engineering design documents. We consider the definition of an XML-based language to consist of a syntax definition, given by means of a schema language, and of a set of additional static semantics constraints, given by means of a constraint language.

Some of these XML languages tend to evolve over time, for example because the initial requirements for the language have not been fully understood, or because change is inherent in the domain. We actively participate in the definition of the Financial products Markup Language (FpML), a language used to represent financial derivative products. In this domain, new financial products are being invented constantly and as a result FpML is in a constant state of flux. These changes need to be exercised in a controlled way and give raise to the need for version and configuration management of XML languages.

The main contribution of this paper is the observation that the version and configuration management needs for XML languages are different is some respect and more demanding than those of more traditional software engineering artifacts. We define the notion of compatibility between XML language definitions and that in general compatibility is undecidable. We propose a heuristic method that exploits relationships between different versions of a language definition to decide version compatibility. We propose to evaluate the method using different versions of FpML.

The paper is further structured as follows. In Section 2, we give a more detailed motivation for the problem. Section 3, we define the notion of version compatibility both for language grammars and for static semantic constraints and show why compatibility is undecidable in general. In Section 4, we sketch our heuristic method to solve compatibility between versions of the same language.

We review related work in Section 5. We discuss further work and conclude the paper in Section 6.

2   Motivation

Our work on version and configuration management of XML languages is motivated by our participation in the FpML standardisation effort. The FpML language is both large and complex because FpML is used to represent financial derivative products, some of the most complex types of products traded in financial markets.

FpML raises several interesting questions for version and configuration management because it changes quickly over time for the following reasons: Firstly, FpML is being developed in a truly distributed manner by a number of different working groups that work concurrently on the language and therefore need to manage different versions appropriately. Secondly, the standard committee is including in the language support for the various types of financial derivative products gradually, as the interest for FpML grows, rather than attempting to include support for all of them at once. Thirdly, financial organisations constantly invent new products that they will want to represent in FpML either by changing the standard or by adding in-house extensions. Finally, it is inevitable that, as the language evolves, some of its parts will be redesigned to allow further developments or to mend previous mistakes.

The designers of FpML, and of other complex XML languages, may need to make changes to the language while retaining overall compatibility. Intuitively and informally, compatibility demands first changes to the language to obey the syntactic and static semantic rules of the meta languages (such as DTDs, Schemas or constraint languages) and second the continued ability to validate any instance documents against the language. This validation would include both syntactic validation (against the schema of the language) and static semantic validation (against the constraint language).

Thus, the notion of compatibility for XML languages is wider than the one with which software configuration management was traditionally concerned. Unlike in usual software configuration management where the notion of compatibility can be established by examining a well-known and finite set of artifacts (such as design documents, code, deployment descriptors and test data), testing compatibility between XML languages typically involves an unknown and potentially infinite set of instances of that language.

It may be impractical to demand compatibility of language changes at all times. If, however, designers must introduce changes that break language compatibility, they will want to do this deliberately rather than accidentally and they would also need to convert instance documents between versions of the language. If also this is not a viable option, they will need to identify exactly what causes the incompatibility, which instance documents are affected and in what way. And they can do this only with the assistance of appropriate methods and tools, which currently do not exist.

3   Compatibility

The aim of this section is to define more formally the notion of XML language compatibility that is absent from the existing XML specifications [6,12,2,3].

The definition of an XML language is given by a schema that defines the concrete syntax and a set of constraints that define the static semantics for the language. An instance document is *valid* against the language definition if it satisfies all the constraints defined by the language schema and by the constraints. We note that XML schema and existing constraint languages, such as Schematron or xlinkit are XML languages themselves. Thus any modification to the language definition first of all has to be valid against the meta-constraints.

We can obtain several definitions of compatibility by reasoning on the relationship between *extents* of two languages. We borrow the term *extent* from the literature on object oriented databases [1] where it denotes the set of instances of a class. In the context of XML-based languages we use it to denote the set of all possible instance documents valid against a language definition. In most cases that occur in practice, this is an infinite set.

It is reasonable to expect that a language definition includes both syntax and semantics. In practice the semantics of XML-based languages is defined informally, or sometimes it is not defined at all because it is evident from the syntax of the language. It is no surprise that there is no XML standard or technology to define the semantics of XML documents.

For example the FpML specifications do not provide a definition for the semantics. Financial products are described in any good text book on financial derivatives [14,27], in the ISDA documentation, and ultimately by the physical paper contract that an FpML file represents. The FpML specifications assume that users of FpML already know about financial products and that they can univocally associate a meaning to the syntax of instance documents.

Furthermore an XML document does not necessarily have a unique semantics: An XML document represents simply data to which different consumers of the document are free to associate a different meaning. But, in the context of financial documents, we can assume that there is one and only one semantical interpretation of a given syntax, so two documents that are syntactically equivalent are also semantically equivalent.

Our research shall therefore focus primarily on issues regarding syntax (i.e. the document structure, and static semantic constraints) and not on issues regarding pure semantics (i.e. the meaning of documents) because of the absence of a both formal and standard way to define the meaning of XML documents.

3.1   Syntactic Compatibility

We start with syntactic compatibility that only considers the schema. The simplest case of syntactic compatibility is when, taken two languages, the first is compatible with the second one. This happens when all possible instance documents of the first language are valid also with respect to the second language. In other words the extent of the first language is a subset of the extent of the second language. Fig. 1 shows a Venn diagram where the sets A and B represent the extent of the two languages respectively. More formally:

Definition 1. *Let $L(A)$ be the extent of Schema A and $L(B)$ be the extent of Schema B. Schema B is syntactically compatible with Schema A if and only if $L(A) \subseteq L(B)$.*

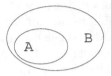

Fig. 1. Instance document sets for compatible languages

The compatibility relation is asymmetric: the fact that Schema B is compatible with Schema A does not imply that Schema A is compatible with Schema B, which would happen only if $L(A) = L(B)$. We can also say that Schema B is *backward compatible* with Schema A when B is a new updated version of A.

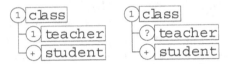

Fig. 2. Compatible schemas

Fig. 2 gives an example of two Schemas A and B where B is compatible with A. This and the following examples in this section assume for simplicity that the schema fully defines the syntax of the language. Schema A defines that instance documents shall have exactly one element called **class** and inside that element there shall be exactly one element called **teacher** and one or more elements called **student**. Schema B is a new version of Schema A. The only difference between the two schemas is the cardinality of element **teacher**, which in Schema B can appear zero or one time. Clearly all valid instance documents for Schema A will be valid also against Schema B, therefore Schema B is backward compatible with Schema A.

On the contrary, two schemas are syntactically incompatible if Definition 1 does not hold. Fig. 3 shows an example of two incompatible schemas. Schema B, as before, introduces inside the **class** element another element called **teacher**, but this time the new element must appear exactly once. All instance documents of Schema A do not have a **teacher** element, whereas all instance document of Schema B are required to have one. Schema B is therefore incompatible with Schema A.

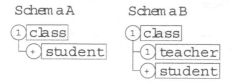

Fig. 3. Incompatible schemas

Language incompatibility is usually an inconvenience, but it can be overcome if the designer can devise a transformation function that converts an instance document for Schema A to a valid instance document for Schema B.

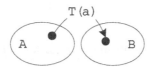

Fig. 4. Instance document transformation

Fig. 4 shows how the transformation function $T(a)$ maps an element of $L(A)$ onto an element of $L(B)$.

Fig. 5 gives an example of an instance document of Schema A to which a transformation is applied to convert it to an instance document of Schema B. The transformation defines to insert an element **teacher** with value "unknown" as a child of the element **class**.

We note that XML languages are context-free languages. This is because they require a push-down parser (rather than a finite state machine) to establish whether or not a document is valid against a schema. Equivalence, containment and empty intersection of context free languages have shown to be undecidable problems. For the proof of this undecidability, we refer to [23,25] and note that therefore syntactic compatibility or incompatibility of general XML languages is undecidable.

Nevertheless, the examples in this section show that it can still be solved, at least in particular circumstances, which we will investigate in Section 4. In our case the languages in question are closely correlated because one is derived as a successor version from the other. We believe that this allows us to find heuristic criteria to determine, in most practical scenarios, if two XML-based languages are compatible.

3.2 Static Semantic Compatibility

The previous subsection has dealt with the language syntax only as it is defined in the schema, but additional constraints are in the general case also part of the

```
Schema A instance document
<class>
  <student>Eric Cartman</student>
  <student>Kyle Broflovski</student>
  <student>Stan Marsh</student>
  ...
</class>

Schema B instance document
<class>
  <teacher>unknown<teacher>
  <student>Eric Cartman</student>
  <student>Kyle Broflovski</student>
  <student>Stan Marsh</student>
  ...
</class>
```

Fig. 5. Instance document transformation (example)

language definition. Examples of such constraints for the FpML language are given in [10]. Nonetheless, Definition 1 still holds.

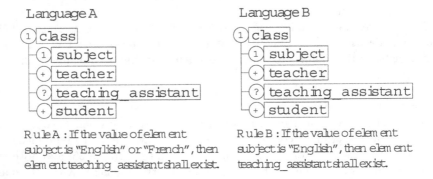

Fig. 6. Compatibility and consistency rules

Fig. 6 shows an example of the evolution of a language definition that comprises a schema and a consistency rule. Rule B is *weaker* than Rule A so Language B is compatible with Language A.

In general, weakening constraints preserves compatibility, whereas strengthening constraints leads to incompatibility. The definition of the terms *stronger* and *weaker* in relation to constraints stems directly from logic:

Definition 2. *Let $c1$ and $c2$ be two constraints, $c1$ is termed* stronger *than $c2$ and $c2$ weaker* than $c1$ *iff $c2 \Rightarrow c1$.*

The static semantic constraints of a language are typically defined by a set of constraints. We can thus extend this definition to constraint sets in the following way:

Definition 3. *Let $\mathcal{A}$ be the set of constraints that determine for Language A and $\mathcal{B}$ be the set of constraints for Language B. $\mathcal{B}$ is static semantically compatible with $\mathcal{A}$ iff $\forall_{b\in\mathcal{B}}\exists_{a\in\mathcal{A}} b \Rightarrow a$.*

Another problem is that consistency rules for a language typically refer to the schema definition of the language, so there is also the problem of keeping them consistent with the schema as the schema evolves. For example if in Schema B the element `teaching_assistant` was renamed `assistant`, then also all rules that refer to that element would need to be updated accordingly. More precisely, the constraints of xlinkit or Schematron use XPath expressions. These expressions express traversals in the DOM tree, the syntax tree that XML parsers establish.

Definition 4. *We say that a static semantic constraint a is well-formed against a Schema A iff it only uses XPaths that are valid in A. We say that a set of constraints $\mathcal{A}$ is well-formed against a Schema A, iff $\forall_{a\in\mathcal{A}}$ a is well-formed against A.*

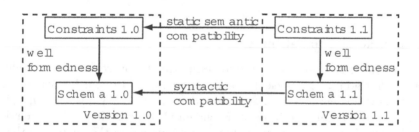

Fig. 7. Language compatibility

We can now summarise our discussion and reformulate the problem of checking compatibility between language versions more precisely by reviewing Fig. 7. An XML language definition consists of a schema that defines the grammar and a set of constraints that are well-formed against the grammar. In order for a new version of the language to be compatible to the previous version the following three conditions must hold:

- The new version of the schema must be syntactically compatible to its predecessor version.
- The new version of the constraint set must be well-formed against the new version of the schema.
- The new version of the constraint set must be static semantically compatible to the predecessor version.

4   Deciding Compatibility between Language Versions

We have already discussed that checking language compatibility is, in the general case, an undecidable problem. We note, however, that the definitions of two versions of the same language are bound to be strongly correlated. Our hypothesis is that it is possible to devise heuristic rules that can be used to establish in most practical cases if one language definition is compatible or not with another.

Checking well-formedness is not strictly speaking a version management problem as well-formedness also needs to be decided for single versions of a language definition. We therefore do not pursue this question further, but note that a well-formedness check needs to be executed when deciding on version compatibility of a change to a language.

For the two remaining problems, we propose the following approach. We establish the differences between both the constraints and the schema. As both the schema and the constraints are written in XML languages, we note that specialist algorithms can be used, such as XMLTreeDiff, which is based on a tree differencing algorithm [16] and delivers more precise results than text-based differencing. We then analyse the sets of differences.

A difference between versions can either be an addition of an element to a schema or a set of constraints, a deletion of an element of a schema or a constraint or a change to a schema element or a constraint. We discuss these separately now.

4.1   Syntactic Compatibility

We start the discussion of syntactic compatibility by reviewing the effect of changes that add or delete elements, the more straightforward cases. The addition of a new element to a schema by itself does not break syntactic compatibility. It may lead to a violation if another schema element is changed to include the new element, but then this case is handled by analysing the change to that element. If a schema element is deleted, it is clear that syntactic compatibility will be broken as instances of these types can then no longer occur in documents that are instances of the new version.

In order to analyse changes to an element of a schema, we can use the finite set of XML schema constructs to classify the change into those that retain compatibility and those that break it. Let us use the example in Fig. 2 for illustrative purposes.

```
Schema A

<xsd:element name="class">
  <xsd:complextype>
    <xsd:sequence>
      <xsd:element name="teacher" type="xsd:string"
                   minOccurs="1" maxOccurs="1" />
      <xsd:element name="student" type="xsd:string"
                   minOccurs="1" maxOccurs="unbounded" />
```

```
    </xsd:sequence>
  </xsd:complextype>
</xsd:element>
```

Schema B

```
<xsd:element name="class">
  <xsd:complextype>
    <xsd:sequence>
      <xsd:element name="teacher" type="xsd:string"
                   minOccurs="0" maxOccurs="1" />
      <xsd:element name="student" type="xsd:string"/>
                   minOccurs="1" maxOccurs="unbounded" />
    </xsd:sequence>
  </xsd:complextype>
</xsd:element>
```

Schema A defines an element called `class` that contains two other elements: `teacher` and `student`. Element `teacher` must occur in instance documents exactly once. Element `student` must occur at least once and the maximum number of its occurrences is unbound. Schema B differs from Schema A only because element `teacher` has been changed to be optional. This particular type of change modifies the cardinality in a compatible way as we can argue that the extent of the language for B includes the extent of A.

In general, we can classify changes into those that retain or violate syntactic compatibility. Examples of changes that retain compatibility include enabling fewer minimal set of elements in a sequence, increasing the number of maximal elements in a sequence, adding non-required attributes to an element, adding, changing or removing default initialisations, changing the order of elements in a choice and so on. Examples of changes to an element that do break syntactic compatibility include addition of a new non-optional sub-element to a sequence, changing the order of elements in a sequence, changing the type of an element or attribute, deleting an element from a sequence and so on.

In order to express changes that do not break compatibility, we can now formalise these as constraints using the xlinkit constraint language at a meta level on XML schemas as follows:

```
<forall var="a" in="/Schema_A//element">
  <forall var="b" in="/Schema_B//element">
    <implies>
      <equals op1="$a/@name" op2="$b/@name" />
      <and>
        <equals op1="$a/@type" op2="$b/@type" />
        <and>
          <lessThanOrEq op1="$b/@minOccurs" op2="$a/@minOccurs" />
          <greaterThanOrEq op1="$b/@maxOccurs" op2="$a/@maxOccurs" />
        </and>
      </and>
```

```
    </implies>
  </forall>
</forall>
```

This constraint states that for all elements of Schema A and Schema B that have the same name, the value of attribute `minOccurs` in Schema B is less than or equal to the value of the corresponding attribute `minOccurs` in Schema A and that the value of the attribute `maxOccurs` is greater than or equal to the value of the corresponding attribute `maxOccurs` in Schema A.

We can formalise rules for changes that would break syntactic compatibility in the same way. We can then use the xlinkit rule engine [21] to decide whether or not a particular version is syntactically compatible to a predecessor version.

4.2   Static Semantic Compatibility

Again we first review addition and deletion of constraints, which are the simple cases. Unless it is a tautology, the addition of a new constraint breaks static semantic compatibility because the new set of constraints will be more restrictive than the ones that were demanded in the predecessor version. The removal of a constraint will preserve static semantic compatibility as any document that was valid against a more inclusive set of constraints will continue to be valid against the smaller set of constraints.

It is possible to change a constraint without changing its meaning at all by using de Morgan's laws. By encoding these laws in a term rewriting system, we can check whether a particular change leads to an equivalent rule. For those rules where this is not the case, we need to establish whether they are weaker or stronger.

To analyse the implication of a change in that respect we can again use a similar approach that uses the constructs of the constraint language to classify whether or not a change weakens or strengthens a constraint. As an example, consider the following two xlinkit constraints, which in fact formalise the constraints shown in Fig. 6.

Rule A

```
<forall var="a" in="//class">
  <implies>
    <or>
      <equals op1="$a/subject/text()" op2="'English'" />
      <equals op1="$a/subject/text()" op2="'French'" />
    </or>
    <exists var="b" in="$a/teaching_assistant" />
  </implies>
</forall>
```

Rule B

```
<forall var="a" in="//class">
  <implies>
    <equals op1="$a/subject/text()" op2="'English'" />
    <exists var="b" in="$a/teaching_assistant" />
  </implies>
</forall>
```

The xlinkit constraint language is rather simple. It can express boolean operators (and, or, implication and not), a few set of operators on DOM nodes (such as equal), as well as existential and universal quantification over a set of nodes identified by XPaths. Thus again we can identify for each possible change to an expression in a constraint whether it strengthens or weakens the constraint and then decide whether the overall change to the constraint breaks static semantic compatibility.

In the above example the change has strengthened the pre-condition of the implication by removing an `<or>` operand, thus making it less likely for the pre-condition to be true. Due to the *ex falso quod libet* rule for implications, this means that it is more likely for the overall formula to be true, which means that this change from version A to version B has weakened the constraint and is therefore statically semantically compatible.

Other examples of weakening a constraint include removing an `<and>` operand, adding an `<or>` operand, changing a universal quantifier into an existential quantifier, and so on. Examples of strengthening a constraint include adding an `<and>` operand, removing an `<or>` operand changing existential into universal quantification and so on.

5 Related Work

The problems of checking compatibility and of tracking version chenges fall into the realm of software configuration management (SCM). According to Jacky Estublier [11], most issues about versioning have already been solved in the general case and the key problem is to incorporate these solutions into SCM tools. Reidar Conradi and Bernhard Westfechtel [8] give a comprehensive overview and classification of versioning paradigms. In their words: "In SCM systems, versioning of the schema is rarely considered seriously. On the other hand schema versioning often does not take versioning of instance data into account". Our approach intends to address both these concerns.

Most XML technologies take a programmer's pragmatic viewpoint and in some respects lack of formal foundation or consistency among them. We have already mentioned that the concept of schema compatibility is absent.

There is also some important work on formal analysis of XML schema languages [7,17,20,18] part of which has been incorporated in XML standards such as Relax NG. However, none of these covers compatibility between language versions.

XML schemas bear clear similarities with database schemas and collections of instance documents can be regarded as a data repository. Understanding of database technology should provide insight on how to approach problems in the XML domain.

The most popular types of database systems are currently relational, object relational, and to a less extent object-oriented for which both the theory and the technology are mature and well documented in many books [24,19,9]. More recently, XML databases have appeared, where XML support is build into the data base management system (DBMS) [4].

We are interested in particular in schema evolution and schema versioning. Ferrandina et al. [13] have proposed a mechanism for schema evolution based on transition functions in the context of object-oriented databases. The difference to our work is that the extent of a class in an object-oriented schema is known – they can work on a closed world assumption, whereas for an XML language the extent is generally unknown and unaccessible.

6   Conclusions and Further Work

This paper identifies a novel area of research in software configuration management that will become increasingly important as the adoption of XML progresses. We have defined the notion of compatibility between different versions of an XML language for both the syntactic and the static semantic constraints of a language. We have observed that the problem of syntactic compatibility is undecidable in general, but have argued that it can become tractable by taking information about differences between versions into account.

Our future work will focus on refining and evaluating the approach for checking version compatibility that we were only able to sketch in this paper. We are in the process of completing the definition of syntactic compatibility rules in the xlinkit constraint language and can then use the existing xlinkit engine for exercising syntactic version compatibility checks. We will have to implement a term rewriting system to apply the de Morgan rules to xlinkit to test for equivalence and implement the strengthening and weakening semantics. To do so, we will again be able to reuse a large portion of the xlinkit rule engine, which to date implements two different semantics for the language in order to generate xlinks and to generate automated repair actions [22].

We have already identified our evaluation case study, which will be to check different versions of the FpML language for compatibility. The International Swaps and Derivatives Association (ISDA) has so far defined three major versions of FpML and for each of these versions a number of minor versions exist that have been in transitional use prior to adoption of the major version. We are actively participating in the standardisation of FpML and have participated in the establishment of a validation working group that will define the static semantic constraints for FpML. Constraints for version 1.0 have already been specified using xlinkit [26] and a working group is currently adding constraints for versions 2.0 and upward.

Acknowledgements

We are indebted to Matt Meinel, Bryan Thal, Steven Lord, and Tom Carroll of UBS Warburg and the members of the FpML Architecture Working Group for drawing our attention to the significant version and configuration managements challenges of FpML in particular and XML languages in general. We would also like to thank Anthony Finkelstein and Chris Clack for their helpful comments on an earlier draft of this paper.

References

1. F. Bancilhon, C. Delobel, and P. Kanellakis. *Building an Object-Oriented Database System: the Story of O_2*. Morgan Kaufmann, 1992.
2. P.V. Biron and A. Malhotra. XML Schema Part 1: Structures. Recommendation http://www.w3.org/TR/2001/REC-xmlschema-1-20010502/, World Wide Web Consortium, MAY 2001.
3. P.V. Biron and A. Malhotra. XML Schema Part 2: Datatypes. Recommendation http://www.w3.org/TR/xmlschema-2/REC-xmlschema-2-20010502/, World Wide Web Consortium, MAY 2001.
4. R. Bourret. XML and Databases. http://www.rpbourret.com/xml/XMLAndDatabases.htm.
5. T. Bray, J. Paoli, and C.M. Sperberg-McQueen. Extensible Markup Language. Recommendation http://www.w3.org/TR/1998/REC-xml-19980210, World Wide Web Consortium, March 1998.
6. T. Bray, J. Paoli, C.M. Sperberg-McQueen, and E. Maler. Extensible Markup Language (XML) 1.0 (Second Edition). Recommendation http://www.w3.org/TR/2000/REC-xml-20001006, World Wide Web Consortium (W3C), October 2000.
7. A. Brown, M. Fuchs, J. Robie, and P. Wadler. MSL - a model for W3C XML schema. In *Proc. of the 10th Int. Conf. on World Wide Web*, pages 191–200. ACM Press, 2001.
8. R. Conradi and B. Westfechtel. Version models for software configuration management. *ACM Computing Surveys (CSUR)*, 30(2):232–282, 1998.
9. C.J. Date and H. Darwen. *Foundation for Object/Relational Databases: The Third Manifesto*. Addison-Wesley, 1998.
10. D. Dui, W. Emmerich, C. Nentwich, and B. Thal. Consistency Checking of Financial Derivatives Transactions. In *Objects, Components, Architectures, Services and Applications for a Networked World*, volume 2591 of *Lecture Notes in Computer Science*. Springer, 2003. To appear.
11. J. Estublier. Software configuration management: a roadmap. In *Proc. of the Conf. on the Future of Software Engineering*, pages 279–289. ACM Press, 2000.
12. D.C. Fallside. XML Schema Part 0: Primer. Recommendation http://www.w3.org/TR/2001/REC-xmlschema-0-20010502/, World Wide Web Consortium, MAY 2001.
13. F. Ferrandina, T. Meyer, and R. Zicari. Implementing Lazy Database Updates for an Object Database System. In *Proc. of the 20th Int. Conference on Very Large Databases, Santiago, Chile*, pages 261–272, 1994.
14. John C. Hull. *Options, Futures and Other Derivatives*. Prentice-Hall International, 2002.

15. R. Jelliffe. The Schematron. http://www.ascc.net/xml/resource/schematron, 1998.

16. K.Tai. The Tree-to-Tree Correction Problem. *Journal of the ACM*, 29(3):422–433, 1979.

17. D. Lee and W.W. Chu. Comparative analysis of six XML schema languages. *SIGMOD Record (ACM Special Interest Group on Management of Data)*, 29(3):76–87, 2000.

18. D. Lee, M. Mani, and M. Murata. Reasoning about XML schema languages using formal language theory. Technical report, IBM Almaden Research Center, November 2000.

19. M. Levene and G. Loizou. *A Guided Tour of Relational Databases and Beyond*. Springer-Verlag, 1999.

20. M. Murata, D. Lee, and M. Mani. Taxonomy of XML schema languages using formal language theory. In *Extreme Markup Languages*, Montreal, Canada, August 2001.

21. C. Nentwich, L. Capra, W. Emmerich, and A. Finkelstein. xlinkit: A Consistency Checking and Smart Link Generation Service. *ACM Transactions on Internet Technology*, 2(2):151–185, 2002.

22. C. Nentwich, W. Emmerich, and A. Finkelstein. Consistency Management with Repair Actions. In *Proc. of the 25th Int. Conference on Software Engineering, Portland, Oregon*. ACM Press, 2003. To appear.

23. V.J. Rayward-Smith. *A First Course in Computability*. Blackwell, 1986.

24. A. Silberschatz, H.F. Korth, and S. Sudarshan. *Database System Concepts*. McGraw-Hill, 2001.

25. M. Sipser. *Introduction to the Theory of Computation*. PWS Publishing, 1997.

26. B. Thal, W. Emmerich, S. Lord, D. Dui, and C. Nentwich. FpML Validation: Joint proposal from UBS Warburg, University College London, and Systemwire. http://www.fpml.org, June 25, 2002.

27. Paul Wilmott. *Derivatives - The Theory and Practice of Financial Engineering*. John Wiley and Sons, 1998.

Using Federations
for Flexible SCM Systems

Jacky Estublier, Anh-Tuyet Le, and Jorge Villalobos

LSR-IMAG, 220 rue de la Chimie, BP53
38041 Grenoble Cedex 9, France
{Jacky.Estublier,Anh-Tuyet.Le,Jorge.Villalobos}@imag.fr

Abstract. SCM products are large and monolithic, difficult to adapt and evolve, with high entry cost. This paper describes a new approach to SCM in which the system is built from, potentially heterogeneous, existing pieces, with assembly mechanisms that enforce high-level properties. The approach does not provide a simple SCM tool, but a family of tools that is easily customized, fits both low-end users (only the required functionalities are present at a very low cost), as well as high-end users (for which very advanced features and/or specific features can be easily added). The paper describes the concepts and mechanisms of federations, and shows how our federation technology was used to develop a family of SCM systems.

1 Introduction

SCM systems have evolved over the years to become powerful and mature tools. However, they have also grown to be large, monolithic products, difficult to adapt and evolve, with high entry cost.

From the beginning, SCM tools have been closed worlds, offering features for specific classes of applications with underlying assumptions regarding the development process used, the kind of development, size of teams, size of software, platform and other sorts. These assumptions, often implicit, have profound influences on the design of the major aspects of an SCM system, like its data model, versioning model or workspace model.

These assumptions, altogether, limit the range of applications these tools can handle reasonably well and have large consequences on many aspects including evolvability, adaptability and interoperability. This limited range of applicability is exemplified by the fact that no tool can handle both software and hardware development (system development) precisely because these assumptions are different. It's also unfortunate that because of the very limited interoperability, even between an SCM system and another closely related system, it is either not possible to make an SCM system interoperate with a PDM system [7][16] or, even worse, hardly with another different SCM system.

This interoperability limitation is a very concerning issue since within the virtual enterprise, different companies, with different SCM tools, will have to cooperate in common software projects. This is especially concerning since a customer using a given SCM system cannot change without a huge investment in time, money and

B.Westfechtel, A. van der Hoek (Eds.): SCM 2001/2003, LNCS 2649, pp. 163-176, 2003.

energy; in practice, such a change is so expensive and risky that it is seldom undertaken.

Therefore, customers tend to buy high-end systems, in the hope they will fit their future needs. Consequently, vendors propose systems with a large amount of features supposed to fit any future need for any customer. This leads to another issue: SCM systems are too big, too expensive, and too difficult to master. The entry barrier is too high.

There is a clear need for systems that can grow with the customer needs and that can be tailored to his/her specific requirements. Unfortunately, the underlying SCM system assumptions include the dimension and the kind of features required by customers. SCM systems provide, in a monolithic way, all the features that could be useful for the targeted customers, with very little room for adaptation. Being monolithic and centralized, scalability (in size and space) and adaptability of these systems to our very decentralized and fast evolving world is fairly limited.

This paper describes a new architecture and framework allowing us to easily assemble families of SCM systems, out of heterogeneous pieces. The resulting systems show extreme adaptability, evolvability and interoperability facilities. These properties have been experimented both to realize low-end systems (cheap, simple and efficient), and to propose very advanced features, like our novel concurrent engineering support system. The latter shows the properties of heterogeneity, distribution and scalability of the system, and proposes a novel concept for the explicit formalization of concurrent engineering policies.

2   An SCM Federation

We have been developing federation technology during the last years, exactly for the purpose of creating a new generation of SCM systems to address the drawbacks mentioned above. Currently, however, this technology revealed itself general enough that we consider our SCM system only as an example of application of the federation technology. In this paper, we will shortly present the federation technology, through the example of our SCM system.

A federation is basically an architecture for the interoperability of large heterogeneous software components. The federation allows the construction of new applications by assembling and integrating existing tools and components.

When building a federation, however, we do not reason in terms of tools and components, but at a higher level of abstraction, in terms of interrelated domains. This approach enables us to think of the architectural and interoperability issues at an adequate semantic level, in an implementation independent way, while at the same time keeping the benefits of the component approach at the execution level (a similar approach is presented in [11]).

The concept of domain is fundamental for federations and will be expanded further in section 2.3, but for now, we can define it as a group of tools and code that, altogether, manage a set of related concepts. The SCM federation is defined by several interrelated domains that model the different aspects of an SCM system. Figure 1 shows some of the basic domains and their relationships.

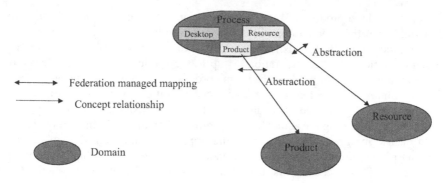

Fig. 1. Abstraction relationship

Consider the nature of the relationship between the process domain and the resource and product domains depicted in figure 1. We label it as an *abstraction* relationship because it links a common concept between the two domains and implies that the source domain only needs limited knowledge of that concept whilst the destination domain is supposed to have full knowledge of the concept and be in charge of handling the actual real entities: the source domain abstracts away a complex concept from the destination domain.

This mapping between domains is explicitly defined in the federation at design time, through a series of models described in section 2.1, and is used at execution time to manage and coordinate the actions of the real tools actually involved.

In our case, the process domain "knows" that it does not "own" the concepts of product and resource, and relies on very limited knowledge of such concepts (actually, their names only). It completely ignores which domain(s) will manage the real products and what is the actual mapping that will be performed, at execution, by the federation from its abstract products to real ones (a related approach in which different aspects of a workflow are defined independently, but mixed at execution, is presented in [18]).

The process domain defines a "product" class that acts like an abstract class; most notably it defines (usually empty) factory methods "load" and "create", which return an ID. The process engine calls these methods whenever an existing or a new product is required in the process; the ID is supposed to be sufficient for the product domain to know, later on, which product is managed by the process. The same applies for resources.

The approach has the advantage that almost any product manager and resource manager can be connected to, and interoperate with, the same process manager, and that the federation mapping is flexible enough to impose almost no constraints on the interface and actual concepts of product and resource in their specific managers.

Indeed, in our implementation, the process domain is implemented by the Apel Process Engine [6], where a product is defined as an atomic entity with a name (a string), a type (a string) and attributes. Our actual Product Manager defines a product as a potentially complex hierarchy of directory and files, having predefined (file system) and user defined attributes, which can be in turn common (whose value is shared by all that product's instance versions) or versioned attributes (whose values are specific to each version of that product).

For example, a product of type "configuration" is an atomic entity in the process domain, but in the product domain it may actually be a real and complete software configuration, with thousands files, associated documents, attributes and so on. The actual definition of a "configuration" is up to the Product Manager in charge of the "configuration" type of product. The same process (say a change control process) can be used almost irrespective of the actual configuration manager to which the type "configuration" is mapped. This allows us to define business processes in a virtual enterprise disregarding the actual SCM system used by the different companies.

In classic integration technologies, the approach, which consists of composing existing pieces of code, has been tried many times and has constantly shown major weaknesses. This is because the usual composition mechanism is the method call: a class calls another class. It requires strict compatibility between method signatures, there is no semantic control; the only property available (imposed) is that method calls are synchronous. In short, there is no matching support.

The major difference between our approach and usual component composition approaches lies in the fact that the mapping between domains is handled by the federation, based on a set of models, established by a "federation designer" who is in charge of composing an application (an SCM system in our case) from a set of existing tools and domains. These models provide flexibility for adapting different domains.

2.1   Domain Mapping Models

Three mapping models drive the federation-managed mappings: a concept mapping model, a functional contract model and a non-functional contract model.

The concept mapping models expresses the semantics of the relationship which links the common concept between the two domains. This model is split in three parts: the meta model mapping, the model mapping and the behavior mapping.

The meta model mapping expresses the relationship itself, at *type* level; which attribute relates with each other attribute in the other domain, along with the transformation function, if any. Note that being an abstraction relationship, few attributes are to be related.

The model mapping expresses the constraints on the *entities* modeled, including existential and referential constraints. In our case, what does mean creating/deleting a product in the process domain, with respect to the real product manager. Indeed, deleting a product in the process does not delete it really; it is simply "out of process"; it can be brought again in a process at a later time. This mapping also expresses the functions allowing to translate an ID from a domain to another.

The behavior model mapping expresses the correspondence between *actions* in the abstract domain to other equivalent action(s) in the concrete domain. This is needed since the abstraction relationship means that actions on the abstract entity are "dummy" actions, they must be translated into real actions on the real products. The correspondence may not be trivial, and may require some computing if the semantic matching between concepts is not direct. In our case, it expresses what it mean, for the product domain, that a product is transferred between two activities in the process domain. It is interesting to mention that this model provides more capabilities than traditional component composition (method calls). In our case, the simple language we propose includes synchronous and asynchronous calls, parallel and sequential execution, as well as local and distributed calls.

The functional contract model expresses the logical constraints under which the mapping is considered valid or not. Most notably, the concept of success is explicit. This model expresses the initial conditions for an abstract action to be valid: a valid mapping can be found in the actual state of both the abstract and concrete domains. Once the mapping is executed, the contract model checks if the resulting state, in both domains, is valid or not. If valid, post conditions can be asserted (in both domains), if not valid, the original action and all the mapped actions are undone and alternative actions can be undertaken or exceptions returned to the caller of the abstract action.

The non-functional contract model expresses properties that have to associated with the above mappings. It can be compared to the concept of a "container" in component-based systems. Indeed, it is in this model that domain distribution, transactions, domain persistency, (communication) security, life cycle and other properties are formally expressed.

It is of uttermost importance to realize that these mappings are external to both domains, which allows much better reusability. The federation framework provides specialized editors for each one of these models and addresses also the static as well as the dynamic evolution dimension.

2.2   The Abstract Architecture: Composition Relationships

Our technology provides much more flexible composition facilities than traditional ones, but the *abstraction* relationship is not sufficient. Other domain relationships have been established and are handled in our system: *refinement, extension* and *specialization*. Figure 2 shows different usages of these relationships in our SCM federation.

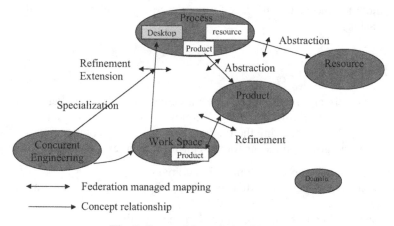

Fig. 2. Composition relationships

A concept from one domain is *refined* when another domain adds structural or behavioral properties to that concept, in a transparent way, to the original domain. In our case for example, the concept of desktop, in the process domain, has been refined to the concept of workspace. *Extension* means that a concept from a domain is related to another different concept in another one, like desktop (from process) and site (from workspace). Indeed, very often refinement and extension come together.

The process domain is therefore very simple and lightweight. *Refinement* and *Extension* are the mechanisms we have used to add state transition diagrams, collaboration, and interoperability with other process support systems in a fully transparent way; precisely the functionalities that were provided monolithically in the previous Apel system [6]. This new Apel System is about 10 times smaller and runs 10 times faster than previous Apel one (V4), not talking about complexity and maintainability.

The process domain ignores the extensions and refinements and does not need them to work. In fact, we could easily contemplate a low-cost entry SCM federation, without the workspace or a sophisticated product domain, in which the process domain is used to define and keep track of the software development process, obviously without automatic workspace or configuration management.

Specialization means that a domain is a specialization of another one, like class and the super class in programming languages. In programming languages, the run-time is in charge of selecting the right methods depending on the situation (type of entity); in a similar way, for federations, it is the mapping that is specialized, and which is in charge of transferring the control to one domain or the other or both. In our example, depending on the process topology, it is either the workspace or the concurrent engineering domains that takes the control, or both.

The same mapping models are used to describe these relationships semantics. Space does not allow a detailed description of these models and mechanisms. Let us simply mention that refinement and extension are similar to Aspect Oriented Programming, except that we handle contracts and that "aspects" are structured according to domains relationships. The underlying technology we use is based on our "Extended Object Machine" that allows us to intercept method calls and add attributes and methods to objects. Our models, for the most part, generate code for this extended object machine.

2.3   Domains

Domains models and meta models are implementation independent; therefore, the different domain relationships are implementation independent composition mechanisms. We are stressing the fundamental role of our composition relationships, because they are powerful means for structuring a complex software application:

Hierarchically: a composed domain is a domain.
Conceptually: refinement, extension, abstraction and specialization are structuring concepts.
Technically: domains are implemented independently.

We emphasize also the fact that the composition models and mechanisms are external to the domain they compose, enhancing their reusability potential. Finally we emphasize the fact that domain definition and composition mechanisms are both model based and implementation independent. These characteristics are those at the base of the OMG Model Driven Architecture (MDA) initiative [4][19] , allowing us to claim that our domains are similar to MDA PIMs (Platform Independent Models), and that our solution is MDA compliant.

In contrast with MDA, however, a domain is said to be abstract only because it manages abstract concepts, but it is always represented as a piece of code which makes concrete the meta model. In the simplest case it is the set of empty classes generated by XMI from the MOF meta model; in other cases it is the program which corresponds to the meta model. In our example, the process domain is associated with the Apel engine, the product domain with our product manager and so on.

A the abstract level, a federation is a set of domains related by our semantic relationship; a execution, these domains execute, and the federation is in charge (among other things) to interpret the relationships defined between the domains, thus coordinating the domains and makings the complete (abstract) execution consistent. However, this execution is still abstract. The real tools and the real execution are still not performed.

2.4   The Implementation Relationship

A domain can also be associated with a set of tools (COTS or legacy) and specific pieces of code, which together make *concrete* the abstract domain (or interpret the domain model). The major goal of a domain is to encapsulate how the abstract domain "execution", which is platform and tool independent, translates to real platform(s) and tool(s) execution. This "implementation" of the domains is performed in two steps. First, the real tools are abstracted in the form of "roles" and domains are connected to roles through the relationship *implements*. Second roles are connected to real tools or specific code.

It is striking to see that actual composition mechanisms including components, EAI, and process based approach like BPM and even the most recent ones [20] are only at this implementation level.

Abstract Tool Mapping. A *role* models a part of a tool or a component functionality. Technically, a role is very similar to a component interface; it is defined by a (java) interface (facets), the set of produced and consumed events, and the set of the domain methods the role can call (receptacles). A tool is therefore modeled under the form of functional interfaces represented by the set of its roles.

The implementation of a role is always a "component". Indeed, our federation engine includes a complete component framework supporting full life cycle support, transparent distribution support and component's interface discovery and dynamic connection between roles. This framework is intended for simplifying the implementation of the components which implement a tool set of interfaces, and thus are modeling a tool.

A set of roles define concepts and can thus be seen as a (low level) domain. However, the implementation relationship is different than the other relationship in that concepts managed by the roles and the abstract domain are not at the same level of abstraction; there is, in general, no one to one mapping between the concepts (abstract, refine and extend usually relate pair of concepts). Thus, it is common that an abstract concept be related to many low level ones, and therefore, that an abstract operation involve many low level operations.

Another difference between the abstract and implementation domains, is that the meta-meta level is object oriented for the former (classes, inheritance, links), but the later also includes the federation component model (interfaces, life cycle, connection protocols etc), the concepts of connector, the mapping role/connectors.

Roles being implemented in Java (in our platform), the "programming" (modeling) of these additional concepts is done outside the role implementation, through specialized editors producing the non functional mapping models similar to "containers" for component models. We emphasize the fact that many difficult technical issues are handled in that way, and therefore removes from role implementation its most tricky issues. It is the federation engine which executes these non functional models.

Concrete Tool Mapping. Still, this implementation domain layer is abstract, the real tools are still not involved. The concrete tool mapping is in charge of connecting the roles to the actual associated tools.

This mapping is specific to role / tool connection. From one side it is simpler than the other mapping, since we have the strict relationship role / tool, and because roles are purposely built as abstraction of the tool. From another side, this mapping is more complex because, in the general case :

Tools are not located on the federation machine,
Tools use heterogeneous technologies and run on heterogeneous platforms
Tools are autonomous, and sometimes interactive
Tools do not expose their interfaces nor their meta model

For COTS, there is in general a need to write a "wrapper", in charge of both observing, and command the tool. Observe because an interactive tool may act "by itself", and thus show initiative, at unpredictable time and unpredictable ways. The wrapper is in charge of notifying to the federation these behaviour, at least when they are relevant from the federation point of view. Command, because the federation need to ask the tool to perform tasks required by the federation, and the way to ask a tool to perform a task is very dependent on the tool, platform and technology used.

Because of the distribution issue, wrapper and roles implementations are on different machines. Worse, in many cases, the same tool (say the client version manager or an IDE), may need to be present and executed on different machine depending on the execution context. Worse, the same role may need to be filled by different real tools depending on the context (the platform of the nature of the entities, or anything else). For example, the IDE to invoke may depend on the programming language, the platform, or the user preference; from the federation point of view, this must be transparent : "the" IDE has to be called on the "current user" workspace.

For all these issues, the meta non functional model provided by the federation for this mapping includes a taxonomy of tools (local, remote, client/server, web Service, EJB, etc), it fully supports distribution handling, multiples copy and dynamic location handling, network error recovery (dynamic restarting / reconnection of wrappers and tools), fire wall and security handling and so on.

The definition and development of this non-functional model and its support was very much time and energy consuming, but it removes from wrapper and role implementations most of its complexity. Even if writing a wrapper is not (necessarily) simple, we already have experimented that this non-functional model, and its automatic management by the federation engines, is a major help in defining and implementing federations.

3   The SCM Federation Implementation

In our system, a domain must have an explicit *domain meta model*, in the form of an XML schema, and zero or more associated *domain models*, in the form of xml files. The *abstract domain* is constituted of the domain model, reified in the form of java entities (the execution view)[1], plus, optionally, other objects if needed to manage the model objects. In the most degenerated case, the abstract domain is simply a java program.

Take for example the process domain. The meta model is an XML schema defining concepts of activity, desktop, product (a name only), resources and so on. The process model is an Apel model, produced using our graphical process editor, and stored in an XML file. The abstract domain is the Apel engine, including the entities (activity instances, product instances) that reify the model entities.

The abstract product and resource domains are limited to the corresponding reified entities, and code to manage them (the real humans for example).

Compositions Editors
A federation instance is defined at three levels. At the meta level, its definition is the domains involved, their meta model and the relationship between domains. At the execution level, it is the set of executables for the domains, and the set of associated tools. At model level, it is the set of models for the domains to work with.

In our example,

the meta level is roughly represented in fig 2.
the execution level is the domain code (apel engines, ...), plus the tools (e.g. CVS and its wrappers (or Zip tool or whatever version manager) for the version manager abstract tool), and so on ...
at the model level, we must indicate which process models are involved (change control, concurrent engineering, development process ...), the products involved (configurations, change control document, tests ...), the resource model (which employees and roles are involved).

We provide graphical editors for each one of these three levels. These editors generate the code and scripts required for the corresponding execution.

It is very interesting to consider that a fairly large family of SCM systems can be built only "playing" at the model level, using only the graphical domain model editors to define the various models. End users can therefore deeply customize their system

---

[1] We use the Castor package (from exolab) to translate between xml and java.

without any knowledge of the technology involved. In our example, they only need to model their processes, resources and products, not a single line of code is required.

At the execution level, our execution composition editor allows to select, for each domain, the different executables, for the domain itself, for the roles it requires, and for each role, the tools that play the role.

If the vendor provides different possible tools for the roles, the user can simply select the one it prefers. If the user wants to use its tool instead, say its preferred version manager, it has to write the wrapper and role implementation for the tools to play the roles required in the federation; and everything else will work as always. This has to be compared with the deep rework required when the data model or the versioning model is changed in an SCM tool.

At the meta level, it is possible to add domains and to define its relationships with the existing domains; everything else is left unchanged. For example, when it came to add our concurrent engineering tool, we only had to add a relationship "specialization" to the actual system to get the new one. That relationship definition is about 15 lines long. This is again to be compared with the rework it would require in a classic architecture to include such a demanding system, which makes interferences with the process, the data model, the resources and so on. Nevertheless the CE system is also, without change a stand alone tool usable without the federation control.

Domain Model Editors
In our SCM system family, we have developed model editors for each domain (process, product, workspace, resource). These editors first ask the user for which federation composition to work with. Once this is known, the editor can ask the federation engine what are the available dependent entities available in this federation composition. For instance, the process editor only shows, and allows, the products types and user roles available in this federation composition. A level of consistency is enforced.

Similarly, the model composition editor checks if all dependencies between models are solved. It acts, for models, like a link editor for binaries; which is no surprise since our federation system, to a large extend, translates to the model level the techniques and feature traditionally found at code level.

4   Experience and Validation

The federation approach sketched above has been used to design and implement an SCM system in radical different terms. The first use was to design lightweight and efficient SCM systems, easily customized to user needs and using the tools already in use in the company. This family of SCM systems is structured in a similar way as described above, in 4 domains.

The second work we have done was to show that it is possible to extend significantly such an SCM system without any need to rework it. In order to make the exercise very significant, we have included a high level concurrent engineering system. Such a system interacts deeply with the data model, the process, and the resources and of course the workspaces. Integrating such a system in a traditional architecture would require a deep rework of the architecture, and changes of code everywhere. And, of course, any change in the CE features would potentially affect any other parts of the system, making difficult to adapt such a system to user specific needs.

Indeed, we have been even surprised to see how light weight is has been to integrate such a demanding system. Indeed the system currently exhibits 4 different kinds of versioning, each handled in a different domain, and implemented independently the on from the other:

the process systems support a king of cooperative versioning,
the workspace supports simple historical versioning,
the concurrent engineering supports another cooperative versioning based on groups and policies,
the product manager supports a logical versioning for a single branch.
we are in the process of adding logical versioning on multiple levels.

We do not know anything, even close, that can make cooperate, in safe way, these many different versioning, along with their different data models, with high capabilities to add/change/remove some of them easily.

On the negative side, the experience also shows that the new development we have made, on domain relationships, require support to reduce the complexity of their use. To this end we have developed the three composition editors, but more work is required in this direction. We envision a system where composition is fully supported, but this requires major research work, under way currently in the team.

This paper presents shortly the current state of a long work seeking to find fundamentally new ways to develop SCM systems, and other complex systems, avoiding the monolithic nature of today solutions.

The early concepts about federations were first published in [9], the first prototype was running in 2000 [21]. The first attempt to put a federation into industrial production was done in 2001, but showed conceptual and technical deficiencies. The domain concept was not present, nor the domain composition relationships and their associated mapping models, nor the editors supporting these model definitions not the composition editors, of course. From a technical point of view, efficiency, availability and stability were not sufficient. Error recovery, evolution and firewall were not supported. A complete re-implementation was undertaken and the current system supports industrial production since the end of 2002.

New federations, not related to SCM, are under development and should be put into production in 2003, among others a federation for the interoperability of transport back-offices (highways, trains, and tunnels), and a federation for the support of System On Chip (SOC) design. A larger use of this technology in industry is forecasted.

So far, our claims about flexibility and evolvability have been fully supported by experience. For example, the integration of the concurrent engineering domain involved only the definition of a *specialize* relationship whose mapping model is 20 lines long.

Conversely, it took us a long time to understand the concept of domain and to establish the nature of the composition relationships; this process is not finished at time of writing; more support is needed in this process of domain composition.

5   Conclusion

It is a permanent goal in computer sciences, to find ways to compose applications from existing elements. Unfortunately, so far, the existing technologies, including the object paradigm, components, EAI and BPM, have shown too insufficient capabilities, both conceptually and technically. This paper presents the current state of our work in attempting to overcome the difficulties involved in application design and building.

The first lesson we learned is that there is little room for solution at the code level. There is a need to reason, design and implement at the much higher, implementation independent, level of domains. Domains are model driven and exhibit meta models and models.

The second lesson is that composing domains requires specific concepts and tools. Direct mapping are generally impossible. Composition, in our approach, is based on the identification of semantic relationships between domains and the associated mapping models provide an explicit definition of the relationship; including concept mapping, functional and non-functional contract models.

Composition through semantic relationships allows one to

Compose a new domain based on existing domains, at different levels of abstraction: refinement, abstraction, extension and specialization relationships.

Structure the solution since a composite domain is itself a domain, allowing us to define domain hierarchies. These contrasts with classic technologies that allow only flat structure.

Implement a domain, using the implementation relationship.

It is important to mention that each of these relationships fulfils a different semantic purpose and constitute complementary fundamental conceptual guideline for both designers and implementers, but they all rely on the same technical mechanisms, and on almost the same mapping models: concept mapping, functional contract mapping and non-functional contract mapping. This contrasts with the usual composition technologies where only direct method mapping is supported.

Domain implementation relies on the *implementation* relationship and its associated mappings and also on the role concept, which provides an additional independence between tools and domain. This contrasts with the usual composition technologies where only the tool level of abstraction is supported, i.e. a very low level.

The experience in building an SCM system, using this technology, supports the above claims. The system we have built does not claim to be a complete and state of the art solution on all dimensions, but shows that simple, practical and efficient solutions can be built on demand, at a very low cost, and reusing existing elements.

We have shown that the solution is easily extensible and can interoperate easily with third party systems. This is a feature no system can provide currently.

Finally, we have shown, with our concurrent engineering system, that very advanced and state of the art features can be included easily in the system. We think that the original claim of finding a system which can lower the entry barrier (cost as well as complexity), which can grow with the customer needs, which can interoperate with other heterogeneous systems (SCM or other), and which can accommodate the advanced features the user needs (and only these), is no longer a dream. We believe this is major progress.

But, as claimed in [5], this requires us to completely redesign our systems with these new paradigms in mind and using a new generation composition framework. Our system is an early implementation, and may be the first, of this new framework generation.

References

[1] Jean Bezivin and Sébastient Gérard. A Preliminary Identification of MDA Components

[2] Desmond D.Souza, Model-Driven Architecture and Integration Opportunities and Challenges. White paper. http://www.kinetium.com/

[3] P. Dourish and V. Belloti: "Awareness and Coordination in Shared Work Spaces". Proceedings of the ACM Conference on Computer Supported Cooperative Work (CSCW'92)

[4] Dsouza, D. Model-Driven Architecture and Integration: Opportunities and Challenges Version 1.1, document available at http://www.kinetiuym.com/, February 2001

[5] J. Estublier: "Distributed objects for Concurrent Engineering". 9th International Symposium on System Configuration Management in the European Software Engineering Conference. Toulouse, France, September 1999

[6] J. Estublier, S. Dami, and M. Amiour. "APEL: A graphical yet Executable Formalism for Process Modelling". Automated Software Engineering, ASE journal. Vol. 5, Issue 1, 1998

[7] J. Estublier, J.M. Favre, and P. Morat. "Toward an integration SCM / PDM". SCM8, Brussels, 20-21 July 1998. In LNCS 1439, Springer Verlag

[8] Jacky Estublier and Anh-Tuyet LE. Design and development of Software Federation. ICSSEA 2001, Paris, 4-6 December 2001

[9] Jacky Estublier, Pierre-Yves Cunin, and Noureddine Belkhatir. An architecture for process support interoperability. ICSP 5, Pages 137-147. 15-17 June 1998 Chicago, Illinois, USA

[10] M. Franklin, M, Carey, and M. Livny: "Transactional Client-Server Cache Consistency: Alternatives and Performance". ACM Transactions on Database Systems, Vol. 22 No. 3. September 1997

[11] A. Gokhale, D.C. Schmidt, B. Natarajan, and N. Wang: "Applying Model-Integrated Computing to Component Middleware and Enterprise Applications". Communications of the ACM, Vol. 45, No. 10. October 2002

[12] C. Godart, F. Charoy, O.Perrin, and H. Skaf-Molli: "Cooperative Workflows to Coordinate Asynchronous Cooperative Applications in a Simple Way.". 7th International Conference on Parallel and Distributed Systems (ICPADS'00). Iwate, Japan, July 2000

[13] P. Molli, H. Skaf-Molli, and C. Bouthier: "State Treemap: An Awareness Widget for Multi-Synchronous Groupware". 7th International Workshop on Groupware (CRIWG'01). September 2001

[14] OMG. A UML Profile for Enterprise Distributed Object Computing Joint Final Submission. 21 November 2002

[15] OMG Model Driven Architecture A Technical Perspective Architecture Board MDA Drafting Team Draft 21st February 2001

[16] A. Personn, I. Crnkovic, M. Larsson: "Managing Complex Systems – Challenges for PDM and SCM". 10th International Workshop on Software Configuration Management, in the International Conference on Software Engineering. Toronto, Canada, May 2001

[17] John Poole. Model-Driven Architecture: Vision, Standards And Emerging Technologies. ECOOP 2002

[18] R. Schmidt and U. Asmann: "Extending Aspect-Oriented-Programming in order to flexibly support workflows". Aspect Oriented Programming Workshop in the International Conference on Software Engineering. Kyoto, Japan, April 1998

[19] Soley, R. and the OMG staff Model-Driven Architecture. White paper, Draft 3.2, document available at www.omg.org, November 2000

[20] G. Valetto and G. Kaiser. Using Process Technology to Control and coordinate Software Adaptation. ICSE, Portland May 2003

[21] Herve Verjus. PhD Thesis. Chambery 2000

Dissecting Configuration Management Policies

Ronald van der Lingen and André van der Hoek

School of Information and Computer Science
University of California, Irvine
Irvine, CA 92697-3425 USA
{vdlingen,andre}@ics.uci.edu

Abstract. A configuration management policy specifies the procedures through which a user evolves artifacts stored in a configuration management system. Different configuration management systems typically use different policies, and new policies continue to be developed. A problem in the development of these new policies is that existing policies (and their implementations) typically cannot be reused. As a basis for a future solution, this paper presents a new configuration management system architecture that focuses on modularly specified policies. In particular, policies consist of a set of constraint modules, which enforce the desired repository structure, and a set of action modules, which govern the desired user interaction. New policies can be developed by combining relevant existing modules from existing policies with new modules that specify the unique aspects of the new policy. We demonstrate how several quite different configuration management policies can be effectively constructed this way.

1 Introduction

Building a new configuration management system is a daunting undertaking. The Subversion project [13], for example, initiated in May 2000, currently comprises over 100,000 lines of code, and has iterated over 14 alpha releases to date. Its first beta release is not scheduled until early next year, and still a number of known issues are yet to be addressed. This is all the more surprising, because the goal of Subversion is merely to provide a better implementation of CVS [2] that addresses a relatively small number of functional "annoyances" in the process [14].

A significant portion of the effort lies in the fact that Subversion is a carefully architected, open, and pluggable implementation with extensive error handling and distributed operation. The inherent non-reusability of the configuration management policy of CVS, however, also played a role. Because the policy of CVS is interwoven throughout its implementation, functionality related to its policy (such as the rules for updating a version tree or selecting artifacts) could not be easily extracted for reuse and had to be reimplemented in Subversion.

A number of projects have attempted to address this issue. EPOS [8] and ICE [21], for instance, provide logic-based infrastructures upon which to implement new con-

B.Westfechtel, A. van der Hoek (Eds.): SCM 2001/2003, LNCS 2649, pp. 177-190, 2003.
© Springer-Verlag Berlin Heidelberg 2003

figuration management systems by specifying their policies as logical constraints. Another approach, NUCM [16], provides a programmatic approach that reuses a generic repository and supports implementation of specific policies via a standard programmatic interface. While successful in making the development of new configuration management systems easier, we observe that all of these approaches only focus on reuse of a generic configuration management model. In particular, the infrastructures provide generic data modeling facilities that are reused for expressing policies, but the policies themselves are not reused.

This paper introduces a new configuration management system architecture that focuses on policy reuse. It is loosely based on the generic model of NUCM, but additionally recognizes that policies can be modularly specified and implemented. In particular, a policy is defined by a set of *constraint modules*, which enforce the desired repository structure on the server side, and a set of *action modules*, which govern the desired user interaction on the client side. Four types of constraint modules exist: storage, hierarchy, locking, and distribution. They are complemented by four types of action modules: selection, evolution, concurrency, and placement. A policy is formed by choosing relevant implementations of each type of constraint module and action module. Reuse occurs when new policies are formed by combining one or more existing modules with newly developed modules that capture the unique aspects of the new policy. A single constraint or action module, thus, can be used in the specification of multiple policies.

Below, we first introduce some background information to form the basis for the remainder of the paper. We then introduce our new architecture and discuss the available constraint and action modules in detail. We continue by showing how several quite different configuration management policies are constructed using our approach. We then briefly compare our architecture to existing architectures and conclude with a discussion of the potential impact of our work and an outlook at our future plans.

2 Background

To understand our approach, it is necessary to clearly delineate a configuration management *model* from a configuration management *policy*. The two are often intertwined, which is not surprising given that a typical CM system requires only a single model tuned to a single policy. As a result, terminology has not been quite clear and early papers on configuration management policies, for instance, referred to them as models [6].

Here, we define a configuration management model as the data structures used to track the evolution of one of more artifacts and a configuration management policy as the procedures through which a user evolves the artifacts stored in those data structures. For example, the version tree model is generally used in conjunction with the check-in/check-out policy [12]. As another example, the change sets policy [11] generally uses specialized data structures to capture and relate individual change sets.

While efficiency reasons may prescribe the use of a customized model in support of a particular policy, research has shown how certain policies can be emulated with other models. For instance, the change sets policy can be supported using the model for the change package policy [20]. Generalizations of this approach provide generic models that support a wide variety of policies [1,16,19,21]. In sacrificing efficiency for generality and expressiveness, these generic models can be used for the exploration and evaluation of new policies [15]. Once a desired policy has been determined, it may need to be reimplemented in an optimized fashion with a specialized model should efficiency be of great concern. Evidence shows, however, that effective systems can be built directly on top of the generic infrastructures [16,21]. Still, reuse of policies themselves remains difficult, a problem we tackle in this paper to make the construction of new configuration management systems even easier.

3 New System Architecture

We base our approach on the observation that configuration management policies do not have to be treated as single, monolithic entities. Rather, they can be dissected into smaller modules, each governing one aspect of one or more policies. As illustrated in Figure 1, we distinguish constraint modules from action modules. Constraint modules are placed on the server side of a configuration management system, and enforce the desired repository structure. The purpose of a storage constraint module, for instance, is to limit the potential relationships among a set of baselines and changes. Among others, those relationships may be restricted to form a linear structure, a version tree, a version graph, or even an arbitrary graph.

Action modules govern the desired user interaction on the client side of a configuration management system. Part of the purpose of a concurrency action module, for example, is to determine which baselines and changes must be locked before a user starts making changes. Example strategies could be to lock all baselines and all changes, only baselines and changes on the current branch, or no baselines or changes at all.

Our architectural decision to place constraint modules on the server side and action modules on the client side is a deliberate choice. While both types of modules could have been placed together on either the server or client side, separating them as in Figure 1 has two significant advantages. First, it places constraint checking at the level of the server, which reduces the need to send state information from the server to a client every time other clients commit changes. Second, it has the advantage of being prepared for a future in which different clients operate with different policies.

Different constraint and action modules can be associated with different artifacts. This allows the architecture to support policies that treat different artifacts differently (e.g., the policy underneath CVS [2] supports file versioning but does not support directory versioning). To avoid having to individually associate modules with every single artifact, default constraint and action modules can be specified.

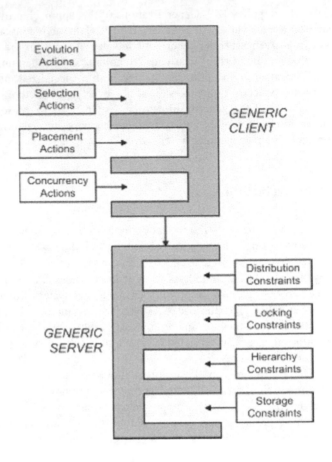

Fig. 1. New configuration management system architecture

3.1 Constraint Modules

The architecture supports four types of constraint modules: storage, hierarchy, locking, and distribution. These types were selected because they represent the common dimensions along which current configuration management policies vary. As our research continues, we will be exploring adding additional dimensions as necessary.

An important aspect of the architecture is that each constraint module is specified independently from the others, making it possible to replace one of the constraint modules without influencing the operation of the others. Of note is also that the sole purpose of a constraint module is to simply enforce the desired repository structure. As such, each constraint module only verifies if a particular operation adheres to the specified constraints. The standard, generic part of the architecture interprets the results of each constraint module and either commits the operation (if all constraints are satisfied) or aborts the operation (if one or more constraints are violated).

Below, we briefly discuss the role of each type of constraint module.

3.1.1 Storage Constraint Module

The architecture is built on baselines and changes. At the storage layer, a baseline represents a version of a single artifact (containment is supported by the hierarchy layer, see Section 3.1.2), as stored in its complete form. A change represents an incremental version, and is stored using a delta mechanism.

The purpose of a storage constraint module is to limit the number of baselines and changes that may be created by a user, as well as to limit the potential relationships that may exist among those baselines and changes. For example, directories in CVS cannot be versioned. The storage constraint module for those directories, therefore, would limit the generic server to only be able to store one baseline of a directory at a time. Files, on the other hand, can be versioned in CVS and are stored as baselines and changes that are related in a directed graph. The storage constraint module for files, therefore, would allow a directed graph but still disallow parts of that graph to be disconnected.

To understand the role of storage constraints, Figure 2 presents the structures that result from applying a number of different storage constraint modules. Figure 2a, for instance, shows a baseline-only structure that results from a very conservative storage constraint module. Figure 2b shows the traditional version tree that results from allowing intermittent baselines and changes that each have a single parent. The version graph in Section 2c is the result of slightly different constraints that allow a single

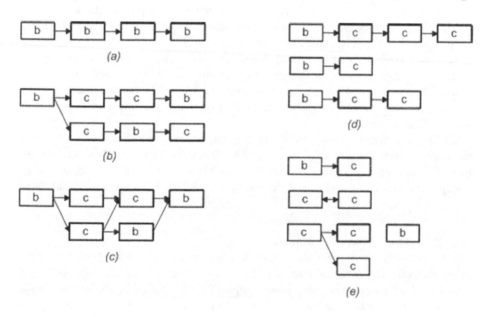

Fig. 2. Structures resulting from different storage constraint modules

baseline or change to have multiple parents, as long as no cycles result. The examples of 2d and 2e show disconnected graphs, as suited for change package [20] and change set [11] policies, respectively.

3.1.2 Hierarchy Constraint Module
The purpose of a hierarchy constraint module is to limit a user in forming potentially arbitrary hierarchal structures. The dimensions along which different policies vary are threefold: (1) whether or not the hierarchical composition of artifacts is allowed, (2) whether or not a single artifact can be part of more than one higher level artifact, and (3) whether or not cyclic relationships are allowed. We have defined and implemented a hierarchy constraint module for each of the meaningful combinations of these three dimensions.

Individually, hierarchy constraint modules are not very powerful. Combining them with storage constraint modules, however, makes for a storage facility that is more generic than its predecessor (i.e., the storage model of NUCM [16]). In particular, our new architecture supports containers that: (a) have actual content in addition to containment information and (b) explicitly distinguish baselines from changes.

3.1.3 Locking Constraint Module
The mechanisms that different configuration management policies use for concurrency control vary. So me are optimistic and rely on automated merging[7] for conflict resolution. Others are pessimistic and rely on locking to avoid conflicts altogether. In terms of persistent state that must be preserved over some timeframe, locks are the only entities that must be stored. Therefore, concurrency-related decisions are made by a concurrency action module (see Section 3.2.1), but locking related checks are performed by a locking constraint module. In particular, a locking constraint module determines whether a request carries the correct set of locks.

Several different locking constraint modules exist that range from not enforcing any locking at all (e.g., in case of a change set policy) to enforcing the simultaneous locking of all baselines and all changes (e.g., in case of a policy like the one in SCCS [10]). Perhaps the most commonly used strategies are to either lock a single node, or to lock a node and its branch.

Locking constraints are specified independently from any hierarchy constraints and therefore cannot cross different levels in the storage hierarchy. Nonetheless, attaching the appropriate locking constraint to each level, combined with the use of an appropriate concurrency action module (see Section 3.2.1), will provide such functionality.

3.1.4 Distribution Constraint Module
The last type of constraint module pertains to the distribution of artifacts over multiple different servers. Different configuration management systems differ in their policies in a number of different ways. First, some support no distribution at all. Second, those that support distribution may support distribution of an artifact as a whole or of individual baselines or changes. Finally, a policy may support replication of artifacts as a whole or of individual baselines or changes.

The purpose of a distribution constraint module, then, is to ensure that the appropriate distribution policy is followed by a user (e.g., a request to replicate a single baseline cannot be honored if only an artifact as a whole can be replicated). Again, a distribution constraint module operates on a single artifact. If the distribution of hierarchically organized artifacts needs to be coordinated, a placement action module can do so.

3.2 Action Modules

In addition to the constraint modules, four types of action modules exist: selection, concurrency, evolution, and placement. Action modules represent the decision points in a configuration management policy. They, for example, make sure to lock the right set of artifacts or to establish appropriate parent relationships when a user merges two or more branches.

Action modules augment the basic user interaction protocol that is supported by the architecture. This interaction protocol consists of two requests. First, a user populates a workspace with artifacts and indicates whether they want read or write access. Second, after the desired changes have been made, they place the changes back in the repository. The actual behavior of the system in response to these requests depends on the particular modules that are "plugged in". For example, if a concurrency action module is plugged in that supports simple locking, populating a workspace results in the artifacts being locked and placing changes back in the repository results in them being unlocked. As described below, each type of action module provides a range of options from which different configuration management policies are composed.

3.2.1 Selection Action Module

A selection action module interprets a request for populating a workspace and automatically incorporates other artifacts as necessary. Particularly important dimensions in this process are whether or not a request is hierarchical (i.e., whether a request for a collection additionally leads to populating of the workspace with constituent artifacts), whether or not latest versions should be selected (i.e., the policy of DVS [3] is to select by default the latest version of any constituent artifact), and whether or not additional selection criteria should be interpreted (i.e., attribute selection or configuration specifications [4]).

The power of the selection action module lies in it being a counterpart to the hierarchy constraint module. If hierarchical artifacts are permitted, the selection action module makes it easy for a user to meaningfully obtain a set of hierarchically related artifacts with a single request.

Note that the selection action module does not actually populate a workspace, but rather only determines the artifacts with which it should be populated. The generic client takes care of taking the list of artifacts and actually placing them in the workspace. This has two advantages. First, new selection action modules become simpler to implement and require fewer details concerning the internals of the architecture. Second, it provides another form of reuse as the generic client implements the mechanisms for obtaining artifacts from the server.

3.2.2 Concurrency Action Module

Similar to the way the selection action module complements the hierarchy constraint module, the concurrency action module serves as a complement to the locking constraint module. When a user requests write access to an artifact that is being placed in their workspace, the concurrency action module determines the appropriate set of baselines and changes that must be locked. As described in Section 3.1.3, the set may be empty in case a change set policy is desired, but it also may involve locking multiple baselines or changes.

A concurrency action module also takes care of determining the set of baselines and changes to be unlocked when a user commits their changes to the server. Normally, of course, this will be the same set that was locked in the first place.

In order to support concurrency policies at the hierarchical level, a concurrency action module specifies two Booleans: the first determines whether locking a container artifact should lead to locking of its constituent artifacts and the second whether locking an artifact should lead to its parent artifacts being locked. Both cases of transitive locking, although rare, are present in certain configuration management policies. Note that the Booleans only indicate a desired behavior. The actual child or parent artifacts are locked according to their own concurrency action modules.

A few configuration management systems incorporate concurrency policies that involve direct workspace-to-workspace communication [5,18]. At the moment, we consider this out of scope since we focus on policies in the setting of client-server based configuration management systems. Our eventual goal, however, is to support such peer-to-peer interaction.

3.2.3 Evolution Action Module

While a storage constraint module limits the relationships that may exist among baselines and changes, certain choices still must be made. For example, when a user wants to create a new version of an artifact, that version must receive a version number, it must be determined whether it should be stored as a baseline or change, and it must be determined what relationships are desired with the other baselines and changes. An evolution action module, guided by appropriate user input, takes care of these kinds of decisions.

Evolution policies range from simply replacing the current version of the artifact in case the artifact is not versioned to storing the new version of the artifact as an independent change in case of a change set policy. Perhaps the most common policy is to add a new version to the end of the branch from which it originated, unless a newer version already exists, in which case a new branch is created. In effect, this policy creates a version tree.

If a version graph is desired, selection information kept in the workspace will help in determining when merge arcs are needed. In particular, if a user requested a workspace to be populated with a version that represents the merging of two branches (simply by asking for those two versions, the architecture automatically merges the two), this information is kept in the workspace and fed into the versioning policy by the standard client.

Because the layers in our architecture are orthogonal, the evolution of hierarchical artifacts (containers) is performed in the same manner as the versioning of atomic artifacts. The only exception to this rule is that, again, an evolution action module can specify two Booleans to determine whether committing a new version of a collection should lead to the committing of parent and/or child artifacts.

3.2.4 Placement Action Module

The last action module in our architecture is the placement action module, which makes decisions regarding the distribution of artifacts, or versions of artifacts. In particular, when a user commits an artifact, the placement action module determines the location where the new baseline or change has to be stored. Normally, that will be the server from which the artifact originated, but it is also possible for a policy to store and or even replicate artifacts on servers that may be closer to the user that is currently making modifications. Again, we note that this module only determines where an artifact will be stored, the actual mechanism of doing so is provided by the generic server implementation.

Just like the concurrency and evolution action modules, the placement action module has two Booleans determining whether parent and/or child artifacts should be co-located with the artifact being manipulated. This way, a policy can restrict a subtree of artifacts to be located at a single server.

4 Examples

In order to demonstrate the use of our new architecture, we have studied which constraint and action models are needed to model some of the more prolific existing configuration management policies. Below, we first demonstrate how to construct a policy similar to the policy of RCS [12]. We then demonstrate how to construct a policy similar to the policy of CVS [2], and show how variants of that policy can be easily constructed. As an example of a rather different kind of policy, we then show how to model the change set policy [11].

In all of these examples, it is important to note that user interaction with the configuration management system remains the same. Users request artifacts for reading and/or writing, and place modified artifacts back into the repository. By plugging in different constraint and action modules, the configuration management system adjusts its behavior to the desired policy. This may result in some user actions to be prohibited (for example, the policy of RCS does not support hierarchical composition), but generally a user will notice little difference.

4.1 RCS

Table 1 illustrates how one would build a configuration management system with a policy similar to RCS. This policy is a relatively simple one and focuses on versioning of individual artifacts in a non-distributed setting. As a result not all features of our architecture are used. In particular, the hierarchy constraint module disallows any hierarchical composition and the distribution constraint module prevents distribution of artifacts over multiple repositories. Consequently, the placement action module is empty, since no decisions regarding placement of artifacts have to be made. Similarly, the value of the Boolean indicators that determine whether the remaining three action modules operate in a hierarchical fashion should be set to false.

Versions are stored in a connected graph of bas elines and changes, which in effect forms a version tree in which branching is allowed. A new version is stored on the branch from which it was created, unless an earlier version was already stored on the branch, in which case a new branch is started. When a user selects two versions of an artifact to put in the workspace, the result is a merged artifact and a merge link in the version graph when the result is placed back in the repository. Locking is per baseline or change, and arbitrary nodes can be locked.

Table 1. Policy of RCS as constructed in our architecture

Module	Implementation
Storage constraint	Acyclic, fully connected graph of baselines and changes
Hierarchy constraint	No hierarchical composition
Locking constraint	At least a single node at a time
Distribution constraint	No distribution
Selection action	At most two versions at a time
Concurrency action	Lock/unlock a single node
Evolution action	Store on existing or new branch
Placement action	No placement

4.2 CVS

The policy that CVS uses differs from the policy of RCS in several ways. First, whereas RCS has a pessimistic policy that resolves around the use of locks to prevent con-flicts, CVS has an optimistic policy that relies on the use of merging to resolve con-flicts as they occur. Second, CVS supports the construction of hierarchal artifacts via the use of directories. Directories themselves, however, cannot be versioned.

Table 2 presents the modules one would use to model the policy of CVS using our architecture. Quite a few modules are different from those of the previous policy in Table 1. In particular, the locking constraint module is now void, as is the concurrency action module. Hierarchical composition is enabled, but restricted to single parents in order to only allow a strict tree of hierarchically structured artifacts. In addition, a new storage constraint module is introduced to handle directories, which can only be stored as a single baseline.

The storage constraint module for files remains unchanged, but the accompanying evolution action module has been modified slightly. Rather than automatically creating a branch if a newer version of an artifact exists (if the artifact is a file), the evolution action module will fail and inform the user they have to res olve the conflict. This is in concordance with CVS, which allows parallel work but puts the burden of conflict resolution on those who check in last. Directories are not versioned in CVS, therefore the evolution action module for directories simply replaces the one existing baseline.

Although the number of modules that were changed in comparison with the RCS policy may be surprising, we observe that the development of a module is a relatively simple task. In fact, we plan to have all of the modules discussed thus far available as standard modules distributed as part of the architecture.

Table 2. Policy of CVS as constructed in our architecture

Module	Implementation
Storage constraint	Acyclic, fully connected graph of baselines and changes for files; single baseline for directories
Hierarchy constraint	Hierarchical composition, single parent
Locking constraint	No locking
Distribution constraint	No distribution
Selection action	At most two versions at a time
Concurrency action	No locking
Evolution action	Store on existing branch if no conflict for files; replace existing baseline for directories
Placement action	No placement

Changing from a CVS-like policy to a Subversion-like policy is trivial with our architecture. Simply applying the existing storage constraint module for files to directories turns our CVS implementation into a Subversion implementation. Compared to the scenario presented in Section 1, this is a significant difference in effort.

Similarly, the effort involved in making the CVS policy distributed is also small. Since distribution is orthogonal to the other modules, the other modules are simple reused and do not need to be changed. For instance, to replicate artifacts or move artifacts to the repository closest to a user, one would plug in the appropriate distribution constraint and placement action modules.

4.3 Change Set

The change set policy does not use a version tree, but instead stores individual baselines and changes independently. Individual versions are constructed in the workspace by applying a set of changes to a baseline. Because changes are considered completely independent, locking is not necessary.

Table 3 shows the modules used to construct the change set policy with our architecture. Because the change set policy stores baselines independently from each other, the storage constraint module allows disconnected graphs. Because changes are always based on a baseline, however, the storage constraint module enforces dependencies from changes on baselines. The evolution action module is slightly different from its counterpart for the CVS policy, since it only establishes relationships between changes and the baselines upon which they are based.

Our change set policy reuses the hierarchy constraints from the CVS policy, and similarly has no locking and no concurrency action module. Should distribution be desired, the same distribution constraint and placement action modules can be reused from the CVS policy, showing the strength of our architecture in separating concerns and promoting reuse.

Table 3. Change set policy as constructed in our architecture

Module	Implementation
Storage constraint	Acyclic graph of baselines and changes that depend on baselines
Hierarchy constraint	Hierarchical composition, single parent
Locking constraint	No locking
Distribution constraint	No distribution
Selection action	Arbitrary baselines and changes
Concurrency action	No locking
Evolution action	Store new version as an independent change depending on the baseline
Placement action	No placement

5 Related Work

Several previous projects have explored the issue of easing the development of new configuration management systems. ICE [21], EPOS [8,19], and NUCM [16] were among the first to provide a generic (also called unified) configuration management model upon which to build new configuration management systems. ICE and NUCM, however, have the problem that a configuration management policy is treated as a single monolithic unit. Some reuse is possible, but neither approach explicitly promotes it. The approach of EPOS is better in that regard, since its architecture explicitly separates different parts of a policy in different layers. Due to strong interdependences among the different layers, however, significant amounts of policy reuse remain elusive.

Parisi and Wolf [9] leverage graph transformations as the mechanism for specifying configuration management policies. While certain compositional properties are demonstrated with respect to configuration management policies, the policies they explore are so closely related (e.g., those underneath RCS [12] and CVS [2]) that it is unclear how the approach may apply to more diverse policies (e.g., change set [11]).

Finally, the unified extensional model [1] is an attempt at creating a generic model that is solely tailored towards extensional policies. While advantageous in providing specific support for building such policies, the approach is limited with respect to policy reuse since it focuses on reuse of the model, not policies.

6 Conclusion

We have introduced a new configuration management system architecture that explicitly supports policy reuse. Key to the approach is our treatment of configuration management policies as non-monolithic entities that are modularized into sets of constraint and action modules. We are currently implementing the architecture. While we still have some significant implementation effort in front of us, early results are encouraging in that the architecture can be faithfully implemented and supports policy modularization.

The initial goal of the project is to reduce the time and effort involved in implementing a new configuration management system. Especially when it is not clear which policy is best suited for a particular situation, our architecture has benefits in speeding up the exploration and evaluation process.

In the long term, our architecture has the potential of making significant impact on two long-standing problems in the field of configuration management. First, we believe the architecture is a step forward towards building a configuration management system that can be incrementally adopted. An organization would start with relatively simple policies, but over time relax those policies and introduce more advanced capabilities as the users become more familiar with the system. For instance, the use of branches (a notoriously difficult issue [17]) could initially be prohibited with a restrictive storage constraint module. Later on, when the users have a good understanding of the other aspects of the desired policy, the original storage constraint module is replaced with a storage constraint module that allows the use of branches.

The second problem that the architecture may help to address is that of policy interaction. Existing configuration management systems typically enforce a policy on the client side. Our architecture, on the other hand, enforces policy constraints on the server side. This represents a step towards addressing the problem of policy interaction, since it allows a server to continue to enforce the original policy as associated with an artifact.

Acknowledgements

This research is supported by the National Science Foundation with grant number CCR-0093489. Effort also sponsored by the Defense Advanced Research Projects Agency, Rome Laboratory, Air Force Materiel Command, USAF under agreement numbers F30602-00-2-0599 and F30602-00-2-0608. The U.S. Government is authorized to reproduce and distribute reprints for governmental purposes notwithstanding any copyright annotation thereon. The views and conclusions contained herein are those of the authors and should not be interpreted as necessarily representing the official policies or endorsements, either expressed or implied, of the Defense Advanced Research Projects Agency, Rome Laboratory or the U.S. Government.

References

1. U. Asklund, L. Bendix, H.B. Christensen, and B. Magnusson. *The Unified Extensional Versioning Model*. Proceedings of the Ninth International Symposium on System Configuration Management, 1999: p. 100-122
2. B. Berliner. *CVS II: Parallelizing Software Development*. Proceedings of the USENIX Winter 1990 Technical Conference, 1990: p. 341-352

3. A. Carzaniga. *DVS 1.2 Manual.* Department of Computer Science, University of Colorado at Boulder, 1998

4. R. Conradi and B. Westfechtel, *Version Models for Software Configuration Management.* ACM Computing Surveys, 1998. 30(2): p. 232-282

5. J. Estublier. *Defining and Supporting Concurrent Engineering Policies in SCM.* Proceedings of the Tenth International Workshop on Software Configuration Management, 2001

6. P.H. Feiler. *Configuration Management Models in Commercial Environments.* Software Engineering Institute, Carnegie Mellon University, 1991

7. T. Mens, *A State-of-the-Art Survey on Software Merging.* IEEE Transactions on Software Engineering, 2002. 28(5): p. 449-462

8. B.P. Munch. *Versioning in a Software Engineering Database - the Change-Oriented Way.* Ph.D. Thesis, DCST, NTH, 1993

9. F. Parisi-Presicce and A.L. Wolf. *Foundations for Software Configuration Management Policies using Graph Transformations.* Proceedings of the Third International Conference on Fundamental Approaches to Software Engineering, 2000: p. 304-318

10. M.J. Rochkind, *The Source Code Control System.* IEEE Transactions on Software Engineering, 1975. SE-1(4): p. 364-370

11. Software Maintenance & Development Systems Inc. *Aide de Camp Product Overview.* 1994

12. W.F. Tichy, *RCS, A System for Version Control.* Software - Practice and Experience, 1985. 15(7): p. 637-654

13. Tigris.org, *Subversion,* http://subversion.tigris.org, 2002

14. Tigris.org, *Subversion Frequently Asked Questions,* http://subversion.tigris.org/project_faq.html, 2002

15. A. van der Hoek. *A Generic, Reusable Repository for Configuration Management Policy Programming.* Ph.D. Thesis, University of Colorado at Boulder, Department of Computer Science, 2000

16. A. van der Hoek, A. Carzaniga, D.M. Heimbigner, and A.L. Wolf, *A Testbed for Configuration Management Policy Programming.* IEEE Transactions on Software Engineering, 2002. 28(1): p. 79-99

17. C. Walrad and D. Strom, *The Importance of Branching Models in SCM.* IEEE Computer, 2002. 35(9): p. 31-38

18. A.I. Wang, J.-O. Larsen, R. Conradi, and B.P. Munch. *Improving Coordination Support in the EPOS CM System.* Proceedings of the Sixth European Workshop in Software Process Technology, 1998: p. 75-91

19. B. Westfechtel, B.P. Munch, and R. Conradi, *A Layered Architecture for Uniform Version Management.* IEEE Transactions on Software Engineering, 2001. 27(12): p. 1111-1133

20. D. Wiborg Weber. *Change Sets versus Change Packages: Comparing Implementations of Change-Based SCM.* Proceedings of the Seventh International Workshop on Software Configuration Management, 1997: p. 25-35

21. A. Zeller and G. Snelting, *Unified Versioning through Feature Logic.* ACM Transactions on Software Engineering and Methodology, 1997. 6(4): p. 398-441

Improving Conflict Detection in Optimistic Concurrency Control Models

Ciaran O'Reilly, Philip Morrow, and David Bustard

School of Computing and Information Engineering
University of Ulster, Coleraine
BT52 1SA, Northern Ireland
{ciarano, pj.morrow,dw.bustard}@infc.ulst.ac.uk

Abstract. Configuration Management is required in all software development processes. To support 'agile' methodologies, an approach is desirable that allows developers to work as independently as possible and yet be aware of each other's activities. Optimistic concurrency control provides good support for independent working but is less supportive of communication. This paper looks at the relationship between the optimistic approach and the needs of the agile philosophy. In particular, it examines support facilities provided by the Concurrent Versions System (CVS) and identifies possible improvements in conflict detection to aid communication. The design and construction of a prototype extension to CVS, implementing some of these enhancements, is described.

1 Introduction

Agile methodologies are having an influence on the way that all aspects of software development are now perceived. Cockburn [5] describes the agile approach as a "frame of mind" rather than a fixed set of rules. In essence, it emphasises communication, productiveness and response to change over that of supporting tools, processes, documentation, contracts and planning.

Superficially, software configuration management (SCM)–a control mechanism that is often perceived as bureaucratic–may seem in conflict with the agile approach. In practice, however, many of the functions of SCM [4], [6] are fundamental to all software development processes and are frequently mentioned, or implied, in the literature describing agile techniques [1], [13], [18] and [16]. In particular, because the agile approach involves greater iterative development the need for effective version control is increased.

Version control systems generally take either a pessimistic or optimistic approach to managing concurrent access to shared files [2]. The traditional approach is pessimistic, using some form of reserved checkout model to give sole update access to the person who has checked out a file. Examples of control systems based on this model include MKS [21] and RCS [19].

In contrast, the optimistic approach uses an unreserved checkout model, allowing all files to be modified as local copies, only checking for conflict when the files are committed back to the central version control repository or when updates

B. Westfechtel, A. van der Hoek (Eds.): SCM 2001/2003, LNCS 2649, pp. 191–205, 2003.

from the central repository are applied to a person's local copy. A merge process is then used to handle any conflict detected [8]. Examples of systems supporting the optimistic approach include ClearCase [24] and CVS (Concurrent Versions System) [3].

The distinction between pessimistic and optimistic systems is perhaps not that clear as pessimistic systems can be used in an optimistic way. For example, increased parallel activity can be achieved by using branching [12] or simply maintaining locks on the repository for the time it takes to resolve and check-in changes. As a general rule, however, it is assumed that control systems should be directly supportive of the development process involved, otherwise such tools can be laborious and error prone.

An agile approach to software development requires an optimistic strategy to permit as much independent parallel development as possible [11]. This, however, must also be balanced with another tenet of the agile philosophy, namely that developers should work closely together and be aware of how one person's work affects another. With the optimistic approach, conflict is only detected at the check-in stage, leaving responsibility for merging to the person finding the problem. In addition, the time delay between when a conflict occurs and its detection could be significant. To support the agile philosophy it would be better if potential conflicts could be identified as soon as possible, leaving it to developers to decide how to react. This is particularly important because there is a significant correlation between the number of parallel changes and related defects [17].

This paper considers how the optimistic SCM strategy might be extended to improve communication for agile working. To fix ideas, the work is based on CVS, a popular SCM tool supporting the optimistic model. Section 2 of the paper provides an overview of CVS, summarising its facilities for optimistic concurrency control and identifying where it might be extended to help improve communication. Section 3 presents the design and construction details of the *Night Watch* system, an experimental prototype implementing some of these extensions. Suggestions for future work are included in the conclusion.

2   Extending The Optimistic Model to Aid Communication

There are many version control systems that implement the optimistic concurrency control model. CVS was selected as the representative system for this study because it is open source and freely available. Indeed, it is the most widely used version control system on open source projects [22]. It supports version control, basic workspace management, and provides several hooks to permit customisation within a specific working environment.

2.1   Overview of CVS

CVS actually supports three different models for controlling concurrent access to files. The unreserved and reserved checkout models have already been described above in terms of optimistic and pessimistic mechanisms, with unreserved check-outs being the default. The third model supported is *watches*, which lies between the optimistic and pessimistic methods. Briefly, the watches mechanism permits users to request notification of edit, un-edit and commit actions on files managed by CVS that originate from other users. These requests for notification are made explicitly by each user (*'cvs watch add...' and 'cvs edit...'*), CVS does not provide a mechanism for automatically setting up watches. However, the *'cvs watch add...'* command does permit a user to specify their desired watch policy on a directory which then applies to any artifacts added to the directory, this also applies recursively to subdirectories.

Essentially, *watches* operate the same way as the unreserved checkout model but permit users to be notified of events that indicate potential conflict. Figure 1 and Figure 2 illustrate the use of watches, through a pair of UML sequence diagrams [7]. These figures depict a CVS repository that has been set up to use watches. At the beginning of these two sequences of events, user 'A' and user 'B' have identical working directory copies of the repository on their local machines.

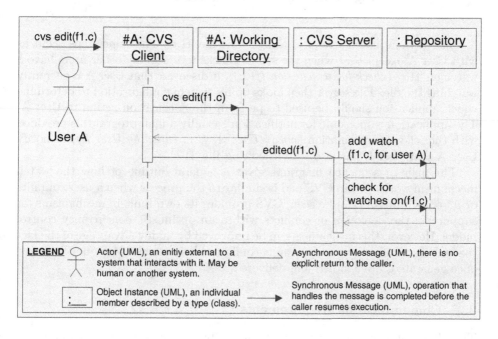

Fig. 1. Sequence diagram of user A's events

User A makes a request to edit the file 'f1.c' (*cvs edit (f1.c)*), which causes the file in User A's working directory to become editable while notifying the server that User A is intending to edit the file (*edited(f1.c)*). The server places a watch in the repository for User A on file 'f1.c' (*add watch(f1.c, for User A)*) and then checks to see if any other users are watching the file (*check for watches on (f1.c)*). At this point no one is doing so.

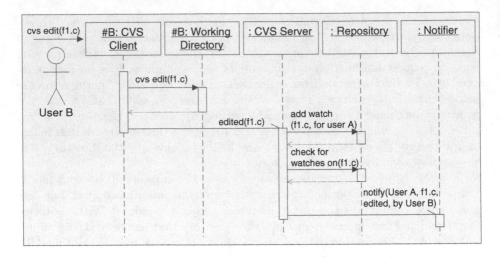

Fig. 2. Sequence diagram of user B's events

User B then makes a request to also edit file 'f1.c'. The same steps occur as with User A except that when the server checks to see if any other users have a watch on 'f1.c' (*check for watches on (f1.c)*), it discovers that User A is currently watching the file. The server then looks up its system configuration to determine which application should be used to perform the notification action to User A. The application responsible for notification (usually a mail program) is provided with the relevant information (*notify(User A, f1.c, edited by User B)*) to notify User A that User B has also started editing file 'f1.c'.

This pair of sequence diagrams gives a general outline of how the watch mechanism works within CVS and is similar to the process when a user commits or un-edits a file. As can be seen, CVS provides its own built-in mechanisms for supporting the detection of conflicts within an optimistic concurrency control model. However, this mechanism can be improved by taking advantage of the fact that CVS's notification mechanism is configurable in terms of how notifications, once generated, are handled and delivered.

2.2   Communication Requirements

The CVS watch facility, if used systematically and correctly goes a significant way towards meeting the needs of SCM for agile development. The main diffi-culty, which is substantial, is assuming that developers will be disciplined and consistent in their use of the facilities provided. Requiring such discipline is also against the spirit of agile development when these responsibilities can be taken away with suitable tool support. That is the approach taken here. The objec-tive is to allow developers to have free access to system components but keep them informed of potential conflicts or possible activity of interest. Relevant events can be either direct or indirect. The direct case is where, for example, two developers modify the same component in parallel. The indirect case concerns knock-on effects. For example, a developer may modify a component that requires other dependent components to be adjusted. In this paper the main focus is on providing automatic notification for direct conflicts and activities of interest, all relating to the basic acts of creating, modifying and deleting files. A 'direct conflict' in the context of this paper is considered to be two or more people working on the same revision of an artifact simultaneously.

In CVS terms, the changes are as follows:

(1) Notification of Change. The effectiveness of CVS's watch mechanism is reduced if the user within a working directory fails to use the edit, un-edit and release commands provided. In this scenario the user changes permissions on files manually or deletes them directly within their working directory. When this is done no notification of these actions is forwarded to the server to inform other interested users that edit or un-edit actions on these files have occurred. This potential gap in receiving events of interest can be closed by monitoring the user's working directory for file updates. If updates occur to files that should have been forwarded to the notification mechanism on the server the local monitor on the working directory can do so. This removes the need to insist that all developers use the edit, un-edit and release commands.

(2) Notification of Creation. The CVS watch mechanism does not have a notification mechanism for files that have not yet been added to the repository. When new work is begun it is possible that two or more developers start working on similar functionality unknowingly within their independent working directories. By monitoring the addition of new files to working directories it may be possible to detect conflicts in advance of the newly developed work being added to the repository.

(3) Self Notification. CVS does not notify users of their own changes. This is based on whether the user name of the person taking the action matches the user name of the person receiving notification [3]. Thus, if the user has multiple working directories they will not be notified of potentially conflicting changes they are making in their separate copies of the repository. Notifying users of all their own changes would address this problem. As the notification component called by CVS is not involved in this decision process the user could receive these types of notifications from components operating within their working directories. These components would also collaborate in determining whether or not conflicts were occurring amongst themselves independently of CVS's mechanisms.

(4) Notification of State. Considering the sequence of events described in Figure 2 it can be seen that an issue exists in terms of who is made aware of the potential for conflict. In this case, User A is notified that User B has edited the file 'f1.c', however, User B was not notified of the fact that User A is already editing the file. It would be preferable that when a user starts working with an

artifact in their workspace that they be brought up to date with respect to the current state of work in other users' workspaces.

The addition of these improvements to CVS's existing conflict detection mechanism would help to greatly reduce the period of time that conflicts remain undetected during parallel development. No additional actions on behalf of the developer are required apart from responding and considering relevant notifications that are provided to them. This helps to reduce the overhead a developer would incur if attempting to perform these types of checks manually.

2.3   Adding Additional Notifications

To support the additional monitoring described in the previous section, our approach is to generate new types of notifications to extend those already provided by CVS. These along with CVS's existing notifications are listed in Table 1, with indications as to which notifications are intended to support the notification cases identified.

   The notifications are derived from the nine different file statuses that CVS specifies that a file can be in within a working directory. These are, *Up to Date*, *Locally Modified*, *Locally Added*, *Locally Removed*, *Needs Checkout*, *Needs Patch*, *Needs Merge*, *Conflicts on Merge* and *Unknown*. The Up to Date status is ignored as it indicates the file within the working directory is identical to that in the repository. The Needs Checkout and Needs Merge file statuses are treated as one type of notification as they are logically equivalent. The Unknown file status is specialised into *Unknown added, removed* and *updated*.

   Scenario one is supported by the Locally Updated, Needs Checkout, Needs Merge and Conflicts on Merge notification types. If, as described in scenario one, an end user fails to use the edit, un-edit and release commands provided by CVS, they will not receive edit and un-edit notifications. However, with the addition of these four notifications, they will be notified of the fact that (a) another user has modified a copy of a file that they themselves have updated or that (b) other users who have updated a file which a user has committed are still inconsistent with the committed revision (the remaining three notifications). All four of these notifications show the state of the modifications that have been made within a user's working directory that notifies other users of actual, ongoing updates to a file of interest.

   Scenario two is supported by the Unknown Added, Unknown Removed and Unknown Updated notification types, all of which are based on CVS's Unknown file status. All of the new notification types support in part the goals of scenarios three and four.

3   Night Watch

Based on the name of CVS's watch facility, *Night Watch* was the name given to the collection of components that were developed to support the scenarios dis-

Table 1. Additional Notification Types

Notification	Scenario	Description
Locally Added	(2), (3, 4)	The file has been added to the working directory, pending commit to the repository.
Locally Removed	(2), (3, 4)	The file has been removed from the working directory, pending commit to the repository.
Locally Updated	(1), (3, 4)	The file in the working directory is based on the head revision in the repository but has been updated in the working directory.
Needs Checkout	(1), (3, 4)	The file in the working directory is not the same revision as the head revision in the repository.
Needs Merge	(1), (3, 4)	Same as 'Needs Checkout' except that the file in the working directory has been updated.
Conflicts on Merge	(1), (3, 4)	A merge was performed on a file in the working directory but conflicts occurred.
Unknown Added	(2), (3, 4)	A file has been added to the working directory that does not exist in the repository.
Unknown Removed	(2), (3, 4)	A file has been removed from the working directory that does not exist in the repository.
Unknown Updated	(2), (3, 4)	A file has been updated in the working directory that does not exist in the repository.
Edit *	N/A	Received when another user edits a file that the recipient is watching.
Un-Edit *	N/A	Received when another user un-edits or releases a file that the recipient is watching.
Commit *	N/A	Received when another user commits a file that the recipient is watching.

*An Existing CVS Watch Notification

cussed. The *Night Watch* system is based on the notion of intelligent agents where emphasis is placed on defining software components that exhibit characteristics of autonomy, reactivity, pro-activeness and social ability [23]. It operates within a loosely coupled federation of cooperating components which makes it easier to introduce its capabilities into a pre-existing software development environment without being overly intrusive on existing infrastructure and processes [15].

3.1   Design Overview

Three main components comprise Night Watch's functionality. They are a *Night Watch Status Monitor* a *Notification Manager* and a *Notification Catcher*. An overview of these components and their dependencies is presented in Figure 3.

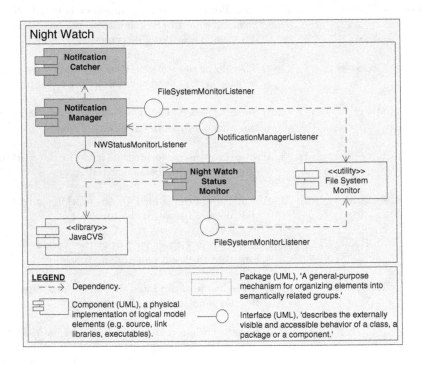

Fig. 3. The Night Watch component model

The Night Watch Status Monitor is a component that runs on each user's development machine, monitoring the working directory using the *File System Monitor* utility (which detects if files are added, removed or updated on the underlying file system). It is responsible for identifying changes within the working directory, checking them with the central repository, and determining if they should be forwarded to a *Notification Manager* associated with the repository. The Notification Manager is responsible for determining from those notifications which should be forwarded to objects that have registered interest in receiving them. Notifications can be received from the CVS repository via standard watch notifications and from the Night Watch Status Monitors with which it is registered.

The final component is the *Notification Catcher*, which is responsible for forwarding notifications received from the CVS Server to the Notification Manager. The CVS Server's generic mechanism for calling an external notification application involves executing a process for each notification and passing information to it via the standard input. It is therefore more appropriate to use a lightweight process (the Notification Catcher) to forward the notifications received to the long lived Notification Manager server process.

3.2   Construction Details

These components have been implemented in the Java programming language using the JavaCVS library [10] to communicate with CVS where appropriate. Each of the components developed follow guidelines presented in the Java Platform's component model specification [9]. To illustrate how the notifications that the Night Watch system supports are implemented, two scenarios are described below, the first detailing how integration with CVS's existing notification mechanism is achieved and the second indicating how the new notifications generated by Night Watch are managed.

Supporting CVS's Existing Notification Mechanism. The point at which the Night Watch System integrates with CVS's watch facility is its notification mechanism. The Notification Catcher and Manager components are responsible for picking up and distributing these existing CVS notifications to the appropriate users via their locally running Night Watch Status Monitors. The Notification Manager is a long lived process as it handles notifications from Night Watch Status Monitors residing on individual developer machines as well as from the CVS Server; therefore receipt of a notification from a CVS Server is delegated to a Notification Catcher. The Notification Manager, when receiving a notification from a Notification Catcher, determines which Night Watch Status Monitors should receive the notification and then forwards it so that the recipient monitors may present the notification to the end user.

Supporting the New Notification Types. The general mechanism by which the additional notifications provided by Night Watch are handled is shown in Figure 4. This indicates how the additional notifications are triggered and distributed.

In this scenario the users initially have identical copies of the repository in their local working directories. User A updates a file 'f1.c' within their working directory (*1: update(f1.c)*). A File System Monitor detects the update to this file and notifies the Night Watch Status Monitor on whose behalf it is acting (*1.1: updated(f1.c)*). The Night Watch Status Monitor obtains the status of the file from the CVS Server (*1.1.1: cvs status(f1.c)*), which indicates that the file is Locally Updated. A Locally Updated event notification is then created by the Night Watch Status Monitor and forwarded to the Notification Manager (*1.1.2: statusNotification(f1.c)*). The Notification Manager checks whether or

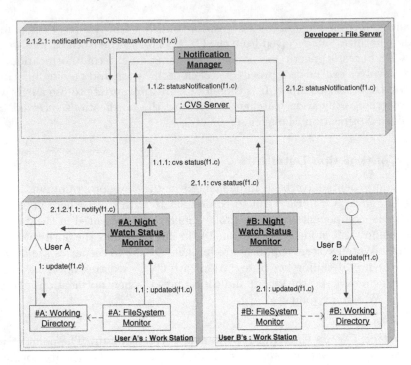

Fig. 4. Collaboration diagram of Night Watch's general notification mechanism

not other Night Watch Status Monitors have indicated activity on an equivalent revision of the file (for this scenario none are detected). User B then updates an equivalent revision of the file 'f1.c' within their own local working directory (*2: update(f1.c)*), following the same sequence of steps as with User A until the Notification Manager detects that other Night Watch Status Monitors have had activity on the file (*2.1.2: statusNotification(f1.c)*). In this instance, User A's Night Watch Status Monitor is noted as having had activity pertaining to the same file. The Notification Manager then notifies the Night Watch Status Monitor that another monitor has had activity against a related revision of file 'f1.c' in their working directory (*2.1.2.1: notificationFromCVSStatusMonitor(f1.c)*). The Night Watch Status Monitor then notifies the end user via an appropriate mechanism (*2.1.2.1.1: notify(f1.c)*) that a conflict has been detected between their work and that of another user. In this way the end-user is only required to address the issue of conflicts being detected as opposed to also being concerned with whether or not conflicting work is occurring.

Managing Notifications. The distribution of notifications is managed by the Notification Manager. For each notification received relating to a revision of an artifact the Notification Manager monitors the state and degree of interest that has been shown across workspaces. The mechanism by which the Notification Manager determines who gets notified is outlined in Figure 5.

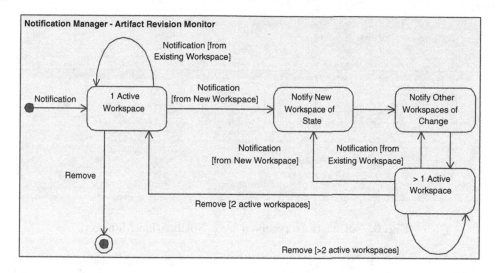

Fig. 5. State transition diagram of how notifications are managed

When a notification is received for a particular revision of an artifact the notification manager sets up a monitor to handle subsequent related notifications. Additional notifications from the same workspace have no impact until another workspace sends a notification related to the same artifact and revision. When this occurs the new workspace is notified of the existing workspace's state of interest in the artifact followed by the existing workspace being notified with the state of the new workspace. This basic mechanism repeats itself until all workspaces have removed interest in receiving notifications related to the specified artifact and revision being monitored.

Night Watch in Action. The following two figures show the Notification Manager and Night Watch Status Monitor notification receipt screens. They emphasise the client server relationship between Night Watch Status Monitors and a Notification Manager.

In addition to receiving notifications from the CVS Servers watch facility, the Notification Manager receives notifications from all Night Watch Status Monitors that have registered with it. It is the responsibility of the Notification Manager to filter these notifications to determine whether or not a conflict has been detected across developer workspaces. On detection of a conflict an appropriate notification is forwarded to the applicable Night Watch Status Monitors that are monitoring the workspaces in which the conflict was detected.

Figure 7 shows notifications received by a Night Watch Status Monitor from a Notification Manager. Each of these notifications is an indication of possible conflicts across workspaces. This figure highlights the two types of notifications and also the differences in details that can be forwarded by a Notification Manager. That is, those that originated originally from a CVS Server (top half of

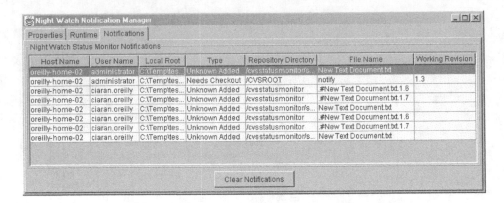

Fig. 6. Notifications received by a Notification Manager

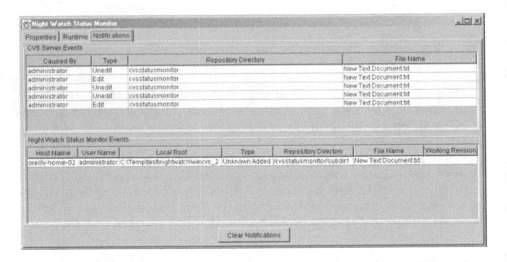

Fig. 7. Notifications received by a Night Watch Status Monitor

Figure 7) and those that originated from other Night Watch Status Monitors that show activities against the same files as the receiving Night Watch Status Monitor.

It can be seen from Figure 7 that the information contained in the notifications from a CVS Server are missing the host name, local root and working revision details which are present on the Night Watch Status Monitor notifications (the CVS Server does not provide this information when calling a notifier). This difference in information is related to scenario *'(3) Self Notification'* outlined in Section 2.2, which to support properly requires this additional information to correctly identify the workspaces and related artifacts involved.

4   Related Work

The work presented here is similar to that of Sarma and van der Hoek [20] with respect to their discussion of non-intrusively breaking the isolation of workspaces by observing check-in and check-out actions. Their work is broader in that it addresses issues related to presentation and indirect conflicts. It also contains a relevant discussion of related work in the field of Computer Supported Cooperative Work (CSCW). The main difference with our work, is in the granularity of the notifications received from a workspace. The work presented here explores the use of finer grain notifications in order to detect potential conflicts as early as possible.

More closely related work with respect to granularity of notifications is that of Molli et al. [14]. The main difference that exists between the level of granularity of notifications supported, is that here, support for artifacts that do not already exist within the repository is considered.

5   Conclusions

All software tools are intended to provide support for stated or assumed ways of working. In providing SCM support for the emerging agile philosophy the two main concerns are to help maximise independent working while at the same time keeping everyone informed of relevant activity by others. This paper has described a first step towards providing such support. It takes the optimistic strategy for SCM as its starting point, extending CVS with Night Watch. This provides automatic monitoring and notification facilities to report relevant file changes to collaborative developers.

Night Watch avoids the need for users to identify their interests or activities explicitly and so helps support independent working. It also aids communication by keeping everyone informed of file changes that may be relevant to them. An evaluation of Night Watch has not yet been conducted to determine how beneficial its usage is within a cooperative development environment. However, based on the observations documented in [17] and the authors' own experiences it is believed that during the phases of architectural flux, implementation of cross-cutting concerns and maintenance, the degree of conflict and miscommunication experienced by developers is significant enough to warrant the need for such a mechanism.

Night Watch is part of a loosely coupled federation of cooperating components where registration of interest and distribution of events is handled by the underlying infrastructure. The advantage of this approach is that it permits new features to be developed independently and then integrated into the CVS environment. However, Night Watch itself is coupled to CVS in its conception and implementation. If it were to be used with another SCM system CVS's watch mechanism would need to be subsumed by Night Watch's notifications either by adding them or inferring their existence from existing notification types (e.g. an edit is treated as a locally updated notification). Secondly, some of Night Watch's notification types may need to be re-cast (e.g. Locally Added and Removed notifications may be unsupportable across SCMs). Finally, in order to obtain the status of an artifact from an SCM system a customized adapter would need to be built for each system. As long as the SCM system uses the underlying filesystem to store individual artifacts the trigger mechanism for deriving notifications should be sufficient.

Night Watch provides good support for direct changes. The next stage of development will be to consider indirect semantic dependencies among components. This will generate additional notifications reporting possible knock-on effects and provide more targeted information on the nature of the changes that have occurred. This is obviously a difficult area to handle generally as it is substantially dependent on the nature of the components under SCM control.

Another important area of development is in the presentation of information to developers. As the Night Watch system considers each change to an artifact within a workspace as a trigger for generating a notification, multiple notifications relating to the same artifact can be generated from the same source. This needs to be made more flexible to allow developers to tune the type of notification provided to their individual tastes, in a non-obtrusive way. Semantic analysis will also enable a greater filtering of notifications. Throughout, the agile philosophy will be used as a guiding influence on the design and assessment of this work.

Acknowledgements

The authors are very grateful for the detailed constructive comments from the anonymous referees. The development of this paper was supported by the Centre for Software Process Technologies (CSPT), funded by Invest NI through the Centres of Excellence Programme, under the EU Peace II initiative.

References

1. Abrahamsson, P., Salo, O., Ronkainen, J., Warsta, J.: Agile Software Development Methods. [Online]. Available:
   http://www.inf.vtt.fi/pdf/publications/2002/P478.pdf [2002, Nov 27]
2. Bischofberger, W.R., Matzel, K.U., Kleinferchner, C.F.: Evolving a Programming Environment Into a Cooperative Software Engineering Environment. Proceedings of CONSEG 95 (1995)
3. Cederqvist, P., et al.: Version Management with CVS for CVS 1.11.2. [Online]. Available: http://www.cvshome.org/docs/manual/ [2002, Nov 7]
4. Clemm, G., Conradi, R., van der Hoek, A., Tichy, W., Wiborg-Weber, D., Estublier, J. (ed.), Leblang, D. (co-ed.): Impact of the Research Community for the Field of Software Configuration Management. Proceedings of the 24th International Conference on Software Engineering (2002) 634–644
5. Cockburn, A.: Agile Software Development. Pearson Education, Inc., United States of America (2002)

6. Dart, S.: Concepts in Configuration Management Systems. Proceedings of the 3rd International Workshop on Software Configuration Management (1991) 1–18

7. Eriksson, H.E., Penker, M.: UML Toolkit. John Wiley & Sons, Inc., United States of America (1998)

8. Estublier, J.: Software Configuration Management: A Roadmap. International Conference of Software Engineering - Proceedings of the Conference on The Future of Software Engineering (2000) 279–289

9. JavaBeans API Specification. [Online]. Available: http://java.sun.com/products/javabeans/docs/spec.html/ [2002, Nov 7]

10. JavaCVS. [Online]. Available: http://javacvs.netbeans.org/ [2002, Nov 27]

11. Lovaasen, G.: Brokering with eXtreme Programming. 2001 XP Universe Conference Papers. [Online]. Available: http://www.xpuniverse.com/2001/pdfs/EP201.pdf [2002, Nov 27]

12. MacKay, S.A.: The State of the Art in Concurrent, Distributed Configuration Management. Proceedings of the 5th International Workshop on Software Configuration Management (1995)

13. Millington, D., Stapleton, J.: Developing a RAD Standard. IEEE Software, Vol. 12 Issue. 5 (1995) 54–55

14. Molli, P., Skaf-Molli, H., Bouthier, C.: State Treemap: an Awareness Widget for Multi-Synchronous Groupware. Proceedings of the Seventh Intenational Workshop on Groupware (2001)

15. O'Reilly, C.: Proactive Cooperative Software Development with Visualisation. MSc Disseration, University of Ulster Coleraine (2002)

16. Paulk, N.C.: Extreme programming from a CMM Perspective. IEEE Software, Vol. 18 Issue. 6 (2001) 19–26

17. Perry, D.E., Siy, H.P., Votta, L.G.: Parallel Changes in Large-Scale Software Development: An Observational Case Study. ACM Transactions of Software Engineering and Methodology (TOSEM), Vol. 10 Issue. 3 (2001) 308–337

18. Pollice, G.: Using the Rational Unified Process for Small Projects: Expanding upon eXtreme Programming. [Online]. Available: http://www.rational.com/media/products/rup/tp183.pdf [2002, Nov 27]

19. RCS Man Pages. [Online]. Available: ftp://ftp.cs.purdue.edu/pub/RCS/rcs-5.7.tar.Z [2002, Nov 27]

20. Sarma, A., van der Hoek, A.: Palantir: Coordinating Distributed Workspaces. Proceedings of the Workshop on Cooperative Supports for Distributed Software Engineering Processes (CSSE) (2002)

21. Source Integrity Enterprise Edition User Guide. [Online]. Available: http://www.mks.com/support/productinfo/docs/SIE83_UserGuide.pdf [2002, Nov 27]

22. van der Hoek, A.: Configuration Management and Open Source Projects. Proceedings of the 3rd International Workshop on Software Engineering over the Internet (2000)

23. Wooldridge, M.J.: Agent-Based Software Engineering. IEEE Proceedings of Software Engineering. Vol. 144 Issue. 1 (1997) 26–37

24. Working in Base ClearCase. [Online]. Available (Requires Rational Membership): http://www.rational.com/docs/v2002/cc/cc_dev.win.pdf [2002, Nov 27]

Data Topology and Process Patterns
for Distributed Development

Darcy Wiborg Weber

Telelogic Technologies North America
9401 Jeronimo Road
Irvine, CA 92618
darcy@telelogic.com

Abstract. This paper describes data topology patterns and development process patterns for distributed development across multiple locations and teams. It describes the strengths and weaknesses of these patterns and for which types of software project they are well suited. It also provides brief case studies for several companies who have implemented these patterns. Finally, the paper provides some best practices for distributed development based on the lessons learned in the case studies.

1 Introduction

Distributed development is the process of developing software in multiple locations, possibly with multiple teams. In the context of this paper, distributed development also refers to the process of tracking change requests across multiple locations and multiple teams, since software change management is an integral part of advanced software configuration management.

This paper discusses patterns found in the data topology for distributed development. A pattern is a model for a solution to a particular type of problem. In object-oriented software development, the word pattern describes a standard way of documenting a solution, including its strengths and weaknesses [1]. In this paper, the term pattern is used more loosely; it describes solutions for distributed development and discusses their strengths and weaknesses, but does not use a standard format for describing them.

First, different types of software development are described; then patterns for data topology and distributed development methodologies are discussed. Finally, this paper documents several case studies of companies doing distributed development using Telelogic tools [2].

The following assumptions are made about distributed development:

- The term *repository* (or database) refers to the physical location of the data. Although there is a notion of a virtual repository [3], data can be distributed between different physical repositories.
- A repository has full versioning and CM capabilities for different types of data.

B.Westfechtel, A. van der Hoek (Eds.): SCM 2001/2003, LNCS 2649, pp. 206-216, 2003.
© Springer-Verlag Berlin Heidelberg 2003

- Not all of the data in one repository needs to be distributed. For example, part of the data in repository A may be only in database A, part may be distributed to repository B, part to repository C, and both parts to repository D. This concept is shown in Figure 1.
- Although a specific version of an object or file can be modified in only one repository at a time, dat a shared between two repositories can be updated in both locations. For example, users can check out parallel versions of the same file in two different repositories.
- Distribution of changes between two databases can be uni-directional or bi-directional.
- Software change management (i.e., change requests) can be distributed, as well as the software itself [4].

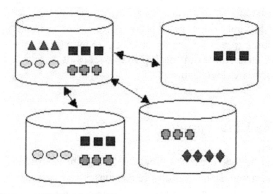

Fig. 1. Granular data distribution

2   Types of Software Development

Several different types of team interaction or collaboration are common in software development. This paper refers to two broad categories as co-development and component development.

2.1   Co-Development

Multiple developers collaborate on a common set of source files to develop the same software. Note that this characteristic does not imply that all of the developers are in the same location or physical repository.

2.2   Component Development

The software is split into components or modules that can be reused. A team (or individual) is responsible for the development of a component, and teams may use components developed by others. Component sharing has several forms [5]:

Black Box Components
Only the end products are published for use by other developers or teams; examples of black box components include an executable, a DLL, or a jar file. A black box component may also include some configuration files or include files that are needed to configure or access the functionality of the component.

Source Components
Rather than publishing only the end products, some teams share components as source code. The entire source tree is reused by other developers or teams.

The patterns and case studies in the following sections are discussed in the context of these types of software development.

3   Patterns for Data Topology

Data topology describes the locations where project data is stored; for example, it can be stored in a single database or in multiple databases.

The following patterns are common for data topology: single repository and multiple repositories. The multiple repository pattern can be further broken down into two topologies: point-to-point, and hub-and-spoke [2].

3.1   Single Repository

The simplest case is the one where all of a team's project data is stored in a single repository. This pattern is a good fit for a team who is located in a single location or remote team members have high-speed network access (e.g., distance working) [6].

This pattern may be necessary if the team is using a CM tool that does not support distributed development. The benefit of this pattern is low cost of administration.

3.2   Multiple Repositories

Data is transferred between multiple discrete repositories. This pattern is appropriate if some team members reside in locations that do not have high-speed network access or do not even share a network This pattern is a good fit for teams who are doing black box component development; since they can distribute only the components without the source, there is less data to transfer and little need for collaboration on source code. However, this pattern can also be used for co-development.

Multiple repositories have a higher cost of administration, since the replication between repositories must be planned and managed.

Teams who distribute data across multiple repositories have the choice of several topologies for data transfer: point-to-point, and hub-and-spoke. [2]

Point-to-Point

Data is transferred directly between repositories as needed. This method is flexible and is the quickest technique for data propagation. This method is well suited for co-development of the same software in different locations, since changes can be transferred quickly. However, this method does not scale well for distribution between many repositories. An example of the point-to-point data topology is shown in Figure 2.

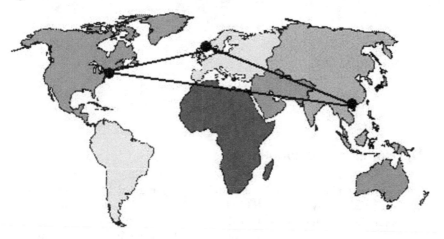

Fig. 2. Point-to-point data topology

Hub-and-Spoke

Data is transferred between development repositories ("spokes") via central repositories ("hubs"). With this method, it may take longer for data to be propagated between two spoke databases, since the data must go through the hub. However, this method is easier to manage, especially for teams with a large number of databases. The hub and spoke topology is well-suited for component sharing and reuse, since the hub repositories provide a good way to organize a central repository of components that may have been developed by different teams in different repositories [2].

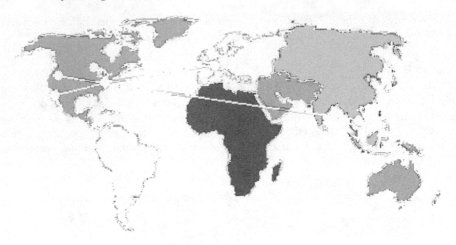

Fig. 3. Hub-and spoke data topology

4   Development Methodology

The CM repository and CM policies are often tightly coupled [7]. Although the end users may not necessarily be aware of the details, the CM administrator must be aware of methodologies for distributing the data between databases, referred to here are the development methodology. Several different development methodologies can be used for distributing data to remote databases: master-and-satellite, publish-and-subscribe, and point-to-point.

4.1   Master-and-Satellite

With the master-and-satellite methodology, components are developed by different teams in different repositories, but must be built, tested, and released together. This methodology might be used for outsourcing, co-located groups, or distributed groups. [6] One repository is designated as the master where components are collected for build, test, and release. The hub-and-spoke data topology is a good fit with this methodology, where the master repository is the hub. [2]

The point-to-point data topology can also be used with the master-and-satellite methodology, as long as the flow of data is well defined. For example, one team may develop component X in database A and transfer component X to database B. In database B, another team develops component Y, and then transfers components X and Y to database C, where the final product is build, tested, and released.

Note that the data transfers may happen only at specific milestones such as once a week, or on an ongoing basis so that the most recent version of a component is available in all databases.

4.2   Publish-and-Subscribe

In the publish-and-subscribe methodology, centralized repositories are set up to contain components. Components are developed and tested in development repositories, then published to a centralized repository. Other repositories subscribe to reuse those components [5]. Again, the hub-and-spoke topology is a good fit, where the centralized repository is the hub [2].

Some development sites that use the publish-and-subscribe methodology have multiple centralized repositories; the topology may be a mix of hub-and-spoke and point-to-point. For example, consider a site with three central component repositories: repository B in Boston, repository L in London, and repository M in Mumbai, India. In addition, each of these three locations has several local databases where different components are developed; the components are published to the local central repository. In turn, the three central repositories exchange components so that all components are available at all sites.

4.3   Point-to-Point

With the point-to-point methodology, software is exchanged between repositories as needed. Each repository builds and tests its own software. The point-to-point methodology is a good fit for distributed groups who are co-developing the same source code; however, this methodology does not scale well as the number of databases increases [2].

5   Case Studies

The following case studies describe teams using Telelogic tools for different types of development. The case studies include examples of the various repository topologies and methodologies described earlier.

5.1   Case Study 1: Single Application Development

Company A develops a commercial software application that is released every 6 to 12 months. The software is organized into components, and is contained in three development repositories: one for the server, one for the client, and one for the business logic. Additionally, the team has an installation repository for gathering the components to build and release the full software application. This installation repository is the hub, collecting component data from the other three repositories as spokes.

In addition, company A has a remote development site in another location. Portions of the server and business logic repositories are replicated between the two locations for co-development. The primary location uses the hub-and-spoke topology, while the server and business logic repositories use the point-to-point topology for sharing data with the remote server and business logic repositories. The data topology is shown in Figure 4.

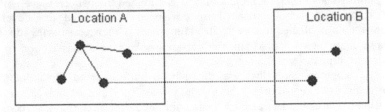

Fig. 4. Repository topology for case study 1

As developers work, the latest changes to the source code are automatically transferred between the peer repositories in different locations every night, prior to the nightly build and integration test. As a part of the automated nightly build process, components in Location A are updated with the latest changes and built in the three local development repositories, then the resulting products (libraries, executables, jar files, configuration files, etc.) are transferred from the local development repositories to the installation repository (i.e., the hub), and packaged for testing.

In addition, the source code is sometimes transferred between the peer repositories in different locations on demand, when the developers need to access each other's recent changes.

This topology and methodology works well for this team. The point-to-point transfer between the peer repositories is flexible and keeps them synchronized, while the hub-and-spoke transfer between the development repositories and the installation repository enables the product to be built and packaged cleanly.

The only problem reported by this team is the occasional occurrence of parallel versions between the peer repositories if developers in different locations should both check out the same file on the same day without knowledge of each other's changes. (The developers are notified when the parallel versions are transferred; however, if the parallel versions were not merged before the end of the day, the nightly build may not include all necessary changes.) This sometimes costs the team one day's delay in integration testing. However, the problem does not occur often because the team is well coordinated.

Lessons Learned

Lessons learned from case study 1 include:

- When co-developing the same source code in distributed repositories, it is important to have a frequent or flexible (i.e., on demand) transfer mechanism because developers often need to see each other's changes.
- If developers change [different versions of] the same code in multiple databases, parallel reporting is critical.
- Distributed development between different locations carries some administrative overhead and can result in occasional project delays that would not occur if all users were local to the same site

- It is a good idea to plan the data topology with the team's development methodology in mind.

5.2   Case Study 2: Component Development in Centralized Repositories

Company B develops embedded software. The company continually releases many different products, but reuses components extensively to build those products. They have development sites in many countries around the world, and have many centralized repositories for storing components. Individual teams publish components to the centralized repositories when the components pass testing. Other teams subscribe to reuse components from the centralized repositories; those components are transferred to their local repositories for reuse.

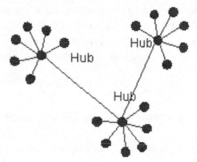

Fig. 5. Repository topology for case study 2

Each team who develops a component is responsible to test and document it before publishing it to the centralized repository. Sometimes the subscriber teams modify the components and publish new versions. It is possible to have many versions of the same component, some published by different teams.

Some of the centralized repositories contain certain types of components, while others are copies, replicated for local network access in a particular location. Each centralized repository acts as a hub to many spoke repositories. For example, a team develops component R1, and publishes it to the local hub. In turn, R1 is propagated to other hubs, where developers in local databases can subscribe to it.

Data transfers between the hubs (central repositories) and spokes (development repositories) are on demand, as components are published or requested. Data transfers between the central repositories and their replicated copies are automated to occur at frequent intervals. Note that the transfers are bi-directional, rather than a master-slave relationship. Spoke repositories can publish to their local copy of the repository, and the new data is replicated to the other copy (and vice versa).

This topology and methodology works well for this team. The primary issue was defining a process for development teams to be able to find the software components to which they want to subscribe. The company solved this by implementing standards for naming and publishing components.

It is worth noting that this company has been developing this topology and methodology for many years, and that they originally started with a point-to-point topology, then moved to a single global hub-and-spoke topology, and finally developed into the combination hub -and-spoke and point-t o-point topology that they use today.

Lessons Learned

Lessons learned from case study 2 include:

- When dealing with many databases on a global scale, it is more efficient to set up multiple local hubs and exchanging data between them. This topology results in more duplicated data, but maximizes performance for local teams and minimizes dependencies on wide area networks.
- Data moves through hub databases more slowly than it does through point -to-point transfers.
- Transfers for component development are less time critical than for co-development, since developers do not need to see each other's ongoing changes. (There are few issues of parallel development in component development.)
- Companies doing component development must consider a standard process for naming and publishing components in order for other teams to find and identify components for reuse.

5.3   Case Study 3: Point -to-Point Software Development

Company C develops network software. They have small development teams in three locations. Each team has a local repository where they develop portions of the code. Some of the code is co-developed by all teams and shared between all repositories, while some code is local to a particular repository.

Fig. 6. Repository Topology for Case Study 3

The data is transferred between repositories continually. New changes are immediately transferred to the other repositories that share the code. Each team is responsible for building certain products.

This process works well for the team; however, they may find that the point-t o-point model does not scale well as they grow and decide to add more sites that reuse most of the same software.

Lessons Learned

Lessons learned from case study 3 include:

- The point-to-point data topology is the best method for getting changes to other sites quickly. A hub-and-spoke model where data needed to pass through one database to another would result in a delay that this team cannot accept.
- As seen in case study 1, if developers change [different versions of] the same code in multiple databases, parallel reporting is critical.

6   Conclusions

Through working with companies who implemented distributed development using various data topologies and methodologies, Telelogic has identified the following best practices [2].

- Plan ahead. A team should consider the following questions when setting up repositories.
  - ➢ How many repositories do you need?
  - ➢ What is the primary purpose of each repository?
  - ➢ Which data will be shared between repositories, and which data is not shared?
  - ➢ Which repository is the master for each set of shared data?
  - ➢ How often is data transferred and what technique is used? (I.e., is it automated or manual, via LAN, WAN, FTP, etc.?)
  - ➢ How is the software tested and built in each repository?
  - ➢ How will the software development requirements change in the coming years, and how will the distributed development process need to scale?
- Use point-to-point repositories when timeliness of data transfer is important.
- Use centralized repositories or hubs in order to scale up to sharing data between large numbers of databases and to maximize performance for local teams. Point-to-point distribution does not scale well with a large number of databases that share the same files, since the number of transfers increases exponentially with each additional database.
- For component reuse, consider setting up standards to organize and name components in a way that makes them easy to find and reuse.
- Teams who are co-developing software in multiple locations should test their local changes before they are incorporated in the master build. In addition, teams may want to be insulated from other teams' changes until they choose to include them.
- For any distributed development project, factor in some extra time for administrative overhead. Be aware that distributed development between different locations can result in project delays that would not occur if all users were local to the same site.

References

1. S. Berczuk. *Configuration Management Patterns.* Proceedings of the 1996 Pattern Languages of Programs Conference. Washington University Technical Report #WUCS-97-07. Available online at http://world.std.com/~berczuk/pubs/PloP9/plop96.html.
2. Telelogic. Distributed CM Guide. 2002.
3. J. Noll and W. Scacchi. Supporting Distributed Configuration Management in Virtual Enterprises. In Proceedings of SCM7 – International Workshop on Software Configuration Management, R. Conradi (Ed.), Boston, MA, USA, May 1997. LNCS, Springer.
4. Telelogic. Distributed ChangeSynergy. 2002.
5. D. Weber. A Framework for Managing Component Development. Available online at http://www.telelogic.com.
6. U. Asklund, B. Magnusson, and A. Persson. Experiences: Distributed Development and Software Configuration Management. In Proceedings of SCM9 – International Workshop on Software Configuration Management, J. Estublier (Ed.), Toulouse, France, September 1999. LNCS, Springer.
7. A. van der Hoek, D. Heimbigner, and A. L. Wolf. A Generic, Peer-to-Peer Repository for Distributed Configuration Management. In Proceedings of the 18th International Conference on Software Engineering. Berlin, Germany, March 1996.

Managing the Evolution of Distributed and Interrelated Components

Sundararajan Sowrirajan and André van der Hoek

School of Information and Computer Science
University of California, Irvine
Irvine, CA 92697-3425 USA
{ssowrira,andre}@ics.uci.edu

Abstract. Software systems are increasingly being built by integrating pre-existing components developed by different, geographically distributed organizations. Each component typically evolves independently over time, not only in terms of its functionality, but also in terms of its exposed interfaces and dependencies on other components. Given that those other components may also evolve, creating an application by assembling sets of components typically involves managing a complex web of evolving dependencies. Traditional configuration management systems assume a form of centralized control that simply does not suffice in these situations. Needed are new configuration management systems that span multiple organizations, operate in a distributed and decentralized fashion, and help in managing the consistent evolution of independently developed, inter-related sets of components. A critical aspect of these new configuration management systems is that they must respect the different levels of autonomy, privacy, and trust that exist among different organizations. In this paper, we introduce TWICS, an early example of such a new configuration management system. Key aspects of TWICS are that it maintains traditional configuration management functionality to support the development of individual components, but integrates policy-driven deployment functionality to support different organizations in evolving their inter-related components.

1 Introduction

Component-based software development has perhaps received the most attention of any kind of software development method to date [13,21]. Based on the premise of component reuse, the hypothesis is that application assembly out of pre-existing components brings with it significant savings in terms of time and cost [26].

While much effort has been put towards developing component technologies via which individual components can be implemented and subsequently assembled into applications (e.g., .NET [18], EJB [7], CORBA [17]), tool support for component-based software development has lagged behind. Exceptions exist (e.g., design notations such

B.Westfechtel, A. van der Hoek (Eds.): SCM 2001/2003, LNCS 2649, pp. 217-230, 2003.

as UML [20], component repositories such as ComponentSource [4], and composition environments such as Component Workbench [16]), but more often than not it is still assumed that existing tools suffice in their present incarnations.

Configuration management systems suffer from this misperception. Although well equipped to support the needs of traditional software development, it has been recognized that they do not meet the unique demands of component-based software development [12,29]. The assumption of centralized control underlying current configuration management systems is at the core of this problem. Since different components typically are developed by different organizations in different geographical locations, centralized control cannot be enforced.

Needed is a new kind of configuration management system that explicitly supports component-based software development. Such a configuration management system must span multiple organizations, operate in a distributed and decentralized fashion, and help in managing the consistent evolution of independently developed, interrelated sets of components. For a component producer, this means that the configuration management system must support development and publication of components. For a component consumer, this means that the configuration management system must support the organization in obtaining components from other organizations, controlling the local evolution of the obtained components independent from their remote schedules of new releases, and publishing its own components with appropriate documentation of their dependencies. In essence, the configuration management system must integrate traditional configuration management functionality with what is known as software deployment functionality: automatically publishing, releasing, and obtaining components and their dependencies [10].

In this paper, we introduce TWICS (Two-Way Integrated Configuration management and Software deployment), an early example of a configuration management system specifically designed to address component-based software development. TWICS is built as a layer on top of Subversion, an existing open source configuration management system that supports the traditional code development paradigm [24]. TWICS adds a component-oriented interface and wraps all the Subversion commands to operate on components as a whole rather than individual source files. Moreover, TWICS adds deployment functionality in the form of an interface through which the release of components and their dependencies can be controlled, and through which remote components can be downloaded and placed in the local repository. Finally, TWICS respects the different levels of autonomy, privacy, and trust that may exist among different organizations. To do so, it allows individual organizations to establish and enforce policies that govern such issues as to whether a component can be obtained in binary or source form and whether a component may be redistributed by other organizations.

The remainder of the paper is organized as follows. In Section 2 we discuss a typical component-based software development scenario and illustrate the difficult issues that it poses for a traditional configuration management system. Section 3 provides a brief background on the disciplines of configuration management and software deployment, which form the basis for our overall approach described in Section 4. Then, in Section 5, we describe the detailed capabilities of TWICS. We conclude with an outlook at our future work in Section 6.

2   Example Scenario

To exemplify the issues raised by component-based development for a traditional configuration management system, consider the scenario depicted in Figure 1. Grey boxes represent different organizations, ovals components developed by each organization, and arrows dependencies among the components. The organization SPELLONE, for example, develops two different components: SPELLCHECKER and DOCFORMATTER. The component SPELLCHECKER depends on the component DICTIONARY as developed by the organization GRAMMAR. The component DICTIONARY has no further dependencies, but the component SPELLCHECKER is used by the component DOC-PROCESSOR as developed by the organization POWERDOC. Many more component dependencies exist, creating an intricate web of distributed, inter-dependent components. Note the use of version identifiers: since each individual component evolves independently from the other components, dependencies must be on a per-version basis.

A first challenge arises because some components may be available solely in binary format, some in source code format, and others maybe even in both. In the case of source code, an organization that obtains such a component may make some local modifications to the component. As newer versions of the component become available, the local changes must be carefully combined with the changes by the original developer in order not to lose any functionality. For example, POWERDOC may be using a locally modified version of GRAMMAR version 2.3. As GRAMMARCORP puts out a new version of the component, version 2.4, POWERDOC must obtain that new version, bring it into the local configuration management system, and ensure that its local changes are integrated in the new version.

A second challenge arises when an organization decides to release its component. At that point, its dependencies on other components must be precisely documented such that anyone obtaining the component knows which other additional components it must obtain. In some cases, an organization may simply document the dependencies. In other cases, it may include the dependencies as part of its release. In yet other cases, a mixed approach may be followed. In all cases, however, it is critical that the dependencies, which may be both direct and indirect, are precisely documented. In the case of POWERDOC, it has to include all of the dependencies of DOCPROCESSOR 2.1, which indeed spans all components by all four organizations in our example. Clearly, this is a non-trivial and error-prone task that often has to be performed manually.

A third challenge arises when organizations have different trust policies between them. A component producer can choose to provide different types of access permissions (source code access or binary access) and redistribution permissions for its components to different component consumers. For example, GRAMMARCORP might be willing to share the source code of its DICTIONARY version 1.0 component with SPELLONE, but may be willing to provide only the binary of GRAMMAR version 2.3 component to POWERDOC. On the other hand, GRAMMARCORP may be willing to allow redistribution of GRAMMAR version 2.3 by POWERDOC, but may not provide similar privileges to SPELLONE for DICTIONARY VERSION 1.0. Clearly, there should be a means for expressing such trust policies between companies and such policies must be incorporated as part of the component's deployment package to ensure they are adhered to.

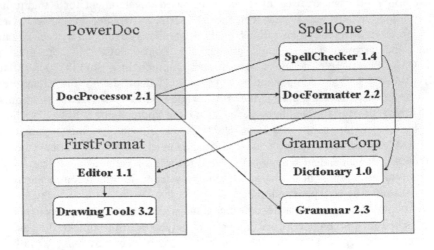

Fig. 1. Example scenario of component-based software development

The above challenges are summarized by the following four questions:

- How can components that are developed by external organizations be efficiently incorporated into the local development environment?

- How can the remote evolution of those components and their influence on the locally developed software systems be controlled?

- How can a component-based software system be effectively deployed as a consistent set of inter-related components?

- How can the issues of autonomy, privacy, and trust of the various organizations be preserved throughout this process?

While it is clear that the availability of a separate configuration management system and a separate software deployment system help in addressing these questions, we observe that a single system that integrates configuration management and software deployment functionality would be more desirable. Such a system, for example, can automatically place deployment information regarding which components were obtained from which other organizations in the local configuration management system. That information can then be used to support the release of a component that depends on those components. TWICS is such a system, and is specifically designed to support scenarios like these.

3 Background

TWICS builds upon work of two areas, namely configuration management and software deployment. We discuss relevant contributions in each of these areas below.

3.1 Configuration Management

Many configuration management systems have been built to date [3,5]. All share the same basic goal: to manage the evolution of artifacts as they are produced in the software life cycle. Most current configuration management systems still follow the model introduced by early systems such as RCS [23] and CVS [2]. Artifacts are locally stored in a repository, can be accessed and modified in a workspace, and, if modified, are stored back in the repository as a new version. To manage concurrent changes, either a pessimistic approach (locking) or an optimistic approach (merging [14]) is used.

Two particular shortcomings of current configuration management systems make it difficult for these systems to support configuration management for component-based software. First, current configuration management systems are very much focused on managing files. While system models have been devised that operate at a higher-level of abstraction [8,9,27], principled use of these system models requires users to manually map them onto source code.

The second shortcoming lies in the fact that current configuration management systems assume centralized control regarding the evolution of artifacts. Only two systems provide support for external components. The first, CM/Synergy [22], provides vendor code management for automatically incorporating new versions of source code from an external source. Similarly, auto bundle [6] supports the incorporation of external components in a local configuration management system and even supports packaging of a resulting set of components.

Both systems are clearly a step in the right direction with respect to the problem of managing component-based software development. However, CM/Synergy only solves one aspect of the problem, namely the incorporation of other components into the local environment. Subsequent deployment is not supported. Similarly, auto bundle assumes that only source code is shared among different organizations. Neither system addresses the different needs of autonomy, privacy, and trust as required by different collaboration policies.

3.2 Software Deployment

Software deployment is concerned with the post-development phase of a software product's lifecycle [10]. In particular, a software deployment system typically supports the activities of packaging, releasing, installing, configuring, updating, and adapting (as well as their counterparts of unreleasing, uninstalling, etc.). Most software deployment systems nowadays inherently support component-based software and handle dependencies among components. Popular examples of such systems are Install-Shield [11], NetDeploy [15], and Tivoli [25].

For our purposes, however, most of these systems fall short in providing the necessary functionality. In particular, dependencies must be manually specified, they often assume all components are released by a single organization, and they provide limited support for managing multiple versions of a single component. SRM [28], the Software Dock [10], and RPM [1,19] are examples of systems that address these shortcomings. They explicitly support distributed and decentralized organization in releasing their components, and also include support for managing different versions of those components. Unfortunately, these software deployment systems operate in a vacuum: they are not connected to a configuration management system. This is detrimental in two ways: (1) they cannot obtain components from the configuration management system to release them and (2) they cannot "install" components into the configuration management system to bring them into the development environment. As a result, much manual effort is still required.

4   Approach

The key insight underlying our approach is depicted in Figure 2. Rather than a traditional model in which a component is first developed in a configuration management system and then deployed using a *separate* software deployment system, our approach is based upon a model in which a single configuration management system integrally supports both the development of a component and its deployment to other organizations. This allows both types of functionality to take advantage of each other and provides users with a single, integrated solution.

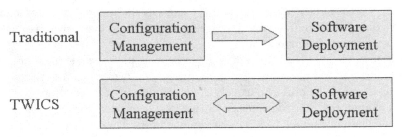

Fig. 2. Traditional separation of CM and deployment functionality versus TWICS

To support this integration, TWICS builds upon an existing configuration management system, Subversion [24], and overlays it with functionality for explicitly managing and deploying components. In particular, as described in detail in the next section, TWICS organizes the configuration management repository in a component-based fashion and adds three extra modules for managing the resulting artifacts.

- A *producer package manager*, which supports a developer in publishing a component;

- A *component publisher*, which supports other organizations in downloading a component; and

- A *component downloader*, which downloads a component and places it under local configuration management control.

All these modules take into account the possibility of dependencies. Additionally, they collaborate in establishing and enforcing different trust policies as they exist among different organizations.

The resulting architecture of TWICS is shown in Figure 3. The *policies* component plays a key role in this architecture. It contains the declarative data describing the trust policy of a particular organization. For instance, in case of the organization FIRSTFORMAT of Section 2, its *policies* component may state that the organization SPELLONE may download but not redistribute its components. Upon a download request, the *component publisher* consults the *policies* component to ensure that only trusted parties are able to download the components.

Of note is that it cannot be expected that all organizations use the same configuration management system (e.g., Subversion). TWICS is therefore built on top of a generic API (see Figure 4). Given a bridge from this API to a particular configuration management system, TWICS can operate on top of that configuration management system. We purposely kept the API small such that TWICS can easily be ported onto new CM systems.

5 Implementation

We have implemented a prototype version of TWICS according to the architecture described in Section 4. Below, we discuss each of the three major components in the architecture, namely the *producer package manager, component publisher,* and *component downloader.* Before we do so, however, we first discuss how TWICS structures the normally unstructured repository of Subversion such that it provides a component-based orientation.

5.1 Repository Structure

TWICS configures the repository structure of its underlying configuration management system in such a way as to enable a transparent development and deployment of both internal and external components. The resulting repository structure is shown in Figure 5. TWICS partitions the available versioning space into two parts: a separate module called "TWICS", in which it stores all the data pertaining to its own operation, and the remaining versioning space, in which actual development takes place.

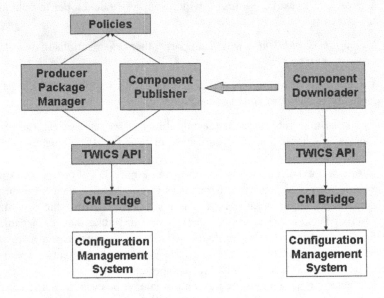

Fig. 3. Architecture of TWICS

Producer side API:
// Method to create source and binary packages and place them on the TWICS side
createComponent(String componentName, String componentVersion);
// Method to add dependency and metadata information for a deployable package
addMetaData(String componentName, String componentVersion);
// Method to get the package to be deployed from the TWICS repository
getPackage(String componentName, String componentVersion, String accessAllowed, String redistributionPermissions);
// Method to configure the CM repository to accommodate TWICS
configureSVN( );

Consumer side API:
// Method to deploy an external component in the local TWICS repository
putComponent(String componentName, String componentVersion);
// Method to read the metadata of an external component and know its dependencies
getMetaData(String componentName, String componentVersion);

Fig. 4. TWICS internal API

To preserve integrity, users should not directly manipulate the TWICS part of the

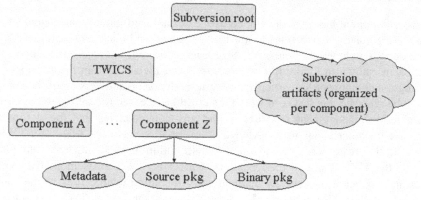

Fig. 5. TWICS repository structure

repository, but use the TWICS user interface instead. The remaining versioning space, however, can be manipulated at will, provided that users adhere to a naming scheme in which each Subversion module represents a component.

The TWICS part of the repository serves as a controlled store for packaged components. These components may have been developed locally, in which case they are stored for download by remote organizations. They may also have been developed remotely, in which case the controlled store serves as a staging area from which components are unpacked and brought into the development side of the repository. Components are stored as archives, and may be available as a source archive, a binary archive, or both. The metadata of a component is stored alongside the component itself, containing both data describing the component (e.g., name, version, authoring organization, dependencies) and data concerning the trust policy to be applied (e.g., organizations permitted to download the component, redistribution permissions).

Using the native versioning mechanisms of Subversion, different versions of a component can be stored in the TWICS repository. This allows different versions of a locally developed component to be available for download, and furthermore supports an organization in obtaining and separating multiple versions of an externally developed component.

Separating the TWICS repository from the actual development area helps to separate the remote evolution of an external component from any local changes that may have been made. When a new version of such an external component is downloaded, placing it in the TWICS repository does not disturb any local development. At a later time, suitable to the local organization, can the remote changes be merged and integrated into the local effort.

Note that, under this scheme, different instances of TWICS in effect act as peers to each other. Each can simultaneously serve as an instance that makes components available to other instances and as an instance that downloads components from other instances.

5.2 Producer Package Manager

Once a component has been developed using normal configuration management procedures (e.g., using Subversion), it must be packaged and made available for release.
To do so, a developer uses the TWICS *producer package manager* component. This
component, shown in Figure 6, first requests some metadata from the developer describing the component. In particular, it requests the name and version of the comp o-
nent to be released, the server to which it should be released (defaulted to the current
configuration management repository), and any dependencies that the component
may have on other components. After this information has been filled out, TWICS
automatically creates a source and a binary distribution for the comp onent and places
them on the TWICS side of the repository. Currently, TWICS assumes Java comp o-
nents and creates a package by automatically including source files in the source
package and class files in the binary package. Future versions of TWICS will extend
this capability significantly.

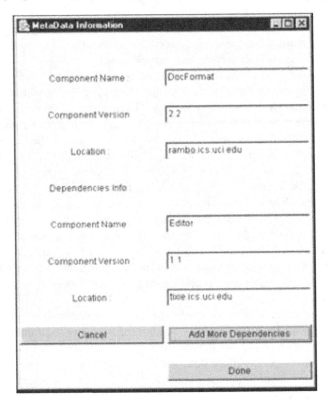

Fig. 6. Releasing a component

The second step that a developer must take is to attach a deployment policy to the
newly released component. As shown in Figure 7, a developer can specify (on a per-
organization basis, if needed) the level of access and redistribution rights of outside
organizations. This includes whether the comp onent may be downloaded in source

and/or binary form as well as whether the component may be modified and/or redistributed directly by the outside organization. Note that if redistribution is disallowed, the outside organization can still use t he component and upon release of its own components establish a remote dependency.

Component Name	Version	Client Company	Access Level	Redistribution Rights	Accept Modified Version
Editor	1.1	WordWorks Inc	Bin	None	No
DrawTools	3.2	WordWorks Inc	Bin	Bin	No
Foo	4.4	FooRequester Inc	Src	Bin	Yes
ArchWren	1.1	ComponentWorks Inc	All	None	Yes
Manage	3.2	Architects Inc	Bin	Bin	No
WebDav	3.2.1	First Solutions Inc	Bin	Bin	No
ArchEdit	5.6	Architects Inc	Src	Bin	Yes

Fig. 7. Specifying trust p olicies

5.3 Component Publisher

Once the trust policy has been specified, the component is available to other organizations for download. The download process itself is governed by the *component pub-lisher* component, whose sole respons ibility is to make sure the consumer is allowed the request they are making. If not, the component cannot be downloaded. If the request can be granted, the component, along with its metadata, is shipped to the consumer.

5.4 Component Downloader

The *component downloader* component eases the process of obtaining remotely developed components. Based on the input received from the user, the component downloader sends a deployment request to the producer of the requested component. If the user is indeed allowed to download the comp onent, an archive will be received from the producer and placed on the TWICS side the configuration management repository. After that, the component downloader checks the metadata of the comp o-nent and automatically fetches any required dependencies. This process is performed recursively, until all the dependencies are obtained and placed in the local enviro n-ment. Note that if a component that is a dependency is already at the co nsume r site, it will not be downloaded again.

After the components have been downloaded, TWICS supports a user in automati-cally unpacking the archives and placing the components on the development side of the repos itory. From there on, a user can start using the components.

Note that if a user locally modified a component for which they are now downloading a new version, TWICS currently requires them to manually integrate the two (perhaps with assistance from the standard merge ro utines in Subversion). While TWICS makes sure to not overwrite any changes, automated support for detecting and resolving these situations is certainly desired (see Section 5.5).

5.5 Discussion

TWICS is a work in progress. The prototype described above represents only the beginnings of our efforts. While it demonstrates the basic feasibility of the idea of merging configuration management and software deployment functionality into a single system, functionality wise the system is still in its infancy. At the forefront of our efforts at improving TWICS are the following:

Incorporate extensive deployment support. TWICS should leverage systems such as SRM [28], for automatically tracking and managing dependencies, and the Software Dock [10], for supporting the configuration of newly downloaded components. Currently, those tasks have to be performed by hand, which is cumbersome and time consuming.

Support the specification and enforcement of advanced trust policies. At the moment, our use of the word "trust" is somewhat overstated given the simplicity of the policies involved. In future, we plan to extend TWICS to incorporate support for specifying, in much more detail, the particular relationships between different organizations. Additionally, we will enhance the TWICS infrastructure to guarantee the desired properties. At present, for example, a consumer can circumvent a "do not redistribute" mandate by taking a component out of the configuration management repository and storing it under a different name. Such functionality should be disallowed.

Enhance the packager and unpackager components. Currently, these components have limited functionality and make a number of simplifying assumptions. We would like to enhance the packager by providing a user interface for creating rules according to which files should be chosen to be incorporated in a package. Similarly, we would like to enhance the unpackager by incorporating some tracking support that: (a) maintains the version number originally assigned by the component producer, (b) detects if the consumer has made any local changes, and (c) automatically integrates the new version with any local changes.

6   Conclusion

TWICS represents a first attempt at building a configuration management system that addresses the problem of managing the evolution of distributed, inter-related components. Set in the world of decentralized collaborating organizations, TWICS supports component-based software development via an integrated configuration management and software deployment system that establishes bi-directional communication among the organizations that produce components and the organizations that consume those components. A key aspect of TWICS is that it treats producers and consumers in the same way, and that its underlying repository structure is the same for both. In effect, producers and consumers serve as peers to one another in a distributed, loosely coupled, federated configuration management repository.

Although TWICS is a limited prototype, it is worth noting that it provides an answer to each of the questions posed in Section 2. By incorporating deployment functionality directly in the configuration management system, components that are developed by external organizations can be brought into the local development environment. By providing a controlled store separate from the development versioning space, the remote evolution of components is separated from their local evolution. By supporting the specification of dependencies and always maintaining the metadata alongside a component, a component-based software system can be effectively deployed. And finally, by establishing trust policies among the different configuration management repositories participating in a federation, we can address the autonomy, privacy, and trust issues that are key to effectively provide configuration management for decentralized component-based software development. We intend to continue developing TWICS to further address these questions.

Acknowledgments

Effort sponsored by the Defense Advanced Research Projects Agency (DARPA) and Air Force Research Laboratory, Air Force Materiel Command, USAF, under agreement number F30602-00-2-0599. Effort also partially funded by the National Science Foundation under grant number CCR-0093489. The U.S. Government is authorized to reproduce and distribute reprints for Governmental purposes notwithstanding any copyright annotation thereon. The views and conclusions contained herein are those of the authors and should not be interpreted as necessarily representing the official policies or endorsements, either expressed or implied, of the Defense Advanced Research Projects Agency (DARPA), the Air Force Laboratory, or the U.S. Government.

References

1. E.C. Bailey, *Maximum RPM*. Red Hat Software Inc., 1997
2. B. Berliner. *CVS II: Parallelizing Software Development.* Proceedings of the USENIX Winter 1990 Technical Conference, 1990: p. 341-352
3. C. Burrows and I. Wesley, *Ovum Evaluates Configuration Management.* Ovum Ltd., Burlington, Massachussetts, 1998
4. ComponentSource, http://www.componentsource.com/, 2002
5. R. Conradi and B. Westfechtel, *Version Models for Software Configuration Management.* ACM Computing Surveys, 1998. 30(2): p. 232-282
6. M. de Jonge. *Source Tree Composition.* Proceedings of the Seventh International Conference on Software Reuse, 2002
7. L.G. DeMichiel, L.U. Yalcinalp, and S. Krishnan, *Enterprise Java Beans Specification, Version 2.0*, http://java.sun.com/products/ejb/docs.html, 2001
8. J. Estublier and R. Casalles, *The Adele Configuration Manager*, in Configuration Management, W.F. Tichy, Editor. 1994: p. 99-134
9. P.H. Feiler. *Configuration Management Models in Commercial Environments.* Software Engineering Institute, Carnegie Mellon University, 1991

10. R.S. Hall, D.M. Heimbigner, and A.L. Wolf. *A Cooperative Approach to Support Software Deployment Using the Software Dock*. Proceedings of the 1999 International Conference on Software Engineering, 1999: p. 174-183

11. InstallShield, http://www.installshield.com/, 2001

12. M. Larsson and I. Crnkovic. *Configuration Management for Component-based Systems*. Proceedings of the Tenth International Workshop on Software Configuration Management, 2001

13. M.D. McIlroy, *Mass Produced Software Components*. Software Engineering: A Report on a Conference Sponsored by the NATO Science Committee, P. Naur and B. Randell (eds.), 1968: p. 138-155

14. T. Mens, *A State-of-the-Art Survey on Software Merging*. IEEE Transactions on Software Engineering, 2002. 28(5): p. 449-462

15. NetDeploy, http://www.netdeploy.com/, 2001

16. J. Oberleitner. *The Component Workbench: A Flexible Component Composition Environment*. M.S. Thesis, Technische Universität Vienna, 2001

17. Object Management Group, ed. *The Common Object Request Broker: Architecture and Specification*. 2001, Object Management Group

18. D.S. Platt, *Introducing Microsoft Dot-Net*. Microsoft, Redmond, 2001

19. Red Hat, http://www.rpm.org/, 2001

20. J. Rumbaugh, I. Jacobson, and G. Booch, *The Unified Modeling Language Reference Manual*. Addison-Wesley, 1998

21. C. Szyperski, *Component Software - Beyond Object-Oriented Programming*. Addison-Wesley / ACM Press, 1998

22. Telelogic, *CM/Synergy*, http://www.telelogic.com/products/synergy/cmsynergy/index.cfm, 2002

23. W.F. Tichy, *RCS, A System for Version Control*. Software - Practice and Experience, 1985. 15(7): p. 637-654

24. Tigris.org, *Subversion*, http://subversion.tigris.org/, 2002

25. Tivoli Systems, http://www.tivoli.com/, 2001

26. V. Traas and J. van Hillegersberg, *The Software Component Market on the Internet: Current Status and Conditions for Growth*. Software Engineering Notes, 2000. 25(1): p. 114-117

27. E. Tryggeseth, B. Gulla, and R. Conradi. *Modelling Systems with Variability Using the PROTEUS Configuration Language*. Proceedings of the International Workshop on Software Configuration Management: ICSE SCM-4 and SCM-5 Workshops Selected Papers, 1995: p. 216-240

28. A. van der Hoek, et al. *Software Release Management*. Proceedings of the Sixth European Software Engineering Conference together with the Fifth ACM SIGSOFT Symposium on the Foundations of Software Engineering, 1997: p. 159-175

29. D. Wiborg Weber. *Requirements for an SCM Architecture to Enable Component-based Development*. Proceedings of the Tenth International Workshop on Software Configuration Management, 2001

A Lightweight Infrastructure
for Reconfiguring Applications

Marco Castaldi[1], Antonio Carzaniga[2],
Paola Inverardi[1], and Alexander L. Wolf[2]

[1] Dipartimento di Informatica
Universita' dell'Aquila
via Vetoio, 1 67100 L'Aquila, Italy
{castaldi,inverard}@di.univaq.it
[2] Department of Computer Science
University of Colorado at Boulder
Boulder, Colorado, 80309-0430 USA
{carzanig,alw}@cs.colorado.edu

Abstract. We describe Lira, a lightweight infrastructure for managing dynamic reconfiguration that applies and extends the concepts of network management to component-based, distributed software systems. Lira is designed to perform both component-level reconfigurations and scalable application-level reconfigurations, the former through agents associated with individual components and the latter through a hierarchy of managers. Agents are programmed on a component-by-component basis to respond to reconfiguration requests appropriate for that component. Managers embody the logic for monitoring the state of one or more components, and for determining when and how to execute reconfiguration activities. A simple protocol based on SNMP is used for communication among managers and agents.

1 Introduction

This paper addresses the problem of managing the dynamic reconfiguration of component-based, distributed software systems. Reconfiguration comes in many forms, but two extreme approaches can be identified: *internal* and *external*.

Internal reconfiguration relies on the programmer to build into a component the facilities for reconfiguring the component. For example, a component might observe its own performance and switch from one algorithm or data structure to another when some performance threshold has been crossed. This form of reconfiguration is therefore sometimes called "programmed" or "self-healing" reconfiguration.

External reconfiguration, by contrast, relies on some entity external to the component to determine when and how the component is reconfigured. For example, an external entity might monitor the performance of a component and perform a wholesale replacement of the component when a performance threshold has been crossed. Likewise, an external entity might determine when to

B. Westfechtel, A. van der Hoek (Eds.): SCM 2001/2003, LNCS 2649, pp. 231–244, 2003.

upgrade a component to a newer version and perform that upgrade by replacing the component within the application system. Of course, replacing a component is a rather drastic reconfiguration action, but there is little that an external entity can do without cooperation from the component itself.

One common form of cooperation is the provision by a component of reconfiguration parameters; the parameters define what internal reconfigurations a component is prepared to carry out, while an external entity is given the ability to set parameter values and thereby to determine which of the possible reconfigurations is to occur and when. Clearly, any particular approach to reconfiguration is likely to be some blending of the two extreme approaches in conjunction with the use of reconfiguration parameters.

At a level above the individual components, we can consider the reconfiguration of the larger application system, where the dominant concern is the topology of the application in terms of the number and location of its components. What this typically introduces into the problem is the need to carry out a coordinated set of reconfigurations against the individual components. The question then arises, how and where is this coordination activity specified and managed?

The "easy" answer would be some centralized, external entity. However, the viability of such an entity essentially assumes that (a) components are designed and built to cooperate with the external entity and (b) it is possible for the entity to have global knowledge of the state of the application. These assumptions run counter to modern development methodology: we want to build generic components having few dependencies so that they can be reused in multiple contexts, and we want distributed systems to be built without global knowledge so that they can scale and be resilient to failure.

In previous work, we developed the Software Dock software deployment system [11]. The Software Dock is a comprehensive tool that addresses issues such as configuration, installation, and automated update. It also explores the challenges of representing component dependencies and constraints arising from heterogeneous deployment environments [10]. The Software Dock provides an extensive and sophisticated infrastructure in which to define and execute post-development activities [12]. However, it does not provide explicit support for dynamic reconfiguration—that is, a reconfiguration applied to a running system—although its infrastructure was designed to accommodate the future introduction of such a capability.

In an effort to better understand the issues surrounding dynamic reconfiguration, we developed a tool called Bark [21]. In contrast to the Software Dock, which is intended to be generic, Bark is a reconfiguration tool that is designed specifically to work within the context of the EJB (Enterprise JavaBean) [20] component framework. Its infrastructure leverages and extends the EJB suite of services and is therefore well integrated into a standard platform. Of course, its strength is also its weakness, since this tight integration means that it is useful only to application systems built on the EJB model. On the other hand, we learned an important lesson from our experience with Bark, namely that it is both possible and advantageous to make use of whatever native facilities are already provided by the components for the purposes of dynamic reconfiguration. Moreover, the burden of tailoring reconfiguration activities is naturally left to and divided among the developers of individual components, the developers of subsystems of components, and ultimately the developers of the encompassing applications.

Reflecting back, then, on our experience with the Software Dock, we realized that it imposes rather severe demands on component and application developers, above and beyond any necessary tailoring. In particular, the architecture of the Software Dock requires that at least one so-called *field dock* reside on every host machine. The field dock serves as the execution environment for all deployment activities, the store for all data associated with deployment activities, and the interface to the file system on the host. The field dock is also the mediator for all communication between individual components and external entities having to do with deployment activities. Finally, in order to make use of the Software Dock, developers must encode detailed information about their components and applications in a special deployment language called the Deployable Software Description (DSD).

Thus, the Software Dock would lead to what we now consider a "heavy-weight" solution to the problem of dynamic reconfiguration, a characteristic shared by many other reconfiguration systems (e.g., DRS [1], Lua [2], and PRISMA [3]). While such an approach may be feasible in some circumstances, we are intrigued by the question of how to build lighter-weight solutions.

It is difficult to be precise about what one means by "lightweight", since it is inherently a relative concept. But for our purposes, we take lightweight to indicate intuitively an approach to dynamic reconfiguration in which:

- the service is *best effort*, in that it arises from, and makes use of, the facilities already provided by individual components, rather than some standardized set of imposed facilities;
- reconfiguration is carried out via *remote control*, in that the management of reconfiguration is separated from the implementation of reconfiguration, so as to enhance the reusability of components and, in conjunction with the best-effort nature of the service, broaden the scope of applicability; and
- communication is through a *simple protocol* between components and the entities managing their reconfiguration, rather than through complex interfaces and/or data models.

In this paper we describe our attempt at a lightweight infrastructure for dynamic reconfiguration and its implementation in a tool called Lira. The inspiration for our approach comes directly from the field of network management and its Internet-Standard Network Management Framework, which for historical reasons is referred to as SNMP [6]. (SNMP is the name of the protocol used within the framework.) Our hypothesis is that this framework can serve, with appropriate extension and adaptation where necessary, as a useful model for lightweight reconfiguration of component-based, distributed software systems.

In the next section, we provide background on network management and the Internet-Standard Network Management Framework. Section 3 describes

Lira, while Section 4 presents a brief example application of Lira that we have implemented. Related work is discussed in Section 5, and we conclude in Section 6 with a discussion of future work.

2   Background: Network Management

As mentioned above, the design of Lira was inspired by network management approaches. The original challenge for network management was to devise a simple and lightweight method for managing network devices, such as routers and printers. These goals were necessary in order to convince manufacturers to make their devices remotely manageable without suffering undue overhead, as well as to encourage widespread acceptance of a method that could lead to a *de facto* management standard. (Perhaps the same can be said of software component manufacturers.)

The network management model consists of four basic elements: *agents*,[1] each of which is associated with a network node (i.e., device) to be managed and which provides remote management access on behalf of the node; *managers*, which embody the logic for monitoring the state of a node and for determining when and how to execute management activities; *a protocol*, which is used for communication among the agent and manager management entities; and *management information*, which defines the aspects of a node's state that can be monitored and the ways in which that state can be modified from outside the node.

Agents are typically provided by node manufacturers, while managers are typically sophisticated third-party applications (e.g., HP's OpenView [14]). The standard protocol is SNMP (Simple Network Management Protocol), which provides managers with the primitive operations for getting and setting variables on agents, and for sending asynchronous alerts from agents to managers. The management information defines the state variables of an agent and is therefore specific to each node. These variable definitions are captured in a MIB (Management Information Base) associated with each agent.

In our work on Lira, we are driven by the complexity of configurations inherent in today's large-scale, component-based, distributed software systems. Specifically, multiple components tend to execute on the same device, and regularly come into and go out of existence (much more often than, say, a router in a network). Further, the components, whether executing on the same or on different devices, tend to have complex relationships and interdependencies. Finally, domains of authority over components tend to overlap and interact, implying complex management relationships.

In theory, the Internet-Standard Network Management Framework places few constraints on how its simple concepts are to be applied, allowing for quite

---

[1] The term "agent" as used in network management should not be confused with other uses of this term in computer science, such as "mobile agent" or "intelligent agent". Network management agents are not mobile, and their intelligence is debatable.

advanced and sophisticated arrangements. In practice, however, network management seems to have employed these concepts in only relatively straightforward ways. For instance, a typical configuration for managing a network consists of a flat space of devices with their associated agents managed by a single, centralized manager; a manager is associated with a particular domain of authority (e.g., a business organization) and controls all the devices within that domain. It is interesting to note that there have been efforts at defining MIBs for some of the more prominent web applications, such as the Apache web server, IBM's WebSphere transaction server, and BEA's WebLogic transaction server, and more generally a proposal for an "application management" MIB [15]. But, again, the approach taken is to view these as independently managed applications, not a true complex of distributed components.

3   Lira

The essence of the approach we take in Lira is to define a particular method for applying the basic facilities of the Internet-Standard Network Management Framework to complex component-based software systems. To summarize:

- We distinguish two kinds of agent. A *reconfiguration agent* is associated with a component, and is responsible for reconfiguring the component in response to operations on variables defined by its MIB. A *host agent* is associated with a computer in the network, and is responsible for installing and activating components on that computer, again, in response to operations on variables defined by its MIB.
- A manager can itself be a reconfiguration agent. What this means is that a manager can have a MIB and thereby be expected to respond to other, higher-level managers. Such a *manager agent* would reinterpret the reconfiguration (and status) requests it receives into management requests it should send to the agents of the components it is managing. In this way a scalable management hierarchy can be established, finally reaching ground on the *base* reconfiguration agents associated with (monolithic) components.
- We define a basic set of "standard" MIB definitions for each kind of agent. These definitions are generically appropriate for managing software components, but are expected to be augmented on an agent-by-agent basis so that individual agents can be specialized to their particular unique tasks.

It is important to note that Lira does not itself provide the agents, although in our prototype implementation we have created convenient base classes from which implementations can be derived. Rather, the principle that we follow is that developers should be free to create agents in any programming language using any technology they desire, as long as the agents serve their intended purpose and provide access through at least the set of MIB definitions we have defined. For example, in our use of Lira within the Willow survivability middleware system [16], there are agents written in C++ and Java. Furthermore, some of the Willow manager agents are highly sophisticated workflow engines that can coordinate and adjudicate among competing reconfiguration requests [17].

The remainder of this section describes these concepts in greater detail.

Reconfiguration Agent

A base reconfiguration agent directly controls and manages a component. Lira does not constrain how the agent is associated with its component, only that the agent is able to act upon the component. For example, the agent might be part of the same thread of execution, execute in a separate thread, or execute in a completely separate process. In fact, the agent might reside on a completely different device, although this would probably be the case only for complex agents associated with components running on capacity-limited devices.

The logical model of communication between a base reconfiguration agent and its component is through shared memory; the component shares a part of its state with the agent. Of course, to avoid synchronization problems, the component must provide atomic access to the shared state.

A reconfiguration agent that is not a base reconfiguration agent is a manager. It interacts with other base and non-base reconfiguration agents using the standard management protocol. For purposes of simplifying the discussion below, we abuse the term "component" to refer also to the subassembly of agents with which a non-base reconfiguration agent (i.e., a manager agent) interacts. Thus, from the perspective of a higher-level manager, it appears as though a lower-level manager is any other reconfiguration agent. This is illustrated in the example agent hierarchy of Figure 1.

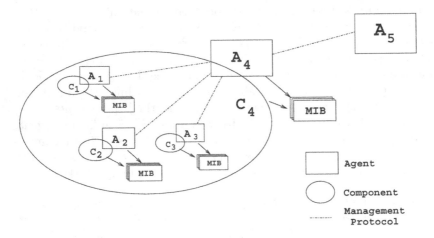

Fig. 1. An example Lira agent hierarchy

In the figure, agents A_1, A_2, and A_3 are base reconfiguration agents acting on components C_1, C_2, and C_3, respectively. Agent A_4 is a manager for A_1, A_2, and A_3, but is treated as a reconfiguration agent by the higher-level manager A_5. In effect, A_4 is responsible for carrying out reconfigurations on a subsystem represented by C_4, and hides the complexity of that responsibility from A_5.

A reconfiguration agent is essentially responsible for managing the lifecycle of its component, and exports at least the following five management functions:[2]

- void START(startArgs)
- void STOP()
- void SUSPEND()
- void RESUME()
- void SHUTDOWN()

The function SHUTDOWN also serves to terminate the agent. Each reconfiguration agent also exports at least the following two variables:

- STATUS
- NOTIFYTO

The first variable contains the current status of the component, and can take on one of the following values: *starting*, *started*, *stopping*, *stopped*, *suspending*, *suspended*, and *resuming*. The second variable contains the address of the manager to which an alert notification should be sent. This is necessary because we allow agents to have multiple managers, but we assume that at any given time only one of those managers has responsibility for alerts. That manager can use other means, not defined by Lira, to spread the alert.

Host Agent

A host agent runs on a computer where components and reconfiguration agents are to be installed and activated, and is responsible for carrying out those activities in response to requests from a manager. (How a host agent is itself installed and activated is obviously a bootstrapping process.) As part of activating a component and its associated agent, the host agent provides an available network port, called the *agent address*, to the reconfiguration agent over which that agent can receive requests from a manager.

Each host agent exports at least the following variables:

- NOTIFYTO
- INSTALLEDAGENTS
- ACTIVEAGENTS

Host agents also export the following functions:

- void INSTALL(componentPackage)
- void UNINSTALL(componentPackage)
- agentAddress GET_AGENTADDRESS(agentName)

---

[2] Lira provides the notion of a "function", described below, as a convenient shorthand for a combination of more primitive concepts already present in SNMP.

- agentAddress ACTIVATE(componentType,componentName,componentArgs)
- void DEACTIVATE(componentName)
- void REMOVEACTIVEAGENT(agentName)

Again, we expect host agents to export additional variables and functions consistent with their particular purposes, including variables described in the Host Resources MIB [24].

Management Protocol

The management protocol follows the SNMP paradigm. Each message in the protocol is either a *request* or a *response*, as shown in the following table:

request	response
SET(*variable_name, variable_value*)	ACK(*message_text*)
GET(*variable_name*)	REPLY(*variable_name, variable_value*)
CALL(*function_name, parameters_list*)	RETURN(*return_value*)

Requests are sent by managers to agents, and responses are sent back to managers from agents. There is one additional kind of message, which is sent from agents to managers in the absence of any request.

$$\text{NOTIFY}(variable\_name,\ variable\_value,\ agent\_name)$$

This message is used to communicate an alert from an agent back to a manager. For instance, an agent might notice that a performance threshold has been crossed, and uses the alert to initiate some remedial action on the part of the manager.

4   Example

We now present a simple, yet practical example to demonstrate how Lira can be used to achieve a dynamic reconfiguration. The example was implemented using Java agents working on components of a pre-existing Java application. Lira has been used in more complex and diverse settings, but this example suffices for illustrative purposes.

The application is an overlay network of software routers for a distributed, content-based, publish/subscribe event notification service called Siena [5]. The routers form a store-and-forward network responsible for delivering messages posted by publishers on one side of a network to the subscribes having expressed interest in the message on the other side of the network. Publishers and subscribers are clients of the service that can connect to arbitrary routers in the network. The routers are arranged in a hierarchical fashion, such that each has a unique parent, called a *master*, to which subscription and notification messages are forwarded. (Notification messages also flow down the hierarchy, from parents to children, but that fact is not germane to this example.) The master of a client is the router to which it is attached. Siena is designed to adjust its forwarding tables in response to changes in subscriptions, and also in response to changes in topology. The topology can be changed through a Siena command called *set master*, which resets the master of a given router.

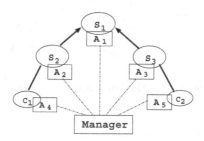

Fig. 2. Topology of an example Siena network

Figure 2 shows a simple topology, where S_1, S_2, and S_3 are Siena routers, and C_1 and C_2 are Siena clients. S_1 is the master of both S_2 and S_3. Each router and client has associated with it a reconfiguration agent. All the agents are managed by a single manager. In addition to the "standard" set of variables, each reconfiguration agent in this system exports a variable MASTER to indicate the identity of its component's master router.

The Siena clients and routers, together with their reconfiguration agents, can each be run on separate computers. Each such computer would have its own host agent. The manager interacts with the host agent to activate a client or router. For example, the manager uses the function

```
ACTIVATE(SienaRouter,S1,
            "-host palio.cs.colorado.edu -port 3333 -log -")
```

to activate Siena router S_1.

Now, notice that if S_1 were to fail, then clients C_1 and C_2 would not be able to communicate. In such a case, we would like to reconfigure the Siena network to restore communication. The manager can do this by reassigning S_3 to be the master of S_2, as shown in Figure 3. The manager will change the value of the variable MASTER of agents A_2 and A_3, sending the request SET("MASTER",S_3) to A_2 and the request SET("MASTER","") to A_3.

Clearly, for the manager to be able to decide on the proper course of action, the state of the Siena network must be monitored. Moreover, the manager must have knowledge of the current topology. This can be done in several ways using Lira, including requests for the values of appropriate variables and the use of the NOTIFY message when an agent notices that a router is unresponsive.

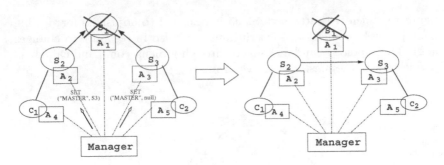

Fig. 3. Reconfiguration in response to the failure of S_1

5   Related Work

Supporting the dynamic reconfiguration of distributed systems has been a goal of researchers and practitioners for the past quarter century, and many techniques and tools have been developed. The work described in this paper is leveraging and integrating the recent maturation of two disciplines, component-based software engineering [13] and network management [6].

Endler divides dynamic reconfiguration into two forms according to when the change is defined: *programmed* and *ad hoc* [8]. The first form is defined at the time the system is designed, and may be compiled into the code of the application. The second form is not predictable and defined only once the application is already in execution. To a certain extent, Lira supports the use of both forms of reconfiguration, the first through planned requests directed at reconfiguration agents, and the second either through replacement of components or through topological reconfigurations at the application level. Of course, the goal of Lira is to automate reconfiguration activities, so the reconfigurations cannot be completely unplanned unless control is given over to the ultimate manager, the human operator.

Endler also discusses a distinction between *functional* and *structural* dynamic reconfigurations [8]. Functional reconfiguration involves new code being added to an application, while structural reconfiguration is topological in nature. Again, Lira supports both.

Several researchers, including Almeida et al. [1], Bidan et al. [4], Kramer and Magee [18], and Wermelinger [25], have tried to address the problem of maintaining consistency during and after a reconfiguration. Usually, the consistency properties of the system are expressed through logical constraints that should be respected, either *a posteriori* or *a priori*. If the constraints are seen as postconditions [26], the reconfiguration must be undone if a constraint is violated. If the constraints are seen as preconditions [8], the reconfiguration can be done only if the constraints are satisfied.

Lira approaches the consistency problem using a sort of "management by delegation" [9], in which it delegates responsibility to agents to do what is necessary to guarantee consistency and state integrity. This is in line with the idea of "self-organizing software architectures" [19], where the goal is to minimize the amount of explicit management and reduce protocol communication. It is also in line with the idea of a lightweight, best-effort service (see Section 1), where we assume that the component developer has the proper insight about how best to maintain consistency. This is in contrast to having the reconfiguration infrastructure impose some sort of consistency-maintenance scheme of its own.

Java Management eXtensions (JMX) is a specification that defines an architecture, design pattern, APIs, and services for application and network management in the Java programming language [23]. Under JMX, each managed resource and its reconfiguration services are captured as a so-called MBean. The MBean is registered with an MBean server inside a JMX agent. The JMX agent controls the registered resources and makes them available to remote management applications. The reconfiguration logic of JMX agents can be dynamically extended by registering MBeans. Finally, the JMX specification allows communication among different kinds of managers through connectors and protocol adaptors that provide integration with HTTP, RMI, and even the SNMP protocols. While JMX is clearly a powerful reconfiguration framework, it is also a heavyweight mechanism, and one that is strongly tied to one specific platform, namely Java.

6 Conclusions and Future Work

Lira represents our attempt to devise a lightweight infrastructure for the dynamic reconfiguration of component-based, distributed software systems. Lira follows the approach pioneered in the realm of network management, providing in essence a particular method for applying the concepts of the Internet-Standard Network Management Framework. Lira is designed to perform both component-level reconfigurations and scalable application-level reconfigurations, the former through agents associated with individual components and the latter through a hierarchy of managers.

A hierachical approach is neither new nor necessary, but it seems to us to be natural and suitable for the purpose, allowing the reconfiguration developer to concentrate on the logic of the reconfiguration rather than on how to coordinate the agents. We are currently investigating more sophisticated approaches to supporting cooperation among agents and, consequently, for making more complex coordinated reconfiguration decisions (see below).

Lira has been developed with the aim of providing a minimal set of functionality. Some desirable capabilities found in more "heavyweight" approaches, such as automated consistency management and version selection, are not provided as part of the basic infrastructure. However, two main strategies can be followed to bridge the gap: (1) advanced capabilities can be used from, or implemented within, individual agents, thus hiding them from managers (i.e., from higher-level agents) or (2) they can be used or implemented at the management level, exploiting variables and functions provided by lower-level agents. It is still an open question as to whether this lightweight approach and its flexible programmable extension is superior to a heavyweight approach and its implicit set of capabilities. We are trying to answer this question through case studies.

We have implemented a prototype of the Lira infrastructure and used it to manage several complex distributed applications, including a network of Siena overlay routers [5] and a prototype of a military information fusion and dissemination system called the Joint Battlespace Infosphere [22]. Based on these and other experiences, we have begun to explore how the basic Lira infrastructure could be enhanced in certain specialized ways.

First, in order to simplify the exportation of reconfiguration variables and functions for Java components, we have created a specialized version of the Lira agent. This agent uses the Java Reflection API to provide mechanisms to export (public) variables and functions defined in the agent and/or in the component. These exported entities are then integrated into the MIB for the agent using a callback mechanism.

Second, in order to provide more "intelligence" in reconfiguration agents, we have created an API to integrate Lira with a ProLog-like language called DALI [7]. The idea is to be able to implement agents that can reason about the local context, make decisions based on that reasoning, and remember (or learn) from past situations. The result of this integration is an intelligent agent we call LiDA (Lira + DALI), which is more autonomous than a basic Lira agent and uses its intelligence and memory to make some simple, local decisions without support from a manager.

Finally, we have created a preliminary version of a reconfiguration language that allows one to define, in a declarative way, application-level reconfiguration activities. We have observed that Lira agents operating at this level follow a regular structure in which their concern is centered on the installation/activation of new components, changes in application topology, and monitoring of global properties of the system. The particulars of these actions can be distilled out and used to drive a generic agent. This echos the approach we took in the Software Dock, where generic agents operate by interpreting the declarative language of the DSD [11].

None of these enhancements are strictly necessary, but they allow us to better understand how well Lira can support sophisticated, programmer-oriented specializations, which is a property that we feel will make Lira a broadly acceptable, lightweight reconfiguration framework.

Acknowledgements

The authors thank Dennis Heimbigner, Jonathan Hill, and John Knight for their helpful comments, criticism, and feedback on the design and prototype implementation of Lira.

This work was supported in part by the Defense Advanced Research Projects Agency, Air Force Research Laboratory, Space and Naval Warfare System Center, and Army Research Office under agreement numbers F30602-01-1-0503,

F30602-00-2-0608, N66001-00-1-8945, and DAAD19-01-1-0484. The U.S. Government is authorized to reproduce and distribute reprints for Governmental purposes notwithstanding any copyright annotation thereon. The views and conclusions contained herein are those of the authors and should not be interpreted as necessarily representing the official policies or endorsements, either expressed or implied, of the Defense Advanced Research Projects Agency, Air Force Research Laboratory, Space and Naval Warfare System Center, Army Research Office, or the U.S. Government.

References

1. J.P.A. Almeida, M. Wegdam, M. van Sinderen, and L. Nieuwenhuis. Transparent Dynamic Reconfiguration for CORBA. In *Proceedings of the 3rd International Symposium on Distributed Objects and Applications*, pages 197–207. IEEE Computer Society, September 2001.
2. T. Batista and N. Rodriguez. Dynamic Reconfiguration of Component-Based Applications. In *Proceedings of the International Symposium on Software Engineering for Parallel and Distributed Systems*, pages 32–39. IEEE Computer Society, June 2000.
3. J. Berghoff, O. Drobnik, A. Lingnau, and C. Monch. Agent-Based Configuration Management of Distributed Applications. In *Proceedings of the 3rd International Conference on Configurable Distributed Systems*, pages 52–59. IEEE Computer Society, May 1996.
4. C. Bidan, V. Issarny, T. Saridakis, and A. Zarras. A Dynamic Reconfiguration Service for CORBA. In *Proceedings of the 4th International Conference on Configurable Distributed Systems*, pages 35–42. IEEE Computer Society, May 1998.
5. A. Carzaniga, D.S. Rosenblum, and A.L. Wolf. Design and Evaluation of a Wide-Area Event Notification Service. *ACM Transactions on Computer Systems*, 19(3):332–383, August 2001.
6. J. Case, R. Mundy, D. Partain, and B. Stewart. *Introduction and Applicability Statements for Internet Standard Management Framework*. RFC 3410. The Internet Society, December 2002.
7. S. Costantini and A. Tocchio. A Logic Programming Language for Multi-Agent Systems. In *8th European Conference on Logics in Artificial Intelligence*, number 2424 in Lecture Notes in Artificial Intelligence, pages 1–13. Springer-Verlag, September 2002.
8. M. Endler. A Language for Implementing Generic Dynamic Reconfigurations of Distributed Programs. In *Proceedings of 12th Brazilian Symposium on Computer Networks*, pages 175–187, 1994.
9. G. Goldszmidt and Y. Yemini. Distributed Management by Delegation. In *Proceedings of the 15th International Conference on Distributed Computing Systems*, pages 333–340. IEEE Computer Society, May 1995.
10. R.S. Hall, D.M. Heimbigner, and A.L. Wolf. Evaluating Software Deployment Languages and Schema. In *Proceedings of the 1998 International Conference on Software Maintenance*, pages 177–185. IEEE Computer Society, November 1998.
11. R.S. Hall, D.M. Heimbigner, and A.L. Wolf. A Cooperative Approach to Support Software Deployment Using the Software Dock. In *Proceedings of the 1999 International Conference on Software Engineering*, pages 174–183. Association for Computer Machinery, May 1999.

12. D.M. Heimbigner and A.L. Wolf. Post-Deployment Configuration Management. In *Proceedings of the Sixth International Workshop on Software Configuration Management*, number 1167 in Lecture Notes in Computer Science, pages 272–276. Springer-Verlag, 1996.
13. G.T. Heineman and W.T. Councill, editors. *Component-Based Software Engineering: Putting the Pieces Together*. Addison-Wesley, Reading, Massachusetts, 2001.
14. Hewlett Packard. *HP OpenView Family Guide*, 1998.
15. C. Kalbfleisch, C. Krupczak, R. Presuhn, and J. Saperia. *Application Management MIB*. RFC 2564. The Internet Society, May 1999.
16. J.C. Knight, D.M. Heimbigner, A.L. Wolf, A. Carzaniga, J. Hill, and P. Devanbu. The Willow Survivability Architecture. In *Proceedings of the Fourth International Survivability Workshop*, March 2002.
17. J.C. Knight, D.M. Heimbigner, A.L. Wolf, A. Carzaniga, J. Hill, P. Devanbu, and M. Gertz. The Willow Architecture: Comprehensive Survivability for Large-Scale Distributed Applications. Technical Report CU-CS-926-01, Department of Computer Science, University of Colorado, Boulder, Colorado, December 2001.
18. J. Kramer and J. Magee. Dynamic Configuration for Distributed Systems. *IEEE Transactions on Software Engineering*, SE-11(4):424–436, April 1985.
19. J. Magee and J. Kramer. Self Organising Software Architectures. In *Proceedings of the Second International Software Architecture Workshop*, pages 35–38, October 1996.
20. R. Monson-Haefel. *Enterprise JavaBeans*. O'Reilly and Associates, 2000.
21. M.J. Rutherford, K.M. Anderson, A. Carzaniga, D.M. Heimbigner, and A.L. Wolf. Reconfiguration in the Enterprise JavaBean Component Model. In *Proceedings of the IFIP/ACM Working Conference on Component Deployment*, number 2370 in Lecture Notes in Computer Science, pages 67–81. Springer-Verlag, 2002.
22. Scientific Advisory Board. Building The Joint Battlespace Infosphere. Technical Report SAB-TR-99-02, U.S. Air Force, December 2000.
23. Sun Microsystems, Inc., Palo Alto, California. *Java Management Extensions Instrumentation and Agent Specification, v1.0*, July 2000.
24. S. Waldbusser and P. Grillo. *Host Resources MIB*. RFC 2790. The Internet Society, March 2000.
25. M. Wermelinger. Towards a Chemical Model for Software Architecture Reconfiguration. In *Proceedings of the 4th International Conference on Configurable Distributed Systems*, pages 111–118. IEEE Computer Society, May 1998.
26. A. Young and J. Magee. A Flexible Approach to Evolution of Reconfigurable Systems. In *Proceedings of the IEE/IFIP International Workshop on Configurable Distributed Systems*, pages 152–163, March 1992.

A Software Configuration Management Course

Ulf Asklund and Lars Bendix

Department of Computer Science, Lund Institute of Technology
Box 118, SE-221 00 Lund, Sweden
{ulf,bendix}@cs.lth.se

Abstract. Software Configuration Management has been a big success in research and creation of tools. There are also many vendors in the market of selling courses to companies. However, in the education sector Software Configuration Management has still not quite made it – at least not into the university
curriculum. It is either not taught at all or is just a minor part of a general course
in software engineering. In this paper, we report on our experience with giving a
full course entirely dedicated to Software Configuration Management topics and
start a discussion of what ideally should be the goal and contents of such a
course.

1 Introduction

In the call for papers for the SCM workshop it says: "The discipline of software configuration management (SCM) provides one of the best success stories in the field of
software engineering. With the availability of over a hundred commercial SCM systems that together form a billion dollar marketplace, and the explicit recognition of
SCM by such standards as the CMM and ISO-9000, the discipline has established
itself as one of the essential cornerstones of software engineering.".

The call furthermore says that "SCM is a well-established discipline". This, however, apparently does not apply to the educational aspects of SCM. To the best of our
knowledge universities only teach SCM as a small part of a more general course in
software engineering – or not at all. If one wants to teach a more extensive course on
SCM topics, there is very little help to get with regards to the contents of such a
course. Most books on the subject, like Berlack [10], Leon [24] and many more, all
follow the traditional way of looking at SCM as consisting of "the four activities":
configuration identification, configuration control, configuration status accounting
and configuration audit. This more formal approach to SCM is, however, in our opinion an experience not quite suited for university students.

At Lund Institute of Technology, we have had the possibility to develop a full
course dedicated entirely to SCM topics. In this paper, we want to report our experience from two years of teaching this course. We also want to start a discussion of
what topics could be included in such a course and how SCM can be taught in a full
course of its own as well as inside a software engineering course.

B.Westfechtel, A. van der Hoek (Eds.): SCM 2001/2003, LNCS 2649, pp. 245-258, 2003.

In the following, we will first describe how our course is given and what is in the course. Then we discuss the considerations that led to the contents that the course has today. This is followed by a discussion of the pedagogical considerations that we have had. Finally, we reflect on the experience we have gained from the first two years of giving the course, describe our plans for future changes to the course and draw our conclusions.

2   Description of the Course

The course we give is at undergraduate level. The students are following the last years of their education and as a prerequisite for following this course they must have taken the project "Program development in groups" in which they in groups of 10 students during a period of 7 weeks develop a software product, thus facing many of the problems addressed by SCM.

What are the goals of the course? Given the amount of resources we have available for this dedicated course, we can be rather ambitious. We can prepare our students for many of the situations that they will meet in industry after they graduate. Most of our students will probably make a career in industry and from an SCM perspective the course should guarantee that they are qualified to cover positions ranging from developer through project leader to SCM expert or manager. The course is optional, so we can count on the students following it out of interest.

If we look at SCM, it is related to many different roles on a company-wide scale. We have distinguished at least the following roles: developers, SCM wizards, project leaders, SCM experts or managers, SCM tool administrators, quality assurance and test, release people, and SCM tool developers. An ambitious SCM course should consider the needs of all these roles. The goals for our course are to provide the developer with knowledge of traditional SCM, comprehension of problems and solutions in development in groups and application of work models including the use of functionality like merge and diff. In addition to what the developer learns, the SCM wizard on a project team should have an analytical insight into problems and solutions in SCM for groups and should reach application level for tasks that are more rarely performed, such as weekly builds, creating branches and doing releases. The project leader needs to have comprehension of the SCM problems and solutions encountered by developers and he should reach application of traditional SCM including CCBs and SCM plans. An SCM expert or manager should ideally know everything. In our course we want to bring the students to a level where they can analyse SCM problems directly related to developers, synthesise one or more possible solutions and evaluate these solutions. In the present course, we choose to leave out the roles of SCM tool administrator and SCM tool developer, the first being too tool specific and the latter too advanced. For the quality assurance and test roles, we consider their needs to be at a usage level and thus a sub-set of the developer's needs. Likewise we consider, in part, the needs of release people to be covered by what is taught for the SCM wizard role.

Our SCM course lasts 7 weeks. Each week we have two lectures, one exercise session and one session in the computer lab – each of the duration of two hours. Each week is entirely dedicated to a specific theme and starts with a lecture that gives the basics of the theme. Then there is an exercise session where the students, based on open questions, discuss the theme of the week in small groups of 3-4 students. This is followed by a second lecture on the theme of the week. This lecture starts with student presentations of their results from the previous exercise session, followed by a in-depth treatment of topics within the theme. Finally there is a session in the computer lab, where the students wo rk in the same groups as during the exercise sessions. The computer labs do not follow the themes, but aim at giving practical hands-on experience with two tools, CVS and ClearCase. There are five computer labs and six exe rcise sessions, which gives a total of 50 hours for the whole course, not including the time the students use for preparation and reading literature.

The themes that are treated in the course are the following:

1. introduction, motivation and overview
2. collaboration (construction site)
3. workspace (study)
4. repository (library)
5. traditional configuration management
6. SCM relations to other domains
7. wrap up, summary and question hour

Theme 1 is introduction, motivation and overview. The first lecture introduces SCM and gives some example scenarios of program development to motivate the students and explain why SCM is important. The exercise session is used for teambuilding, forming the groups that will work together during the rest of the exercise sessions, during the computer labs, and for the examination. We also use the first exercise session to get information about the students' background and their expectations to the course. The second lecture gives an overview of SCM and the rest of the course. The literature used for this theme is chapters from Babich [6].

Themes 2, 3 and 4 all deal with what a developer needs from SCM and to describe these aspects we use three metaphors [9]: a construction site, a study, and a library. A developer needs to collaborate with others (a construction site), to create a workspace where he can work undisturbed (a study), and a place where he and others can store the results of their work (a library). Common for the exercise sessions during these three themes is that we also use the metaphors to facilitate the discussions and that each group has to produce one slide containing the most interesting/surprising result from their discussions to be presented (by them) and discussed briefly during the following lecture.

Theme 2 – the construction site: The first lecture is basics about co-ordination and communication. The exercise session focuses on the importance of planning, co-ordination and communication and the second lecture goes more in -depth with work models and how geographical distribution affects SCM. Literature used is excerpts from [25], parts of [2] and a chapter from [30].

Theme 3 – the study: The first lecture is basics about roles, versioning and work-spaces. The exercise session discusses what a workspace should look like to make it possible for the developer to get his work done. The in -depth lecture is about SCM models and merging. Literature is excerpts from [31], [7], and [19].

Theme 4 – the library: The basics here are repository structures, identification and history. In the exercise session students discuss possible solutions for versioning, branching, selection and representing dependencies. The in-depth lecture covers versioning models and branching patterns. Literature is excerpts from [21], [3], and [1].

Theme 5 deals with the traditional way of looking at SCM as consisting of "the four activities". The first lecture explains configuration identification and configuration control with its main emphasis on the change process and the role and functioning of the change control board (CCB). The second lecture covers the remaining activities of configuration status accounting and configuration audit. Furthermore this lecture covers CM plans and roles. This week's exercise session is not strictly connected to the theme, as the session comes between the two lectures. Exercises are more focused discussion questions than the previous weeks and relate to the identification, structuring and process aspects of themes 2-4 seen in the light of this week's first lecture. As literature we use chapters from [14] and excerpts from [24] and [13].

Theme 6 covers domains related to SCM. We treat product data management (PDM), open source software development (OSS), software architecture (SA), and the use of patterns for SCM. Literature is excerpts from [12] for patterns, [8] for SA, [4] for PDM, and [5] for OSS. During the exercise session this week, the students have to put the previous weeks' work together within the framework of a CM plan. Based on their discussions during the metaphor sessions and with the knowledge they now have about traditional SCM and the purpose and contents of CM plans, they have to construct fragments of a CM plan for an imaginary project. This has to be written up as a 2-3 pages essay that has to be handed in before the examination.

The final theme wraps up the whole course. The pieces that each theme constitutes are put together again to form a whole. We also look back on what we've been through and focus on the relationships there are between the themes instead of looking at them in isolation. The second lecture during the final week is an external lecture. The first time we had an industrial presentation and the second time a PhD defence. Literature is excerpts from [15] and [23].

The computer labs are not strictly connected to the themes followed by the lectures and exercise sessions. Starting week 2 through week 6 there are five labs covering practical work with the tools CVS (3 labs) and ClearCase (2 labs). Labs are a mixture of detailed guidance and open ended experiments. The students work in the same groups as for the exercise sessions.

In the first CVS-lab the students familiarise themselves with the tool. They set up the repository and use it for simple collaboration using turn-taking. In the second lab they continue to explore the support for parallel development and automatic merge. They also make a release that is used in the third lab. The last CVS-lab is focused on the use of branches for maintenance as well as for experiments/variants. Furthermore, they investigate the possibilities for creating awareness within a group of developers. Finally, they have the possibility use tkCVS to compare a graphical interface with a pure command-based tool.

During the ClearCase-labs the students go through roughly the same set of tasks as for the CVS-lab, but now getting experience with a different tool. They do not have to set up the tool and the repository, but they do explore the VOB and the configuration specifications. They create views exploring different collaboration patterns to discover the flexibility and power of ClearCase – and the price paid. They also create a release and turn back to it to create a maintenance branch – and to merge that branch back into the main line of development.

In the week following the last lecture, we have the examination. It is an oral examination which uses the essay produced during the last exercise session, but the examination covers the whole course curriculum. It is carried out in the same groups that the students work in during exercises and labs, it lasts for 15-20 minutes pr. student and is a group discussion more than an interrogation. The students get individual grades.

3   Contents Considerations

The past two years at Lund Institute of Technology, we have had the opportunity to teach a full course dedicated to SCM topics only. This course is an optional course for students in the final years of their masters education in computer science. Usually the problem is to choose what to put into – and especially what to leave out of – one or two lectures about SCM given as part of a more general course in software engineering. Faced with the luxury of a whole course of 50 hours of lectures, exercise and lab sessions we were unsure whether or not we could actually fill all this time with relevant topics. All our doubts proved to be unfounded – quite on the contrary we found such a wealth of topics in SCM that even with a full course we were faced with having to choose between what to include and what to leave out.

With regards to a curriculum for an SCM course we looked around for help, but found very little guidance. There are a number of papers on the concepts and principles of SCM starting with papers by Tichy [29] and Estublier [17] from the very first SCM workshop. These two papers deal with fundamentals like versioning, selection, configurations and builds. Things that are definitely central and should be covered by any kind of SCM course. In fact, these topics are an important part of the contents in our course being treated in themes 2, 3 and 4. However, we do not find the papers themselves suited as literature because of their orientation towards tools and functionality that was of interest for the papers' original audience. This is also the reason why we chose Babich [6], who gives more motivational examples and less technical detail, as literature for theme 1 "Overview and motivation". Later on Leblang [23] wrote an overview paper about the fundamentals of SCM. It treats roughly the same problems as [29] and [17], but sees SCM as part of an overall process and has more bias towards tasks than tool functionality. In fact, this paper has a more general audience and made it into the course literature – serving as the final look back tying things together. More recently Estublier [18] wrote another paper providing a roadmap of the results that had been obtained by the SCM research community at the turn of the millennium. It provides an even broader view by including explicitly also co-operative work and product data management. Topics that are treated in themes 2 and 6 respectively of our course. Because it is a roadmap, it does not go into any detail. Likewise it is more focused on research results than on the actual problems they try to solve. For these reasons we did not find the paper itself suited as literature– though an excellent list of important topics.

We also looked at general software engineering textbooks like [26] and [28]. By nature such textbooks cannot cover everything in each of the topics they treat. Both books provide good overviews of formal as well as more informal aspects of SCM. Being more hands-on oriented they focus on the activities of configuration identification and configuration control for the formal part. The informal parts concerns versioning, releasing and building of systems. We have included both aspects in our course, theme 5 covering the formal aspects and themes 2, 3 and 4 the informal aspects. Most textbooks that deal with SCM only, like [10] and [24], cover the traditional way of looking at SCM as consisting of the four activities of: configuration identification, configuration control, configuration status accounting and configuration audit. We have dedicated an entire theme to these formal aspects of SCM. However, in our opinion these aspects may be important, but in the context of a university course there is much more to SCM than that. This means that we treat all four activities in one theme (two lectures and one exercise session). As such we can cover the most important parts, but do not have the time to go into any level of detail. This also has the consequence that we do not find these books suited as textbooks in their entirety as they convey more details than overview. Two books stand out as exceptions to the traditional treatment of SCM as consisting of "the four activities". Babich [6] and later on Mikkelsen and Pherigo [25] take on the developer's perspective and look at SCM as a set of techniques to handle the individual developer's work and his co-ordination with the rest of the people on a team. Our experience is that students consider these aspects important and we too find that they are central aspects in the practice of SCM. As such they are treated carefully and in detail in themes 2, 3 and 4 – collaboration, workspace and repository respectively. Again neither of these books is sufficient as a stand-alone textbook, as there is more to SCM than just the developer's view – however important it might be.

So far the above references have helped in identifying many topics that should be included in an SCM curriculum. However, none of the references gives any thoughts or advice about how to balance and structure the topics, neither how to prioritise them. If we take all of the above mentioned topics and treat all topics in detail we will have far more material than can be covered even in a course with 50 hours of lectures, exercise and lab sessions. To the best of our knowledge, the only reference that treats the curriculum aspect is the Software Engineering Body of Knowledge (SWEBOK) initiative [27]. It provides an overview of SCM and presents a breakdown of topics along with a description of each topic. It is a very thorough and detailed work that we would very much have liked to follow. However, in our opinion it has the weakness that it considers only traditional SCM, even if it does extend "the four activities" with those of management of the SCM process and release management and delivery. These two extensions are still quite remote from what a developer is usually confronted with. Thus we take note that these six activities are important and should be treated in our course, but do not think that it can serve as the entire curriculum. As an aside, these SCM workshops might not be the best forum for a discussion of the contents of an SCM course as [27] consider these workshops to cover only 5 out of their 44 breakdown topics for SCM.

So we were left with no help when it came down to structuring and prioritising all the topics that we wanted to crowd our course with. In the end we decided to try to come up with what we thought would be a proper curriculum for at university course on SCM. One of the main goals of the course is that the students should master SCM as support for several roles and levels in a company organisation. Fig. 1 depicts four such levels: the individual develo per, the project, the company and the society.

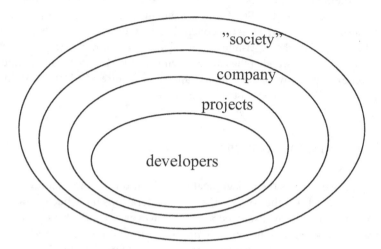

Fig. 1. The different spheres where SCM is practised

We based the structure and contents on these roles and levels presented in the p a-pers [5] and [9]. The students' career in industry is reflected in the spheres seen from Fig. 1, where they start as developers, have to interact with others in a project, will become SCM-wizards on their project, will have to handle their project's SCM-interaction with the company – and other projects, will bec ome SCM experts that can handle the company's SCM -interaction with customers – and other companies – and will eventually become company-wide SCM experts. This is what we try to reflect in the structure of the course – and in the weight we give each topic/s phere. We spend more time on the innermost sphere and treat that before the others because it is the first that our students will meet when they graduate and get a job. We also do it be-cause we find it easier to build traditional SCM on top on that than the other way around. We also spend less time and detail on traditional SCM as most of our students will probably never have to deal with those aspects directly. However, we find it im-portant that they have some knowledge of all aspects of SCM ranging from what a developer needs to get his daily work done most efficiently to what the company needs to do to provide its customers with consistent products – and why these cu s-tomers may have SCM requirements to the company. It will also provide them with a proper foundation to build upon if they want to make a career in SCM.

Based on this we can start to structure the course and to prioritise the topics. There should be a progression from developer to company view with main emphasis on the former aspects. Furthermore, for each theme that we define there should be a progre s-sion from the basics to more advanced topics. The latter progression we try to obtain by treating basic concepts in the first lecture and dedicating the second lecture on a theme to a selected set of more advanced topics to be able to treat them in -depth. For the former progression we have theme 3 (workspace) and in part theme 4 (repository) that covers the developer's individual work. The developer's interaction with the project – and as such also with his fellow developers– are covered by theme 2 (collaboration) and by theme 4 (repository), as such describing SCM at the project level with respect to the developers. The SCM-interactions that exist between a project and the company – and between projects – are covered by theme 5 (traditional SCM) – a theme that in reality also treats the SCM-interactions with the customer. Theme 6 (relations to other domains) serve to broaden the students' view of SCM, how it can be practised in different contexts and how other domains can use or inspire SCM. Parts of this theme (PDM) also caters for the needs at the company level

4   Pedagogical Considerations

In this section, we discuss the pedagogical considerations that influenced the way we organised and structured the course. These considerations have been sub-ordinate to the contents considerations discussed above. However, we still think that these considerations are important, as they convey important information to understand why we did things the way we did. Furthermore, it can help others to tailor the course if they have other restrictions and traditions for schedule, group work and examination form.

Our first consideration was the prerequisites that the students should have to take the course. In reality there is very little that the students have to know in order to follow a course on SCM – in fact if we take the software out of SCM, many of the concepts and principles would change only marginally. So with regards to knowledge the course does not build on anything in specific and could be taught even at an introductory level. However, for the students to appreciate that there are indeed problems in software development and that a great deal of help can be found in SCM they do need a broad cultural background from software engineering topics and experience from "real" projects. A trend in the curriculum for the undergraduate computer science education in Lund is that the number of student projects increases. One of these is a combined course and project on "Program development in group" [20] in which the students, in groups of 10 during 7 weeks, develop a software product. In this way they learn a lot about practical software engineering. Before the actual project there is a course with lectures and computer lab exercises. One lecture and one lab exercise is about SCM, which is just about enough to help them run the project. It does not give them a deeper knowledge of SCM, however it exposes them to many problems and make them aware that SCM exists and can be helpful. We require that students have taken this project (which is on their second year), because it ensures that they have a varied and broad background in software engineering and because it exposes the students to problems that can be handled by SCM. Being an optional course we thus get interested, motivated and hard working students. We use the same principles of project experience and background for the fair number of exchange students – and graduated students– that want to take the course.

One of the reasons for the prerequisites is based on the philosophy of problem-based learning (PBL) as reflected in the learning cycle of Kolb [22]. It says that we get better and deeper learning if we respect the natural cycle of learning. This cycle starts with experiencing a problem in practice, this is followed by a reflection about what could be the causes of the problem, then we conceptualise a possible solution and finally we plan how to carry it out in practice – at which point we can experience new problems and the learning cycle can continue. During their project course they experienced problems and some students even reflected on the possible causes. Now the course on SCM should help them to conceptualise solutions and plan how they can be carried out. The PBL philosophy reappears in the fact that the students actually try out some of their solutions during the computer labs. It is also the reason for starting at the developer level – where they have practical experience – and progressing through to the company level. By the use of metaphors during the exercise sessions we also try to draw on problems students have experienced that are similar in nature to those caused by lack of SCM. Finally, the structure of each theme into a lecture followed by an exercise session and another lecture and finally a computer lab was also implemented to facilitate PBL.

Dreyfus and Dreyfus [16] explain how people progress from novices through advanced beginners, competent and proficient to become experts. We do not claim – or even hope – to turn our students into experts on SCM. When we get them they are a mixture of novices and advanced beginners in the field of SCM. What we can do is to bring them to the level of competence in SCM – they can only obtain the levels of proficiency and expertise through practising SCM and gaining experience. Something that we can never hope to have time for in a university course. However, we find that this philosophy gives support for the existence of the computer labs and also the fact that exercise sessions are based on discussions and aimed at creating solutions rather than just answers. Furthermore, it gives us a way to explain to the student that they are not experts in SCM even though they have just followed a course dedicated to just that subject. The course have made them competent – and experience will make them become experts in time. This avoids that they start a job interview by claiming that they are experts on SCM.

Bloom [11] introduces a taxonomy for levels of understanding that we can use when we want to specify how far the students come with a given topic. He works with six levels of increasing understanding– knowledge, comprehension, application, analysis, synthesis, and evaluation. Working with such a distinction makes it easier to prioritise each topic. The first three levels are sufficient for users of SCM, while higher levels are necessary for people that have to design SCM. The higher up we get in the spheres of Fig. 1, the less likely it is that our students have to practise – or even design – topics at that level. Therefore, it might be sufficient to know that configuration audit exists even though they do not comprehend it let alone are capable of practising it. The contrary applies for levels close to the developer. Our students should be capable of analysing SCM problems at these levels and to design and maybe even evaluate solutions. Themes 2, 3 and 4 that focus on the developer and project levels are structured such that the first lecture gives the basics and the second lecture gives more in-depth and advanced knowledge. Thus the first lecture brings the students to the level of comprehension or application. The discussions during the exercise sessions contribute to preparing them for the analysis and synthesis levels while the second lecture provides them with analytical tools and a wider and deeper background to synthesise solutions. As such it will enable them to become "SCM wizards" in projects right after the course has finished. For the outer spheres of SCM there is no division in basic and in-depth lectures as we aim for only the first three levels of understanding. Also the SWEBOK [27] project at one point applied Bloom's taxonomy to each of their breakdown topics, clearly aiming at people that had to carry out – as opposed to design – the SCM activities (no breakdown topic exceeds the application level and most topics remain at either knowledge or comprehension, which corresponds pretty much to the levels students obtain in our course).

5   Lessons Learned

Reflecting on the experience we have obtained from running this course twice, we want to share some of the lessons that we have learned along the way. What worked and what did not? What are the students' impressions?

The open (metaphor) questions leading to brainstorming like discussions during the exercise sessions works well and is popular among the students. However, it is important to steer them into discussions about more concrete software development problems, i.e. to transfer the metaphor back to the software engineering world (avoid getting stuck in the metaphor). The metaphor is used only in the first phase of the brainstorm – and whenever they get stuck discussing concrete SCM problems/solutions. One way we facilitate the detachment from the metaphor is to insist that they produce a concrete result that they can present for the other groups.

Dividing the course material into themes makes it easy for the students to focus on one aspect at the time and to structure their minds. However, it may also lead to isolated islands of knowledge, which they are not able to combine. Thus, it is very important to actually reserve time to present the larger picture. The overview lecture the first week provides a structure that is then filled out during the rest of the course. The final lecture looks back at the course and makes sure that things are tied together. And finally, the essay that they produce at the last exercise session asks for parts of a "total solution" in order for them to reflect on how all parts work together in practice.

To start with the developer view of SCM works very well. The students are from the beginning well motivated to learn about how to manage situations/problems they have been in themselves. Previous experience from teaching traditional CM, listing the "four activities", is that it bores them to death. However, after three weeks of developer view – bringing them to a level where they are able to analyse different solutions – they are ready to also understand and appreciate the needs and solutions of the manager and the company.

Students gave the computer labs very high ratings in their evaluation of the course. They got a solid understanding of the underlying models for the tools from the mixture of guided exercises and more free experimentation. Even students that had previous self-taught experience with CVS got a deeper insight. Several students wanted labs to be longer than two hours to allow for even more experimentation with the tools. The first lab on CVS was optional and was aimed at student with no previous experience (not having followed the project that was a prerequisite). We believe the fact that they got a solid understanding of ClearCase in just 2x2 hours of labs to be due to a carry-over effect from the CVS labs and we are confident that they would now be able to pick up any CM-tool in 4 hours or less.

Now what about the goals for the course– did we meet them? In our opinion we did not set low standards for passing the course, but still no students were failed. We applied several ways of evaluating the students. During the exercise sessions where the students had to discuss in groups, we were present and circulating between groups taking part in the discussions. This gave us both the possibility to guide the discussions and to make an informal evaluation of the students' level. Furthermore, each group had to shortly present and discuss their findings from the exercises. It is our impression that all students have a very good comprehension of problems and solutions from the developer's perspective. Most students are also very capable of analysing, synthesising and evaluating such solutions. For traditional SCM, students were able to produce fragments of an SCM plan and they were able to evaluate a given SCM plan template with respect to the different roles. We were also present during the lab exercises and could see that students were able to apply and use different work models. We see the fact that they were able to get a solid understanding of ClearCase in just 2x2 hours of lab as an indication of a thorough understanding of the different work models. The final examination was oral and we were able to evaluate in more detail their capability to analyse, synthesise and evaluate SCM problems and solutions. As there were less exercise time for traditional SCM, we were more focused on this aspect during the oral examination. The fact that the examination was done in groups of 3-4 students gave us sufficient time to explore the depth of their learning without sacrificing too much the range of topics.

6 Future Work

We have now run two iterations of the course where we have made only minor changes from the first to the second. In general, our experience is that the course is working fine. The students like it and we do not see any big problems that need fixing. However, before running the third iteration we have some ideas for changes that we want to carry out.

What is it that works very well and should be kept? The exercise sessions with the students working in small groups and discussing open questions is definitely a strong point of the course. The computer labs is also something that attract the students and could even be extended as requested by the students. There is room in the schedule for more computer labs and we contemplate utilising this for one or two more labs. We have not decided whether it should be used for adding a third CM-tool, for digging deeper into one of the tools or for exploring completely new aspects like PDM or problem reporting. The structure with themes that fit into one week of activities is also something that we want to maintain. Thus any changes that are made will have to respect that constraint.

The contents of the course seems to be appropriate and has not created any pro b-lems. However, this is the point where we see the greatest potential for improving and fine-tuning the course. Spending three weeks on topics from the developer and project spheres and one week on topics from the company sphere may seem a bit unbalanced – and we would not disagree. The reason for the present division is in part due to the schedule constraints mentioned above. However, that does not mean that we could not treat topics that are general for all levels – like the change process – at the devel-oper level and thus only deal with the more formal aspects of already seen solutions at the higher levels. We also contemplate writing our own course material. At the present state we use bits and pieces from many different places. Each part in itself is excellent and to the point. However, the overall result of putting them together is rather like a piece of patchwork.

One thing that we are definitely going to change is to make the students even more active and involved than is the case today. Now all lectures are given by the authors and the students read the literature in parallel. Lectures are not exposing the literature, but are exposing the theme and give a "second opinion" on what the students get from the literature. This could work fine for the basics lectures, but for the advanced topics lectures we plan to have the students do the presentation. 2-4 papers would be selected for each advanced lecture session and each paper assigned to a group. This groups would be responsible for presenting the paper – and all the other groups would be responsible for having questions for discussion. This system would have the consequence that the students would work more actively also with the literature. The groups that had to present a paper on an advanced topic would get an even deeper insight than today, and the rest of the groups would probably also work more with the material during reading. Finally, it would transform the lectures from passive listening to active discussion.

Another thing that we will do in the near future it to cast the course in other con-texts. One of the authors has previously given the traditional two lectures on SCM within a general course on software engineering. How could we take the present course and fit it into two or three lectures? Should it be scaled or should we cut it down – and can it be done from our set up or will it have to a course of its own? Fu r-thermore, in the context of a research collaboration with industry, we have to give a one-day course on SCM to future project managers. Again, how can we fit the present 50 hours into one day? Finally, we are considering a post-graduate course on SCM and the above mentioned changes to actively involve students may be one step in turning the present course into a post-graduate course.

7 Conclusions

We have shown that SCM does not have to be confined to a couple of lectures within another course. SCM is rich enough in important topics to fill a whole course on its own. Given more time, the students also reach a higher level of theoretical understand-ing making it possible for them to analyse and reflect about different situations and solutions. Students like SCM – out of a student population of 80-100 we have 15-20 students and 4-6 exchange students taking the course.

We have made a proposal for the structure and contents of such a course. We have gained some experience giving the course twice and have stated some ideas for changes and improvements. Obviously this is not the final word and we welcome suggestions and discussion that can contrast and complement our experience with other experience from the SCM community.

References

1. B. Appleton, S. P. Berczuk, R. Cabrera, R. Orenstein: *Streamed Lines: Branching Patterns for Parallel Software Development*, http://www.cmcrossroads.com/bradapp/acme/branching/streamed-lines.html, 1998

2. U. Asklund: *Configuration Management for Distributed Development – Practice and Needs*, Lund University, 1999

3. U. Asklund, L. Bendix, H. Christensen, B. Magnusson: *The Unified Extensional Versioning Model*, in proceedings of SCM -9, Toulouse, France, September 5-7, 1999

4. U. Asklund, I. Crnkovic, A. Hedin, M. Larsson, A. Persson Dahlquist, J. Ranby, D. Svensson: *Product Data Management and Software Configuration Management – Similarities and Differences*, Sveriges Verkstadsindustrier, 2001

5. U. Asklund, L. Bendix: *A Study of Configuration Management in Open Source Software*, in IEE Proceedings – Software, Vol. 149, No. 1, February 2002

6. W. A. Babich: *Software Configuration Management: Coordination for Team Productivity*, Addison-Wesley, 1986

7. M.E. Bays: *Software Release Methodology*, Prentice-Hall, 1999

8. L. Bendix, P. Nowack: *Software Architecture and Configuration Management*, in 4th Workshop on Object-Oriented Architectural Evolution, Budapest, Hungary, June 18, 2001

9. L. Bendix, O. Vinter: *Configuration Management from a Developer's Perspective*, in proceedings of the EuroSTAR2001 Conference, Stockholm, Sweden, November 19-23, 2001

10. H.R. Berlack: *Software Configuration Management*, John Wiley & Sons, 1992

11. B.S. Bloom (ed.): *Taxonomy of Educational Objectives, Handbook 1: Cognitive Domain*, Addison-Wesley, 1984

12. W. J. Brown, H. W. McCormick III, S. W. Thomas: *AntiPatterns and Patterns in Software Configuration Management*, Wiley, 1999

13. S.B. Compton, G. Connor: *Configuration Management for Software*, Van Nostrand Reinhold, 1994

14. M.A. Daniels: *Principles of Configuration Management*, Advanced Applications Consultants, 1985

15. S. Dart: *Configuration Management: The Missing Link in Web Engineering*, Artech House, 2000

16. S. Dreyfus, H. Dreyfus: *Mind Over Machine: The Power of Human Intuition and Expertise in the Era of the Computer*, Simon & Schuster, 2000

17. J. Estublier: *Configuration Management – The Notion and the Tools*, in proceedings of the International Workshop on Software Version and Configuration Control, Grassau, Germany, January 27-29, 1988

18. J. Estublier: *Software Configuration Management: A Roadmap*, in proceedings of The Future of Software Engineering, Limerick, Ireland, June 4-11, 2000

19. P. Feiler: *Configuration Management Models in Commercial Environments*, Software Engineering Institute, 1991

20. G. Hedin, L. Bendix, B. Magnusson: *Introducing Software Engineering by means of Extreme Programming*, in proceedings of the International Conference on Software Engineering, ICSE 2003, Portland, Oregon, May 3-10, 2003

21. M. Kelly: *Configuration Management – The Changing Image*, McGraw-Hill, 1996

22. D.A. Kolb: *Experiental Learning: Experience as the Source of Learning and Development*, Prentice-Hall, 1984

23. D. Leblang: *The CM Challenge: Configuration Management that Works*, in W. F. Tichy (ed.) Configuration Management, John Wiley and Sons, 1994

24. A. Leon: *A Guide to Software Configuration Management*, Artech House Computer Library, 2000

25. T. Mikkelsen, S. Pherigo: *Practical Software Configuration Management: The Latenight Developer's Handbook*, Prentice-Hall, 1997

26. R.S. Pressman: *Software Engineering: A Practitioner's Approach*, McGraw-Hill, 1997

27. J.A. Scott, D. Nisse: *Software Configuration Management*, in Guide to the Software Engineering Body of Knowledge, Version 1.0, May 2001

28. I. Sommerville: *Software Engineering, Fifth Edition*, Addison-Wesley, 1995

29. W.F. Tichy: *Tools for Software Configuration Management*, in proceedings of the International Workshop on Software Version and Configuration Control, Grassau, Germany, January 27-29, 1988

30. B. White: *Software Configuration Management Strategies and Rational ClearCase: A Practical Introduction*, Addison-Wesley, 2000

31. D. Whitgift: *Methods and Tools for Software Configuration Management*, John Wiley and Sons, 1991

Applications of Configuration Information to Security

Dennis Heimbigner

Computer Science Department
University of Colorado
Boulder, CO, 80309-0430, USA
dennis.heimbigner@colorado.edu

Abstract. Securing software systems against malicious attack, corruption, and subversion has been an ongoing research problem. Novel applications of software configuration technology may provide solutions to these problems. Three interesting problems and potentials solutions are presented. The problems are intrusion tolerance, misuse protection, and cyber-forensics. The first two can be addressed using dynamic reconfiguration to modify the behavior of a software system. The last problem can be addressed using configuration information as a comprehensive framework on which to hang a variety of other information necessary for forensic analysis.

1 Introduction

Securing software systems against malicious attack, corruption, and subversion has been an ongoing research problem. With the advent of the Internet, solving these problems is increasingly seen as essential as use of networked computers continues to pervade every aspect of society.

In the last few years, the Software Engineering Research Laboratory at the University of Colorado has been developing novel applications of configuration information to the problem of computer security. This builds upon a longer history of research into configuration management [1,2,3,4,5].

Our initial work (Section 2) addressed the problem of responding to attacks against software systems once those attacks were detected. In contrast to the large amount of work in intrusion detection, intrusion response had been generally neglected. We recognized that an interesting approach to response was to provide automated modifications to the behavior of software in order to make it more resistant to attacks or to mitigate an ongoing attack. Such behavior modifications clearly required the ability to dynamically reconfigure a software system, and that in turn depended on being able describe a set of run-time configurations that embodied the modified behavior.

Since that initial work, we have begun to identify additional research problems in security for which configuration information may provide an approach for solving those problems. We use the term configuration information broadly to include traditional development-time configuration-management information

B. Westfechtel, A. van der Hoek (Eds.): SCM 2001/2003, LNCS 2649, pp. 259–266, 2003.
© Springer-Verlag Berlin Heidelberg 2003

as well as the post-development configuration information such as deployment information [6] and run-time architecture information [3].

In the remainder of this paper, we identify three interesting problems that we believe can be attacked effectively using configuration information. The first two, intrusion tolerance, and misuse protection, have solutions that rely on the ability to modify the behavior of a software system by dynamic reconfiguration. The last problem, cyber-forensics, can be addressed using configuration information as a comprehensive framework on which to hang a variety of other information necessary for forensic analysis.

2   Intrusion Response

The Willow project was our first application of configuration information to security problems. Willow provides automated responses to attacks against software systems. The problem of responding to attacks has received only limited attention until recently. Currently most responses are manual, and manual procedures - however well designed and tested - cannot react to security breaches in a timely and coordinated fashion.

Willow is a joint effort of the University of Colorado, the University of Virginia, and the University of California at Davis that supports software system survivability by modifying the behavior of the system to improve its defenses or to mitigate the effects of an attack after it has occurred. This is accomplished through an architecture [7] that supports a secure, automated framework for dynamically reconfiguring large-scale, heterogeneous, distributed systems.

The Willow architecture supports reconfiguration in a very broad sense, and reconfiguration in this context refers to any scenario that is outside of normal, "steady-state" operation. Thus, for example, initial system deployment is included intentionally in this definition, as are system modifications, posturing and so on. All are viewed merely as special cases of the general notion of reconfiguration. More specifically, the system reconfigurations supported by Willow are:

- Initial application system deployment.
- Periodic application and operating system updates including component replacement and re-parameterization.
- Planned posture changes in response to anticipated threats.
- Planned fault tolerance in response to anticipated component failures.
- Systematic best efforts to deal with unanticipated failures.

In order to reconfigure a system, it must, of course, be composed of functional components. This in turn presumes that the overall architecture of the system conforms to some component-based mechanism that is capable of supporting reconfiguration. A number of such architectures exist, including EJB (J2EE), CORBA, Web Services (UDDI), and OSGI. We are currently focusing on EJB and OSGI for our target application architectures.

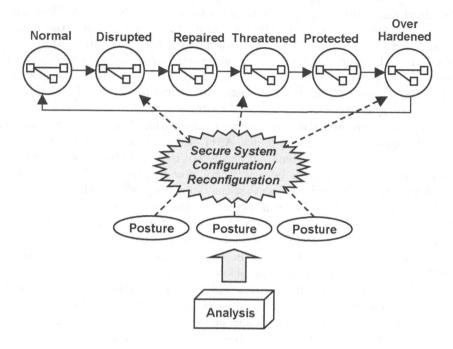

Fig. 1. Intrusion tolerance life cycle

Reconfiguration takes place after a decision is made that it is required. An important element of the Willow approach is the integration of information from sensing mechanisms within the network (such as intrusion detection systems) and information from other sources (such as intelligence data).

Responses are of two kinds: proactive and reactive. Proactive responses attempt to harden a software system before it is attacked. In addition, we view the initial, correct installation of a system and the subsequent upgrades to be a form of proactive reconfiguration because many system failures have occurred purely through the mis-configuration of a system during normal maintenance.

Proactive reconfiguration adds, removes, and replaces components and interconnections, or changes their mode of operation. This form of reconfiguration, referred to as posturing, is designed to limit possible vulnerabilities when the possibility of a threat that will exploit them is heightened. Examples of posturing would be a network-wide shutdown of non-essential services, strengthening of cryptographic keys, and disconnection of non-essential network links. These actions might be initiated by system or security administrators when they are notified of the release of a new worm or are informed about infections that have already been observed elsewhere in the Internet.

In a complementary fashion, reactive reconfiguration adds, removes, and replaces components and interconnections to restore the integrity of a system in bounded time once damage or intrusions have taken place. In Willow, mechanisms are provided for both the detection of penetrations and the recovery from them. As an example, the network might detect a coordinated attack on a distributed application and respond automatically by activating copies of the application modules on different network nodes while configuring the system to ignore the suspect modules. The system would perform this modification rapidly and inform system administrators of the change.

In addition to proactive and reactive configuration, Willow uses reconfiguration to support a return to normalcy. After either a proactive or reactive reconfiguration, the software system is typically not in a state that can be continued as a normal operating state because of the cost in resources. When system or security administrators recognize that the danger is past or perhaps an effective patch is available, then they can invoke reconfiguration to "un-harden" the effects of a potentially expensive proactive reconfiguration, to apply any available patches, and also to repair any residual effects of an attack.

Figure 1 illustrates a simple application scenario using Willow. The bottom of the figure illustrates the analysis before deployment of the specific application to produce the set of specific postures. This analysis is derived from vulnerability analysis and also an analysis of anticipated threats. Operational experience and even intelligence information may also play a part in determining the necessary postures. Note that part of the analysis must deal with the situation in which the nature of the attack is unknown, and one or more "disaster" postures must be produced.

After analysis, the application is deployed and is started under the watch of Willow, as shown in the top half of Figure 1. The application starts in its normal state. Suppose that it is then attacked; this puts it in a disrupted state. Willow is invoked to apply an appropriate posture to reactively reconfigure the application to repair it. Later, the system administrator learns of a threat to the system and so invokes Willow proactively to put the application into a protected (hardened) state. When the threat has passed, then the administrator will again invoke Willow to move it from its now over-hardened state back to its normal state.

3   Misuse Protection

Detecting and controlling misuse of software systems is increasingly recognized as an important problem. This is most often cast as the "insider problem," where a person with legitimate access to a system utilizes that access to subvert the system. Detecting misuse of software may be viewed as a special case of the intrusion detection problem. Unfortunately, it suffers from the same difficulties as many current intrusion detection systems, which have significant problems with false alarms. The term "false alarm" means that some person or mechanism has detected a pattern of behavior that appears superficially to be suspect, but upon further investigation, turns out to be, in fact, benign behavior.

False alarms present serious difficulties for security administrators. When the response to the alarm is performed manually, the responder (typically the security/system administrator) can be overwhelmed by large numbers of false alarms and can miss genuine alarms. For automated responses, false alarms can cause overall system operation to seriously degrade as the system thrashes between normal states and intrusion resistant states.

What is needed is a more controlled sequence of responses to potential misuse that allows for better response to false alarms while retaining the ability to disarm (and later rearm) the software by degrees. Thus, false alarms would be met with more measured responses that provide both time and information necessary to verify the correctness of the alarm. As the seriousness of the misuse is ascertained, more severe responses can be brought to bear. In the event of a false alarm, the response sequence and its effects should be reversible so that normal operation is resumed.

We are addressing this problem by using controlled dynamic reconfiguration to achieve the desired graduated response. In this approach, components and data sets of a software system are systematically and dynamically modified, or replaced, to establish modified or new behaviors for that software system. This work builds on the Willow project to provide the reconfiguration infrastructure. This project is building specific postures for the purpose of explicitly degraded operation.

The key element of our approach is to use configuration information to reconfigure the software system into increasingly informative and increasingly degraded modes of operation. By informative, we mean that the component begins to capture and report more detailed information about suspicious activities. By degraded, we mean that the component begins to modify its outputs and actions to reduce its functionality, or in more extreme case, even practice deception and provide wholly or partially false outputs. This latter use of deception represents a new use for the concepts first introduced by Cohen [8,9].

As with Willow, we assume a reconfigurable application architecture. However, our approach here is to try to be as generic as possible so that this work can support a wide variety of application architectures only limited by the underlying infrastructure.

Degradation of data is as important as degradation of functionality. A closely related project is examining client-side degradation of web browsers. In this project, the goal is to provide a systematic approach for providing modified web content to a client who is potentially misusing the information. This work may also branch out into the degradation of other data sources including office documents, and databases.

The approach we are developing also provides two additional capabilities. The first is self-destruction - the ability to reconfigure the software so that it appears to be working but has in fact had all important information and capabilities destroyed, ideally without immediate knowledge by the misuser. The second is restoration - the ability to reconfigure the software to undo degradation responses; this is a unique capability made possible by our use of dynamic reconfiguration, and is important in the event of false alarms or the external neutralizing of the misuse threat.

4 Cyber-Forensics

Computer forensic analysis is an important element in overall response to cyber-attacks. When a system crashes, it is critically important to quickly identify the cause of the crash in order to determine if it was caused by an attack. It is then important to identify anomalies indicating the attack mechanism and the consequent effects in order to develop a defense against the attack.

Existing analysis tools such as the Coroner's Toolkit [10] are excellent at providing large quantities of information about the state of a crashed computer. Unfortunately, this information is available only at a low level using abstractions provided by the operating system: the processes running and the files that are open, for example.

What is desperately needed is a set of higher level abstractions that can provide more insight into the state of the system so that a forensic analyst can focus on the anomalies and quickly identify the nature of any attack.

We are working on an approach that utilizes various models of software systems to organize and present high level abstractions about the state of crashed systems. In particular, we are using run-time configuration information as the basis for this organization. We plan to provide both the "should-be" configuration and the "as-is" configuration. The former represents the range of legal configurations for which a system was designed. The latter represents the apparent configuration of the system as it was at the time of the crash. These representations provide important structural information about the programs that should be, and are, running and how they relate to each other. They provide a high level framework to which other, related information can be attached to provide a growing complex of information about the state of the crashed system. They will also become the basis for presenting the information in ways that will highlight discrepancies between the expected state and the crash state in order to guide the forensic analyst to potential problems. It should be noted that this approach has much in common with the concepts advanced by van der Hoek [11], where it is proposed that architecture information be used to integrate development time information. We take a similar approach, but are using it at a very different point in the life cycle of a software system. This approach also has a relationship to application-level intrusion detection [12] in which the behavior of the system is monitored to look for anomalies based on a comparison to a model of the system.

Our approach can also address the forensic analysis of distributed systems. Such systems are difficult to analyze with existing forensics tools because those tools find it difficult to relate information from one machine with information from another machine. We can use configuration information about the architecture of a distributed application to help relate information across machines.

Thus, it is possible to indicate that process X on machine 1 is a server that was connected to the client process Y on machine 2.

Another important new research issue raised by this approach involves modeling of system state. Just as with code, the state of a system has substantial structure and may have multiple versions. This project will need to investigate the definition and manipulation of useful configuration models for system state.

We plan to build our research prototype using the University of Colorado Information Integration framework [13]. This framework supports the dynamic integration of a wide variety of information sources, and this is exactly what is needed for forensic analysis. Using this framework, we will explore the following capabilities:

- Maintenance of the "should-be" configuration,
- Bottom-up construction of the "as-is" configuration based directly on analysis of the crash data,
- Integration of the massive amounts of existing (but unstructured) crash analysis data provided by the Coroner's Toolkit.
- Cross-machine relationships for distributed applications.

Over time, this framework can then be extended to include data from additional sources, subsequent analyses of that data, and additional models of the system. We believe that our use of configuration information as the core will produce a forensic analysis system significantly superior to the relatively unintegrated products currently available.

5 Summary

This paper illustrates some new uses for configuration information. Three problems are presented:

1. Intrusion Response,
2. Misuse Protection, and
3. Cyber-Forensics.

For each problem, it is shown how appropriate use of configuration information can significantly contribute to solving the problem. For the first two problems, the information supports behavior changes through dynamic reconfiguration. For the last problem, configuration information is used as a comprehensive framework upon which to coalesce and integrate forensic data.

Acknowledgments

This material is based in part upon work sponsored by the Air Force Research Laboratories, SPAWAR, and the Defense Advanced Research Projects Agency under Contract Numbers F30602-00-2-0608 and N66001-00-8945. The content of the information does not necessarily reflect the position or the policy of the Government and no official endorsement should be inferred.

References

1. Hall, R., Heimbigner, D., Wolf, A.: A Cooperative Approach to Support Software Deployment Using the Software Dock. In: Proc. of the 1999 Int'l Conf. on Software Engineering, ACM (1999) 174–183
2. Heimbigner, D., Krane, S.: A Graph Transform Model for Configuration Management Environments,. In: Proc. of the Third ACM-SIGSOFT Symposium on Software Development Environments, Boston, Mass. (1988) 216–225
3. Rutherford, M., Anderson, K., Carzaniga, A., Heimbigner, D., Wolf, A.: Reconfiguration in the Enterprise JavaBean Component Model. In: Proc. of IFIP/ACM Working Conf. on Component Deployment, Berlin, FRG (2002)
4. van der Hoek, A., Carzaniga, A., Heimbigner, D., Wolf, A.: A Testbed for Configuration Management Policy Programming. IEEE Transactions on Software Engineering **28** (2002) 79–99
5. van der Hoek, A., Heimbigner, D., Wolf, A.: A Generic, Peer-to-Peer Repository for Distributed Configuration Management. In: Proc. of the 18th Int'l Conf. on Software Engineering, Berlin, FRG, (1996)
6. Hall, R., Heimbigner, D., Wolf, A.: Evaluating Software Deployment Languages and Schema. In: Proc. of the 1998 Int'l Conf. on Software Maintenance, IEEE Computer Society (1998) 177–185
7. Knight, J., Heimbigner, D., Wolf, A., Carzaniga, A., Hill, J., Devanbu, P.: The Willow Survivability Architecture. In: Proc. of the Fourth Information Survivability Workshop, Vancouver, B.C. (2002)
8. Cohen, F.: A Mathematical Structure of Simple Defensive Network Deceptions. Technical report, Fred Cohen and Associates Technical Report (1999) http://all.net/journal/deception/mathdeception/mathdeception.html.
9. Cohen, F., D.Lambert, Preston, C., Berry, N., Stewart, C., Thomas, E.: A Framework for Deception. Technical report, Fred Cohen and Associates Technical Report (2001) http://all.net/journal/deception/Framework/Framework.html.
10. Farmer, D., Venema, W.: Coroner's Toolkit Web Page. (1999) http://www.fish.com/tct.
11. van der Hoek, A.: Configurable Software Architecture in Support of Configuration Management and Software Deployment. In: Proc. of the ICSE99 Doctoral Workshop, Los Angeles, California (1999)
12. Ko, C., Brutch, P., Rowe, J., Tsafnat, G., Levitt, K.: System Health and Intrusion Monitoring Using a Hierarchy of Constraints. In: Proc. Recent Advances in Intrusion Detection. (2001) 190–203
13. Anderson, K., Sherba, S., Lepthien, W.: Towards Large-Scale Information Integration. In: Proc. of the 24th Int'l Conf. on Software Engineering, Orlando, Florida (2002) 524–535

Towards Software Configuration Management for Test-Driven Development

Tammo Freese

OFFIS, Escherweg 2, 26121 Oldenburg, Germany
tammo.freese@offis.de

Abstract. Test-Driven Development is a technique where each change to the observable behavior of a program is motivated by a failing test. High design quality is maintained by continuous small design improvements called refactorings. While some integrated development environments support automated refactoring, they do not handle problems that occur if refactorings are used in development teams or on published interfaces. This paper outlines the idea of a specialized software configuration management tool which integrates into a development environment to record the steps of Test-Driven Development as operations. These operations are useful for summarizing local changes, merging parallel changes and for migrating code that uses published interfaces.

1 Introduction

Test-Driven Development (TDD) [3] is the core development strategy of Extreme Programming [2]. The main ideas of TDD are to test a program before writing it, and to continuously maintain a simple design.

Each change of the observable program behavior has to be motivated by a failing test. Seeing the test fail is important, as it verifies that the code does not fulfill the test's expectations. After writing just enough code to meet the new expectations, all the tests have to pass to verify that the new expectation as well as all the old ones are fulfilled. The tests are written by developers in the development language itself using a testing framework like JUnit [10]. The GUI front ends of these frameworks provide visual feedback. A green bar means that all tests passed, while a red one means that at least one test failed. Each development step may be understood as a state transition green–red–green.

Every development step introduces new behavior. The current design is often not fitted to incorporate the new behavior, so it may grow more complex with every change. To keep the design straightforward and easy to understand, it is required to improve it without changing the observable behavior of the code. This is known as refactoring [7]. In TDD, refactoring is only allowed if all existing tests pass. Since refactorings do not change the observable behavior, all tests still have to pass afterwards. Refactoring steps thus may be understood as state transitions green–green. Refactoring steps are typically small. Bigger refactorings are achieved by many small steps. Examples for refactorings in Java are renaming classes, interfaces or methods as well as extracting and inlining methods.

B. Westfechtel, A. van der Hoek (Eds.): SCM 2001/2003, LNCS 2649, pp. 267–273, 2003.

As performing refactorings manually is slow and error-prone, tool support is essential. Some integrated development environments (IDEs) support automated refactoring and thus speed up TDD. However, there are still some shortcomings in using local version histories, merging changes and applying changes to published interfaces.

1.1   Local Version History

TDD is a feedback-driven development style with many small steps. From time to time the development may take a wrong path, so that backtracking is necessary. Common examples are a new test requiring too much code to be written so that the developer does not get back to a green state quickly, or an experimental refactoring route which led to an overly complex or otherwise inappropriate design.

Many IDEs provide undo/redo features, some even provide local histories that allow backtracking to every saved version. However, the huge number of steps in TDD clutters local histories, making it difficult to identify interesting targets for backtracking. An additional problem is that local changes and versions often do not carry additional information, like whether they are refactorings or whether the tests passed. Undo/redo is usually file-related and not project-related, and too fine-grained for backtracking. Common implementations even lose information, since undone development routes cannot be reached again after changes.

1.2   Merging Changes

Commercial software configuration management (SCM) tools usually rely on textual merging [12]. Refactorings often lead to problems when using textual merging. Suppose we have a method x(). While developer A renames the method to y(), developer B implements a new method using the old signature x(). Text-oriented SCM tools will show no merge conflicts, but the resulting code will not compile. Even worse, if both developers rename the same method to different names, textual merging leads to conflicts at every invocation of the method.

Another problem is method inlining. If developer A inlines method x() while developer B invokes it in a new code fragment, no merge conflicts will be shown, although the resulting code will not compile.

1.3   Changing Published Interfaces

Many software development projects work on libraries or frameworks. Changing published interfaces breaks client code and is therefore discouraged. Typical recommendations are to publish as little as possible as late as possible or to make changes additions [8,5]. While following these rules is generally useful, it makes TDD more difficult, since refactorings cannot be applied easily to published interfaces.

2   Software Configuration Management for Test-Driven Development

The main reason for the problems described in section 1 is the missing support for Test-Driven Development in current SCM systems, as they are not aware of the development steps. Our goal is therefore to build a specialized SCM for Test-Driven Development.

2.1   Local Change History

As the SCM should be based on the steps of TDD, these steps have to be recorded. By integration into an IDE, events like saving files, refactorings, compilation success/failure and test success/failure may be gathered. With additional information from the source code, we get a sequence of changes, each of them either a delta for some source files or an automated refactoring. Each change may carry additional information on compilation success (compilable change) or failure (non-compilable change) and test success (green change) or failure (red change). With these changes, a simple mechanism for backtracking may be implemented. Backtracking itself is recorded as a kind of change as well.

The stream of changes contains the complete development path, but it does not provide an overview. To focus on important information, the changes are structured into a tree by organizing changes under new parent nodes. Each parent node is regarded as a change and inherits the additional information from its last child. Parent nodes are introduced for various change sequences:

- backtracking changes with all preceding changes they have undone
- changes where compilation was triggered with all preceding changes that were not compiled
- compilable changes with all preceding non-compilable changes
- changes where tests were invoked with all preceding changes where the tests were not invoked
- a maximal sequence of red changes followed by a green change, i.e. a TDD development step
- a maximal sequence of green changes after a green change, i.e. a sequence of TDD refactoring steps

Figure 1 shows a small example where 11 changes are structured in a tree. In the collapsed form, the tree only shows 3 elements.

2.2   Merging Changes

The local change sequence provides valuable information for merging parallel changes. Our goal is to combine operation-based merging [11] with syntactic software merging [4]. Operation-based merging uses the operations that were performed during development. Syntactic software merging takes the programming language syntax into account.

before aggregation

number	type	compile	test
38	change	F	
37	change		
36	refactoring	S	S
35	refactoring	S	
34	change	S	S
33	change	F	
32	change	S	F
31	change		
30	change		
29	change	F	
28	change		

after aggregation

number	type	compile	test
37–38	non-compilable change	F	
38	change	F	
37	change		
35–36	refactoring step	S	S
36	refactoring	S	S
35	refactoring	S	
28–34	development step	S	S
33–34	green change	S	S
34	change	S	S
33	change	F	
28–32	red change	S	F
30–32	compilable change	S	F
32	change	S	F
31	change		
30	change		
28–29	non-compilable change	F	
29	change	F	
28	change		

S: success, F: failure

Fig. 1. Aggregating changes

For merging parallel changes, we would like to use operation sequences where the code compiles after each change. Thus it is required that the local change sequence starts and ends with compilable code. The operation sequence is created by pruning all the development paths that were undone by backtracking, and combining each compilable change with all its preceding non-compilable changes.

Each operation, then, is either a refactoring or a change to one or more source files. We assume that we have an initial state X of the source code and two operation sequences (transformations in [11]) $T_a = T_{a,n}T_{a,n-1}\ldots T_{a,1}$ and $T_b = T_{b,m}T_{b,m-1}\ldots T_{b,1}$. The typical situation is that a developer (B) would like to release his changes T_b to X into the repository. While he worked on his changes, another developer (A) has released his changes T_a. The result of the release should then be $T_bT_aX = T_{b,m}T_{b,m-1}\ldots T_{b,1}T_{a,n}T_{a,n-1}\ldots T_{a,1}X$. Since the operations T_b were applied to X and not to T_aX, conflicts may occur. The approach followed here is to check each operations of T_b for conflicts with operations of T_a. Conflicts are resolved by modifying the operations of T_b (automatically or manually). The rationale behind this is that T_a is never changed, since it is already stored in the repository.

In merging, the basic assumption for operation-based merging is used: If the result of applying two transformations stays the same after changing their order, the result is a good candidate for merging [11]. For merging two non-refactoring operations, syntactic software merging [4] should be used to minimize conflicts. If a change cannot be applied after a refactoring, it is often sufficient to apply the refactoring on the change itself. The same strategy works for many conflicting refactorings. If this strategy does not work, in most cases the conflict is due to a name clash. An example would be a change operation which adds method x() and a refactoring renaming method y() to x(). These cases may be resolved automatically by either modifying the change operation or the refactoring to use another target name. Remaining conflicts should be solved interactively.

2.3   Changing Published Interfaces

If a library or framework is developed, refactorings on published interfaces have to be applied to dependent code, too. Since the change operations themselves are stored in the SCM, a refactoring script may be created for the operation sequence since the last published version of the library. A migration tool may apply these refactorings on dependent code by using the refactoring capabilities of existing tools. Such a tool is expected to reduce migration costs in these cases drastically, so that the development team may establish more liberate change policies on published interfaces.

3   Related Work

The SCM tool outlined here combines various ideas, among them using the change history in the development process, operation-based and syntactic software merging as well as applying refactorings to code that uses published interfaces. This section summarizes these ideas and relates them to this paper.

3.1   Version Sensitive Editing

In [1], David L. Atkins describes the idea of enhancing the development process by making the change history easily available to the programmer. The tool described there is capable of showing the history for each line of code, thus simplifying the identification of errors introduced earlier. The local change history described in section 2.1 is guided by the same idea, but takes another approach. In TDD, different ideas for a code change are often just tried one after another, so it is important to be able to roll back the whole project to an earlier version. So instead of showing the history of a line of code, the change history here shows the history of the whole project.

3.2   Local Change Histories

Some IDEs ([6,9]) include local change histories which allow rolling back either single methods or files or the whole project to older versions. The local change history proposed here only allows to roll back the whole project. Its advantages are that it simplifies finding interesting targets for backtracking by structuring the development steps, and its awareness for refactoring operations which may later be used in merging.

3.3   Operation-Based Merging

Most SCM tools use state-based merging, as they only have initial and final versions available.

Operation-based merging [11] uses the operations that were performed during development. As refactorings are typical operations in TDD, section 2.2 proposes to use them as operations in merging. All other changes are combined to change operations.

In [11], the operation sequences leading to different versions may both be changed to create the merge result. The approach described here requires that the sequence already in the repository is not changed: All changes have to be applied to the sequence which is not in the repository. As a result, the repository contains a stream of operations from version to version, which may be used for migration of dependent code.

3.4   Syntactic Software Merging

In [4], Jim Buffenbarger provides an overview on methods of software merging, including the idea of syntactic software merging that uses the programming language for merging. Since the source code is compilable before and after each change operation in section 2.2, two non-refactoring operations are good candidates for syntactic merging.

3.5   Refactoring Tags

The strategies for changing published interfaces mentioned in section 1.3 are inappropriate for Extreme Programming, since they focus on avoiding change. In [13], Stefan Roock and Andreas Havenstein describe the concept of special tags for framework development. The tags describe refactorings applied to the framework. They are used by a migration tool to help application developers in migrating their source code to a new version of the framework.

In comparison to the approach described here, the advantage of refactoring tags is their independence of the development environment: They may be used in every IDE or editor. However, the refactoring information is not gathered automatically, but has to be added manually.

4   Current Status and Future Work

The SCM outlined in this paper is currently under development for the Java programming language. It is integrated into the open source IDE Eclipse [6] which provides a huge number of plug-in points which greatly simplify tool integration. At the time of writing (February 2003), the local change history works, and plug-in points for providing local change types as well as building the tree structure for the change sequence are finished. Since Eclipse does not yet provide information on invoked refactorings, we added a related plug-in point, and currently work on creating the operation sequence from the local development steps.

References

1. Atkins, D.L.: Version Sensitive Editing: Change History as a Programming Tool. In: Magnusson, B.: Software Configuration Management: ECOOP'98 SCM-8 Symposium. Springer (1998)
2. Beck, K.: Extreme Programming Explained: Embrace Change. Addison-Wesley (1999)
3. Beck, K.: Test-Driven Development: By Example. Addison-Wesley (2003)
4. Buffenbarger, J.: Syntactic Software Merging. In: Estublier, J. (ed.): Software Configuration Management: Selected Papers SCM-4 and SCM-5. Springer (1995)
5. des Rivières, J.: Evolving Java-based APIs.
   http://www.eclipse.org/eclipse/development/java-api-evolution.html
   (2002)
6. Eclipse home page. http://www.eclipse.org
7. Fowler, M.: Refactoring: Improving the Design of Existing Code. Addison-Wesley (1999)
8. Fowler, M.: Public versus Published Interfaces. In: IEEE Software (March/April 2002)
9. IntelliJ IDEA home page. http://www.intellij.com
10. JUnit home page. http://www.junit.org
11. Lippe, E., van Oosterom, N.: Operation-based Merging. Lecture Notes in Computer Science, Vol. 1000. In: Proceedings of ACM SIGSOFT'92: Fifth Symposium on Software Development Environments (SDE5) (1992)
12. Mens, T.: A State-of-the-Art Survey on Software Merging. In: IEEE Transactions on Software Engineering, vol. 28, no. 5 (2002)
13. Roock, S., Havenstein, A.: Refactoring Tags for automated refactoring of framework dependent applications. XP2002 Conference (2002)

Author Index

Asklund, Ulf   245

Barkstrom, Bruce R.   118
Bendix, Lars   245
Bustard, David   191

Carzaniga, Antonio   231
Castaldi, Marco   231
Chu-Carroll, Mark C.   40
Conradi, Reidar   24

Dolstra, Eelco   102
Dui, Daniel   148

Emmerich, Wolfgang   148
Estublier, Jacky   1, 163

Freese, Tammo   267

García, Sergio   1
Gordon, Dorrit   70

Heimbigner, Dennis   259
Hoek, André van der   177, 217

Inverardi, Paola   231

Kojo, Tero   86

Le, Anh-Tuyet   163
Lingen, Ronald van der   177

Männistö, Tomi   86
Mennie, David   54
Morrow, Philip   191

Ommering, Rob van   16
O'Reilly, Ciaran   191

Pagurek, Bernard   54

Soininen, Timo   86
Sowrirajan, Sundararajan   217

Tosic, Vladimir   54

Vega, Germán   1
Villalobos, Jorge   163

Westfechtel, Bernhard   24
Whitehead, E. James Jr.   70
Wiborg Weber, Darcy   206
Wienberg, Axel   134
Wolf, Alexander L.   231
Wright, James   40

Lecture Notes in Computer Science

For information about Vols. 1–2556

please contact your bookseller or Springer-Verlag

Vol. 2557: B. McKay, J. Slaney (Eds.), AI 2002: Advances in Artificial Intelligence. Proceedings, 2002. XV, 730 pages. 2002. (Subseries LNAI).

Vol. 2558: P. Perner, Data Mining on Multimedia Data. X, 131 pages. 2002.

Vol. 2559: M. Oivo, S. Komi-Sirviö (Eds.), Product Focused Software Process Improvement. Proceedings, 2002. XV, 646 pages. 2002.

Vol. 2560: S. Goronzy, Robust Adaptation to Non-Native Accents in Automatic Speech Recognition. Proceedings, 2002. XI, 144 pages. 2002. (Subseries LNAI).

Vol. 2561: H.C.M. de Swart (Ed.), Relational Methods in Computer Science. Proceedings, 2001. X, 315 pages. 2002.

Vol. 2562: V. Dahl, P. Wadler (Eds.), Practical Aspects of Declarative Languages. Proceedings, 2003. X, 315 pages. 2002.

Vol. 2563: Y. Manolopoulos, S, Evripidou, A.C. Kakas (Eds.), Advances in Informatics. Proceedings, 2001. XI, 498 pages. 2002.

Vol. 2565: J.M.L.M. Palma, J. Dongarra, V. Hernández, A. Augusto Sousa (Eds.), High Performance Computing for Computational Science – VECPAR 2002. Proceedings, 2002. XVII, 732 pages. 2003.

Vol. 2566: T.Æ. Mogensen, D.A. Schmidt, I.H. Sudborough (Eds.), The Essence of Computation. XIV, 473 pages. 2002.

Vol. 2567: Y.G. Desmedt (Ed.), Public Key Cryptography – PKC 2003. Proceedings, 2003. XI, 365 pages. 2002.

Vol. 2568: M. Hagiya, A. Ohuchi (Eds.), DNA Computing. Proceedings, 2002. XI, 338 pages. 2003.

Vol. 2569: D. Gollmann, G. Karjoth, M. Waidner (Eds.), Computer Security – ESORICS 2002. Proceedings, 2002. XIII, 648 pages. 2002. (Subseries LNAI).

Vol. 2570: M. Jünger, G. Reinelt, G. Rinaldi (Eds.), Combinatorial Optimization – Eureka, You Shrink!. Proceedings, 2001. X, 209 pages. 2003.

Vol. 2571: S.K. Das, S. Bhattacharya (Eds.), Distributed Computing. Proceedings, 2002. XIV, 354 pages. 2002.

Vol. 2572: D. Calvanese, M. Lenzerini, R. Motwani (Eds.), Database Theory – ICDT 2003. Proceedings, 2003. XI, 455 pages. 2002.

Vol. 2574: M.-S. Chen, P.K. Chrysanthis, M. Sloman, A. Zaslavsky (Eds.), Mobile Data Management. Proceedings, 2003. XII, 414 pages. 2003.

Vol. 2575: L.D. Zuck, P.C. Attie, A. Cortesi, S. Mukhopadhyay (Eds.), Verification, Model Checking, and Abstract Interpretation. Proceedings, 2003. XI, 325 pages. 2003.

Vol. 2576: S. Cimato, C. Galdi, G. Persiano (Eds.), Security in Communication Networks. Proceedings, 2002. IX, 365 pages. 2003.

Vol. 2577: P. Petta, R. Tolksdorf, F. Zambonelli (Eds.), Engineering Societies in the Agents World III. Proceedings, 2002. X, 285 pages. 2003. (Subseries LNAI).

Vol. 2578: F.A.P. Petitcolas (Ed.), Information Hiding. Proceedings, 2002. IX, 427 pages. 2003.

Vol. 2580: H. Erdogmus, T. Weng (Eds.), COTS-Based Software Systems. Proceedings, 2003. XVIII, 261 pages. 2003.

Vol. 2581: J.S. Sichman, F. Bousquet, P. Davidsson (Eds.), Multi-Agent-Based Simulation II. Proceedings, 2002. X, 195 pages. 2003. (Subseries LNAI).

Vol. 2582: L. Bertossi, G.O.H. Katona, K.-D. Schewe, B. Thalheim (Eds.), Semantics in Databases. Proceedings, 2001. IX, 229 pages. 2003.

Vol. 2583: S. Matwin, C. Sammut (Eds.), Inductive Logic Programming. Proceedings, 2002. X, 351 pages. 2003. (Subseries LNAI).

Vol. 2584: A. Schiper, A.A. Shvartsman, H. Weatherspoon, B.Y. Zhao (Eds.), Future Directions in Distributed Computing. X, 219 pages. 2003.

Vol. 2585: F. Giunchiglia, J. Odell, G. Weiß (Eds.), Agent-Oriented Software Engineering III. Proceedings, 2002. X, 229 pages. 2003.

Vol. 2586: M. Klusch, S. Bergamaschi, P. Edwards, P. Petta (Eds.), Intelligent Information Agents. VI, 275 pages. 2003. (Subseries LNAI).

Vol. 2587: P.J. Lee, C.H. Lim (Eds.), Information Security and Cryptology – ICISC 2002. Proceedings, 2002. XI, 536 pages. 2003.

Vol. 2588: A. Gelbukh (Ed.), Computational Linguistics and Intelligent Text Processing. Proceedings, 2003. XV, 648 pages. 2003.

Vol. 2589: E. Börger, A. Gargantini, E. Riccobene (Eds.), Abstract State Machines 2003. Proceedings, 2003. XI, 427 pages. 2003.

Vol. 2590: S. Bressan, A.B. Chaudhri, M.L. Lee, J.X. Yu, Z. Lacroix (Eds.), Efficiency and Effectiveness of XML Tools and Techniques and Data Integration over the Web. Proceedings, 2002. X, 259 pages. 2003.

Vol. 2591: M. Aksit, M. Mezini, R. Unland (Eds.), Objects, Components, Architectures, Services, and Applications for a Networked World. Proceedings, 2002. XI, 431 pages. 2003.

Vol. 2592: R. Kowalczyk, J.P. Müller, H. Tianfield, R. Unland (Eds.), Agent Technologies, Infrastructures, Tools, and Applications for E-Services. Proceedings, 2002. XVII, 371 pages. 2003. (Subseries LNAI).

Vol. 2593: A.B. Chaudhri, M. Jeckle, E. Rahm, R. Unland (Eds.), Web, Web-Services, and Database Systems. Proceedings, 2002. XI, 311 pages. 2003.

Vol. 2594: A. Asperti, B. Buchberger, J.H. Davenport (Eds.), Mathematical Knowledge Management. Proceedings, 2003. X, 225 pages. 2003.

Vol. 2595: K. Nyberg, H. Heys (Eds.), Selected Areas in Cryptography. Proceedings, 2002. XI, 405 pages. 2003.

Vol. 2596: A. Coen-Porisini, A. van der Hoek (Eds.), Software Engineering and Middleware. Proceedings, 2002. XII, 239 pages. 2003.

Vol. 2597: G. Păun, G. Rozenberg, A. Salomaa, C. Zandron (Eds.), Membrane Computing. Proceedings, 2002. VIII, 423 pages. 2003.

Vol. 2598: R. Klein, H.-W. Six, L. Wegner (Eds.), Computer Science in Perspective. X, 357 pages. 2003.

Vol. 2599: E. Sherratt (Ed.), Telecommunications and beyond: The Broader Applicability of SDL and MSC. Proceedings, 2002. X, 253 pages. 2003.

Vol. 2600: S. Mendelson, A.J. Smola, Advanced Lectures on Machine Learning. Proceedings, 2002. IX, 259 pages. 2003. (Subseries LNAI).

Vol. 2601: M. Ajmone Marsan, G. Corazza, M. Listanti, A. Roveri (Eds.) Quality of Service in Multiservice IP Networks. Proceedings, 2003. XV, 759 pages. 2003.

Vol. 2602: C. Priami (Ed.), Computational Methods in Systems Biology. Proceedings, 2003. IX, 214 pages. 2003.

Vol. 2603: A. Garcia, C. Lucena, F. Zambonelli, A. Omicini, J. Castro (Eds.), Software Engineering for Large-Scale Multi-Agent Systems. XIV, 285 pages. 2003.

Vol. 2604: N. Guelfi, E. Astesiano, G. Reggio (Eds.), Scientific Engineering for Distributed Java Applications. Proceedings, 2002. X, 205 pages. 2003.

Vol. 2606: A.M. Tyrrell, P.C. Haddow, J. Torresen (Eds.), Evolvable Systems: From Biology to Hardware. Proceedings, 2003. XIV, 468 pages. 2003.

Vol. 2607: H. Alt, M. Habib (Eds.), STACS 2003. Proceedings, 2003. XVII, 700 pages. 2003.

Vol. 2609: M. Okada, B. Pierce, A. Scedrov, H. Tokuda, A. Yonezawa (Eds.), Software Security – Theories and Systems. Proceedings, 2002. XI, 471 pages. 2003.

Vol. 2610: C. Ryan, T. Soule, M. Keijzer, E. Tsang, R. Poli, E. Costa (Eds.), Genetic Programming. Proceedings, 2003. XII, 486 pages. 2003.

Vol. 2611: S. Cagnoni, J.J. Romero Cardalda, D.W. Corne, J. Gottlieb, A. Guillot, E. Hart, C.G. Johnson, E. Marchiori, J.-A. Meyer, M. Middendorf, G.R. Raidl (Eds.), Applications of Evolutionary Computing. Proceedings, 2003. XXI, 708 pages. 2003.

Vol. 2612: M. Joye (Ed.), Topics in Cryptology – CT-RSA 2003. Proceedings, 2003. XI, 417 pages. 2003.

Vol. 2613: F.A.P. Petitcolas, H.J. Kim (Eds.), Digital Watermarking. Proceedings, 2002. XI, 265 pages. 2003.

Vol. 2614: R. Laddaga, P. Robertson, H. Shrobe (Eds.), Self-Adaptive Software: Applications. Proceedings, 2001. VIII, 291 pages. 2003.

Vol. 2615: N. Carbonell, C. Stephanidis (Eds.), Universal Access. Proceedings, 2002. XIV, 534 pages. 2003.

Vol. 2616: T. Asano, R. Klette, C. Ronse (Eds.), Geometry, Morphology, and Computational Imaging. Proceedings, 2002. X, 437 pages. 2003.

Vol. 2617: H.A. Reijers (Eds.), Design and Control of Workflow Processes. Proceedings, 2002. XV, 624 pages. 2003.

Vol. 2618: P. Degano (Ed.), Programming Languages and Systems. Proceedings, 2003. XV, 415 pages. 2003.

Vol. 2619: H. Garavel, J. Hatcliff (Eds.), Tools and Algorithms for the Construction and Analysis of Systems. Proceedings, 2003. XVI, 604 pages. 2003.

Vol. 2620: A.D. Gordon (Ed.), Foundations of Software Science and Computation Structures. Proceedings, 2003. XII, 441 pages. 2003.

Vol. 2621: M. Pezzè (Ed.), Fundamental Approaches to Software Engineering. Proceedings, 2003. XIV, 403 pages. 2003.

Vol. 2622: G. Hedin (Ed.), Compiler Construction. Proceedings, 2003. XII, 335 pages. 2003.

Vol. 2623: O. Maler, A. Pnueli (Eds.), Hybrid Systems: Computation and Control. Proceedings, 2003. XII, 558 pages. 2003.

Vol. 2625: U. Meyer, P. Sanders, J. Sibeyn (Eds.), Algorithms for Memory Hierarchies. Proceedings, 2003. XVIII, 428 pages. 2003.

Vol. 2626: J.L. Crowley, J.H. Piater, M. Vincze, L. Paletta (Eds.), Computer Vision Systems. Proceedings, 2003. XIII, 546 pages. 2003.

Vol. 2627: B. O'Sullivan (Ed.), Recent Advances in Constraints. Proceedings, 2002. X, 201 pages. 2003. (Subseries LNAI).

Vol. 2628: T. Fahringer, B. Scholz, Advanced Symbolic Analysis for Compilers. XII, 129 pages. 2003.

Vol. 2631: R. Falcone, S. Barber, L. Korba, M. Singh (Eds.), Trust, Reputation, and Security: Theories and Practice. Proceedings, 2002. X, 235 pages. 2003. (Subseries LNAI).

Vol. 2632: C.M. Fonseca, P.J. Fleming, E. Zitzler, K. Deb, L. Thiele (Eds.), Evolutionary Multi-Criterion Optimization. Proceedings, 2003. XV, 812 pages. 2003.

Vol. 2633: F. Sebastiani (Ed.), Advances in Information Retrieval. Proceedings, 2003. XIII, 546 pages. 2003.

Vol. 2634: F. Zhao, L. Guibas (Eds.), Information Processing in Sensor Networks. Proceedings, 2003. XII, 692 pages. 2003.

Vol. 2636: E. Alonso, D, Kudenko, D. Kazakov (Eds.), Adaptive Agents and Multi-Agent Systems. XIV, 323 pages. 2003. (Subseries LNAI).

Vol. 2637: K.-Y. Whang, J. Jeon, K. Shim, J. Srivastava (Eds.), Advances in Knowledge Discovery and Data Mining. Proceedings, 2003. XVIII, 610 pages. 2003. (Subseries LNAI).

Vol. 2642: X. Zhou, Y. Zhang, M.E. Orlowska (Eds.), Web Technologies and Applications. Proceedings, 2003. XIII, 608 pages. 2003.

Vol. 2646: H. Geuvers, F, Wiedijk (Eds.), Types for Proofs and Programs. Proceedings, 2002. VIII, 331 pages. 2003.

Vol. 2649: B. Westfechtel, A. van der Hoek (Eds.), Software Configuration Management. Proceedings, 2003. VIII, 275 pages. 2003.

Vol. 2656: E. Biham (Ed.), Advances in Cryptology – EUROCRPYT 2003. Proceedings, 2003. XIV, 649 pages. 2003.